A PLUME

GAME BO

MICHAEL KANE is an entertainment featur...        ...rk Post and a former
sports writer and editor at the *Denver H...*        ...ared in *ESPN the
Magazine* and *Sport* magazine. He lives in...

---

"A welcome look at a subculture overlooked by the ...        ...*hronicle*

"Welcome to e-sports, in which real players face off through c... ...rs and become
online celebrities. Fascinating and surprisingly exciting."        —*St. Petersburg Times*

"Mr. Kane de...        **DATE DUE**        ...rs when
they discuss...        ...eo game
players to pro...        ...*Observer*

"Even if you'...        ...oting for
Kane's game...        ...*enthouse*

"An intriguir...        ...b capturing a fledglir...        ...ven non-
gamers [will...        ...ted Press

"Like any go...        ...s in equal
measure."        —*Booklist*

"Michael K...        ...ge makes
you care about the...        ...ccounts of
the heated rivalry make *Game Boys* worth reading."        —*Xbox Magazine*

"A classic underdog-versus-the-establishment sports drama. *Game Boys* is a perfect
example of how competitive gaming could be made to thrill and entertain. Not only
does he manage to turn the geek jargon of tournament-level Counter-Strike into
comprehensible play-by-play, he digs down into the personal lives of the players
and coaches, adding the kind of human-interest depth normally found in the sports
pages."        —1UP.com

"Amazing."

"One part eye-opening look at the world of professional gaming, one part true American underdog story, *Game Boys* is a highly informative, enjoyable read that challenges popular perceptions of the dedicated gamer. Kane's knowledge of the game, and his craft, is such that we are not only never overloaded with new terminology, but also given exactly what we need to appreciate the book's climax. *Game Boys* feels like watching a good documentary." —Gamecyte.com

"*Game Boys* made me actually want to sit down and watch people play videogames against each other. And cheer. And boo. I can't think of a stronger endorsement than that."

—Will Leitch, author of *God Save the Fan* and
founding editor of Deadspin.com

"As someone who never was able to quite handle the leap from Pac-Man to Ms. Pac-Man, I am indebted to Michael Kane for writing *Game Boys* and explaining how far videogaming has come in the years since…and just how far it might go. He'll be the first person I consult when I'm assigned to cover the World Series of Counter-Strike."

—Jim Caple, ESPN.com senior writer and
author of *The Devil Wears Pinstripes*

"Competitive videogaming is ready for prime time. In this excellent book, Michael Kane masterfully draws on the emotion, excitement, and backstage drama that helped e-sports hit the major leagues. Whether you play video games or not, Kane will convince you they could be the main event of the twenty-first century. A fascinating read."

—Matt Mason, author of *The Pirate's Dilemma: How Youth Culture
Is Reinventing Capitalism*

"*Game Boys* is a fascinating, rail-gun ride through the world of competitive gaming. With electric prose and engaging authority, Kane skillfully captures all the drama, angst, and geekery that drove a niche of passionate gamers to forge a subculture, command the respect of corporations, and claw their way into the big time."

—Aaron Ruby, coauthor of *Smartbomb: The Quest for Art, Entertainment,
and Big Bucks in the Videogame Revolution*

# GAME BOYS

**TRIUMPH, HEARTBREAK, AND THE QUEST FOR
CASH IN THE BATTLEGROUND OF COMPETITIVE
VIDEOGAMING**

## Michael Kane

A PLUME BOOK

PLUME
Published by the Penguin Group
Penguin Group (USA) Inc., 375 Hudson Street, New York, New York 10014, U.S.A. • Penguin
Group (Canada), 90 Eglinton Avenue East, Suite 700, Toronto, Ontario, Canada M4P 2Y3
(a division of Pearson Penguin Canada Inc.) • Penguin Books Ltd., 80 Strand, London WC2R 0RL,
England • Penguin Ireland, 25 St. Stephen's Green, Dublin 2, Ireland (a division of Penguin
Books Ltd.) • Penguin Group (Australia), 250 Camberwell Road, Camberwell, Victoria 3124,
Australia (a division of Pearson Australia Group Pty. Ltd.) • Penguin Books India Pvt. Ltd.,
11 Community Centre, Panchsheel Park, New Delhi – 110 017, India • Penguin Group (NZ),
67 Apollo Drive, Rosedale, North Shore 0632, New Zealand (a division of Pearson New Zealand
Ltd.) • Penguin Books (South Africa) (Pty.) Ltd., 24 Sturdee Avenue, Rosebank, Johannesburg
2196, South Africa

Penguin Books Ltd., Registered Offices: 80 Strand, London WC2R 0RL, England

Published by Plume, a member of Penguin Group (USA) Inc. Previously published in a Viking
edition.

First Plume Printing, July 2009
10  9  8  7  6  5  4  3  2  1

3 9082 11307 5785

 REGISTERED TRADEMARK—MARCA REGISTRADA

The Library of Congress has catalogued the Viking edition as follows:
Kane, Michael.
Game boys : professional videogaming's rise from the basement to the big time / Michael Kane.
     p.   cm.
ISBN 978-0-670-01896-3 (h.c.)
ISBN 978-0-452-29544-5 (pbk.)
  1. Computer games—Social aspects.   2. Videogamers as businesspeople.   I. Title
GV1469.17.S63K36 2008
794.8—dc22                    2007044545

Printed in the United States of America
Set in Celeste with Steelfish Outline
Original hardcover design by Daniel Lagin

**To Anna,**
*for letting me talk about videogames*
*for the past two years straight*

# Contents

# List of Illustrations

# Introduction:
## FROM BASEMENT TO BIG TIME

IN SEPTEMBER 2005, I WAS ASSIGNED TO WRITE A STORY for the *New York Post* about competitive videogamers. "You may find this hard to believe," my editor, Stephen Lynch, said at the time, "but these guys make, like, forty grand a year playing videogames. It's hard-core."

I was to preview a gaming tournament at the Hammerstein Ballroom, a three-thousand-seat venue in Manhattan usually reserved for rock concerts. But on that particular weekend, hundreds of gamers would be gathering to compete onstage for $34,000 in prize money.

My story was of the "wacky subculture" variety, and since it would appear in the predictably wisecracking pages of the *Post*, it was assumed I'd be having a bit of fun at the expense of the geekboys manning the joysticks.

"You know," advised my editor, "find out if they do finger exercises to warm up before matches, or whatever."

Being thirty-six years old, I hadn't played videogames since putting away my own Atari in the 1980s, other than the occasional game of Ms. Pac-Man or Galaga at a pizzeria while waiting for a slice. Yet over the years, I had noticed—with slight envy, to be honest—how good today's kids had it, with their incredibly sophisticated games for modern systems like Xbox, PlayStation, and their computers. These new games were *a lot* more realistic. For example, these days when you strike out a baseball player like Derek Jeter in a videogame, he actually grimaces in disappointment. The players in today's football videogames spike the ball after touchdowns. And if you play the games in "season mode," some of your players will actually get hurt.

Back in the good ole Atari days, we had it rough—not like today's pampered kids. We shot a square basketball at a hoop that resembled a lowercase letter *t*. But we were happy to have that, damn it. Until, of course, Intellivision came out and it looked cooler. Then we all wanted that. Then came ColecoVision. Then Nintendo, and on and on.

In the twenty-five years since the earliest Atari and arcade games hit the market, the games have evolved exponentially beyond anything we imagined back in the early 1980s. Today, psychologically absorbing games like The Sims or Grand Theft Auto can make half a day fly by. In their remarkable realism and vast detail, they are fully immersive worlds unto themselves.

As of 2005, approximately 108 million Americans played videogames recreationally. More significantly, the average age of a U.S. gamer was nearly thirty, with twelve years of gaming experience. Nobody quits at sixteen anymore when they get their driver's license and start chasing after girls.

That year, Americans brought home more than $10 billion worth of videogame systems and software, a figure that's been well documented as having eclipsed the money spent at the domestic movie box office.

PriceWaterhouseCoopers estimated that the global videogame market grew to $32 billion in 2006 and predicts it will reach $49 billion by 2011, easily surpassing the recorded-music industry.

In September 2007, the game Halo 3 was released with a record 4.2 million units on store shelves and in its first twenty-four hours set an entertainment industry record with $170 million in sales.

Clearly, videogames aren't just for kids anymore. As the games' visual quality and intellectually stimulating content leapt forward so dramatically in the late nineties and beyond, many from the Atari generation returned to gaming—no doubt plenty of them needled into buying new systems and software by their kids. By the millennium, the industry had boomed. It was common to see lines around the block at Toys "R" Us for the release of megahit titles like the Madden NFL series and Halo. A number of hugely popular games even became movies, like *Tomb Raider, Doom*, and *Resident Evil.*

But regardless of the popularity, who would've believed that the industry would spawn an entire competitive circuit of professional gamers making up to $40,000 a year? Who started paying these guys to play videogames? When did "gamer" become a profession?

Much of what I discovered in my research, for the *Post* article and later for this book, came as a surprise. Most everything I had assumed about gaming was proven false—and very much outdated. (For starters, some of those gamer *guys* were actually girls.)

Gamers weren't pubescent, pimply-faced teenagers. At the elite level, typically they were young men in their early twenties, out of high school and devoting their days and nights almost entirely to gaming. The very best actually pulled salaries and were flown around the world—at the expense of their corporate sponsors—to take the stage and compete at massive, international "e-sports" competitions. In that sense, they were more like pro surfers and skateboarders, traveling the world on someone else's dime and doing what they love.

Well, maybe gamers are not as cool as surfers. But the elite players, at least in their own competitive subculture, are considered every bit as talented and are equally as worshipped.

The e-sports industry bills today's pro gamers as the "cyberathletes" of the future, the stars of the twenty-first century. The first time I heard that term, "cyberathlete," it sounded like a huge stretch—the supposition that these guys were athletes by virtue of precise hand-eye coordination, tireless dedication, and the pressure of competing onstage at gaming tournaments with prize money on the line.

Before attending a gaming event, I'd envisioned something goofy, like two kids sitting in a boxing ring, playing a boxing videogame head-to-head. What I found was something entirely different. In spending time in this world and getting to know the competitors, what I saw turned my cynicism into appreciation. It turned my assumption that I'd be playing this scene for laughs into a desire to convey admiration. In gaming, I found a microcosm of all that's good—and most of what's bad—about modern sports.

I discovered camaraderie and infighting, high-fives and finger pointing, free-agent signings and contract squabbles, cocky all-star players and irrepressible underdogs. I found egos, obsession with statistics, game plans gone awry, shameless cheating and the widespread use of performance-enhancing drugs. In short, I found a world that bizarrely resembled traditional pro sports in almost every way, and least of all because the players possessed exceptional hand-eye coordination.

I also discovered what's true—and just as often false—about the way underground sports are packaged in modern culture, the uneasy balance between substance and style. I found a community desperately clinging to the hope that gaming will become the next Texas hold 'em poker, breaking through to TV and making household names of its biggest stars. And I gained respect for the struggle of the pioneers attempting to lead the first wave of the "next big thing" in entertainment.

But before all that, I found myself at an e-sports tournament, standing behind some kids and looking over their shoulders as they played a PC game called Counter-Strike. The most popular title at gaming tournaments, Counter-Strike is a type of combat-simulation game known as a first-person shooter. Players view the action from the point of view of a participant in a gun battle. In other words, the gamer sees a virtual world through the eyes of the character he controls, right down to looking down and seeing the gun in his hands.

Counter-Strike is the most popular action computer game in the world, with a following of 2.5 million players worldwide. At any given time, day or night, at least 85,000 people are playing Counter-Strike over the Internet. Remember playing army as a kid in the woods behind your backyard, losing all sense of time until you had to come in and wash up for dinner? That's the feeling of a first-person shooter like Counter-Strike. Make-believe is a lot of fun, and very addictive, when it looks real.

What makes Counter-Strike unique is that it's a team game, a shoot-'em-up with two commando squads waging war in a shadowy underworld of mazes and tunnels. It's organized, five on five. To someone from the Space Invaders era, the very concept of a team videogame initially seemed completely foreign and, frankly, absurd.

I thought of ten guys playing an NBA basketball videogame, going five on five. After a dunk inside the game, would they turn and high-five their teammates in real life? Would they pull their chairs together during time-outs and draw up plays on an actual chalkboard? Would one guy sulk because he wasn't getting enough shots? Gaming was so individual and self-contained, the very idea of a team videogame just seemed impossible to take seriously. And yet, as I would soon discover, thousands did. Not just as players, but as entrepreneurs seeking to capitalize on gaming's popularity and turn it into, of all things, a spectator sport. Sound ridiculous, the idea of e-sports as mainstream entertainment? Well, in 1891, when Dr. James Naismith first nailed a peach basket to a gymnasium wall, the same surely would've been said of basketball.

When I was around twenty years old, the same age as today's "cyberathletes," my friends and I never played videogames. We played Frisbee golf every day, rain or shine, at a cemetery down the street from my apartment.

The course was well known to students at the University of Colorado. It was a mapped-out eighteen holes, each represented by a particular grave marking. The first hole was the tombstone marked with the name of the deceased, Murray. If you bounced your Frisbee off the grave in two shots, you'd make par. The second hole was Depalmer. The third hole, Healy, was a lengthy par-three around an oak tree.

I must have played that course two hundred times, my best score a 13-under. Usually, though, I'd mess up a perfectly good round by glancing one off a tree and into the street, out of bounds. On the way home, we'd pass other groups of golfers headed to the cemetery for a round of their own. "How'd you shoot?" they'd holler over.

"Shitty," I'd yell back, furious at myself. "I went off the tree on Healy and then put it in the water on Jensen. Totally screwed up the round."

Then for an hour afterward, I'd sit on my front porch and stew about it.

The point? Sports can be idiotic, or at least it's idiotic to let a double-bogey on a make-believe golf course in a cemetery ruin your afternoon. But is it *that* much more idiotic than NHL players fighting on the ice, or Duke basketball players crying in joy after a stunning victory, or spectators agonizing over a Buffalo Bills loss or watching Olympic table tennis on TV or rooting for a particular dogsled in the Iditarod?

It's not the game itself that's important. It's the fact that people are invested emotionally in it, players and fans alike. That goes for the games we know and love, like football, soccer, and golf, as well as the ones considered niche, like badminton, rhythmic gymnastics, or all the X Games extreme sports. It's simply more fun to care.

In late 2005, as I walked into my first professional videogame competition, I wondered, with skepticism, is "e-sports" really the next evolution of sport? Are "cyberathletes" the athletes of the future? Quickly, I realized it hardly mattered. What proved more important—and more entertaining—was that they think they are.

# GAME BOYS

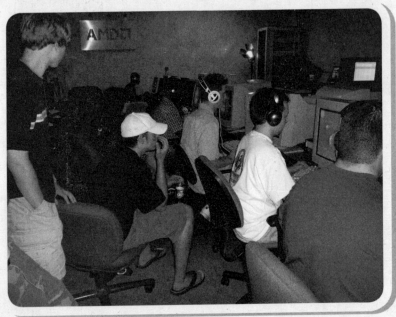

# PART I

## Cellar Dwellers

# Chapter 1

*LICK-CLICK-CLICK.*

*Go ahead, kid. Keep pressing that call button. Your elevator's not getting here any faster. It doesn't matter how many times you rapid fire that glowing arrow. You're stuck, dead to rights, pinned down here at the end of this long stretch of hallway. It's just you, a fake potted floor plant, and an elevator that can't get here soon enough.*

*Feeling kinda antsy, aren't you, kid? Like someone's got a bead on you, got you in the cross-hairs. Next you'll be dazed and defenseless after a flash grenade comes bouncing down the hall and pops under your feet. Bang! The world turns a blinding bright white and that awful, high-pitched wheeeeeee fills your ears.*

*Then comes the burst-fire spray of bullets from an AK-47 assault rifle that pulverizes the plaster walls around you in a chalky shit storm of destruction. Dust swirls and jagged hunks of ceiling panel rain down on your head. The tall, thin window behind you spiders and shatters into fragments, and the fake plastic floor plant at your feet is riddled into a thousand little fake plastic pieces. The tacky turquoise carpet turns squishy like a wet sponge as a widening circle of crimson soaks the floor.*

*It's coming, and you're stuck here, trapped at the dead end of a long indefensible hallway. There's no way out. No way back. No way in hell.*

*Go ahead. Try that button again, kid.*

*Click-click-click-click.*

The gamer steps out of the elevator and makes his way toward the lobby. He looks Scandinavian, or German maybe, all blond hair and blue eyes, like the kind of guy who knows how to put topspin on a crosscourt backhand.

He's about twenty years old, give or take. He wears yellow sneakers with two green slashes. It's an indistinct marking, something Euro. Not Nike or Adidas. Over his dark blue jeans hangs a white hooded sweatshirt covered in words you won't find in any dictionary: BenQ, Gibabyt, Levicom. Those are companies that sponsor his videogaming team, Mousesports, providing them with free keyboards and graphics cards and mousepads. To an outsider, those words may not mean much, but slapped together on a sweatshirt so plastered with sponsorship logos it reminds you of a NASCAR racer's jumpsuit, the meaning is clear: The kid wearing this sweatshirt is a gamer. A good one. And he gets paid to play.

His gelled-up haircut is typical vid-kid style. It's short in the back but hangs extra long in the front. It's halfway between New Wave rocker and Japanese anime. There's no hair over his eyes. That would interfere with seeing the computer screen. Gamer hair is spiked out in every direction. Macabre perhaps, but you might call it "head-shot hair," as if a whizzing bullet from a sniper's rifle plunged into the back of the head and exploded out the front.

Tucked under his right arm are the weapons of his trade: a top-of-the-line laser computer mouse, a headset with earphones and built-in microphone, and a specially designed gaming keyboard all wrapped up together inside a floppy, oversized mousepad.

Although physically unimposing at no more than five-foot-eight, there's a confidence about the gamer kid. It's the self-assurance of a young man who's already figured out what he's good at. And on this particular weekend, in this particular Dallas hotel, there's more than assurance in his step. There's ego.

For these four days in December 2005, the Hyatt Regency is hosting the winter championships of the Cyberathlete Professional League (CPL), the pioneering "e-sports" venture that since its inception in 1997 has drawn kids from around the world to compete for thousands of dollars in prize money playing videogames.

The Hyatt is a futuristic hotel located on the edge of Dallas. It's the lone prominent structure just over the edge of the sprawling north Texas metropolis, on the wrong side of the tracks. That's not a metaphor. It literally is on the wrong side of the tracks, at least for any reasonable pedestrian access. Aside from a largely unmarked underpass, the Regency is cut off from the busy Main Street commercial district by a Union Pacific rail line that carves out an unofficial southwestern boundary of the city.

Fifty yards to the east of the Hyatt, metal railroad cars bearing the words Cosco, Hapag-Lloyd, and Pacer Stacktrain rumble northward and south. Alongside those brawny cargo trains, sleeker Dallas Area Rapid Transit (DART) commuter trains stop and go, in theory letting off and taking on passengers at the Union Station stop. It seems, though, that nobody but the occasional Hyatt guest has much reason to get out here.

Past the tracks to the east, the rest of Dallas is happening. Cars, cranes, buses, skyscrapers. There's a whole city bustling out there, but from the isolation of the Hyatt, you can't hear it. You can't feel it. It's a muted cityscape vague on details, a bit like the half-drawn background of a videogame.

Designed in 1978, the Hyatt Regency has a façade almost entirely of sun-reflecting glass. It doesn't have a roof so much as it has tiers. At the top, it's flat and uneven, like an unbalanced Aztec pyramid or a bar graph indicating an upward trend.

The finishing touch on this monument to seventies sensibilities is, fittingly, a giant disco ball. At the southern end of the hotel, the fifty-five-story Reunion Tower rises to a massive sphere of sparkly lights, inside which a restaurant offers 360-degree panoramas.

The hotel has a pseudo-futuristic feel in the same way that a monorail train or electric toothbrush feels pseudo-futuristic. It's all part of that sparkling clean, no-graffiti future we all imagined before *Blade Runner*.

In 1978, when the Hyatt was built, it was easy to get carried away with dreams of twenty-first-century living. Technology was leaping forward, and in ways that average consumers could wrap their hands around. There were early personal computers like the Apple II and Commodore PET, with its chunky orange keys and built-in cassette deck. There were the first Sony Walkmans and electronic calculators and Mattel handheld football games with a little glowing hyphen starting at tailback. Those primitive entertainment devices were big and clunky and the buttons stuck, but they were more fun than flashlights and walkie-talkies. The future was coming, one gizmo at a time.

Thirty years ago looking forward, the builders of the Hyatt Regency in Dallas probably envisioned a wondrous era beyond the year 2000, when their hotel of the future would be filled with earthlings of all continents milling around the lobby in strange clothing and haircuts and speaking a techno-vernacular into tiny handheld communications units.

So, basically, they were right on the money.

In December 2005, an electric sign on the wall of the Hyatt Regency reads: WELCOME CPL WINTER CHAMPIONSHIPS. Who knew gizmos would come so far?

The Euro gamer kid is headed for Marsalis Hall in the underground level of the hotel, where the CPL Winter tournament is already under way. With gear in hand, he strides purposefully through the halls, which in their own labyrinthine repetition feel something like the claustrophobic hallways of a videogame.

Every corner he turns, there are more hotel doorways to the left and right and more of that tacky teal carpet with its interlocking rune design stretched out ahead. And as in a videogame, every now and again there's a random item to break the visual repetition, a *Dallas Morning News* on the floor or a housekeeping cart parked outside an open door. In the bullet-riddled world of first-person-shooter games, that housekeeping cart, with its stacks of clean white towels, would make fine cover in a firefight—although, the pink and blue bottles of all-purpose cleaning solution hanging off its handle would make a soapy goddamn mess after a strafing from AK-47 fire.

The gamer kid emerges from the hallways and walks quickly through the Hyatt's high-ceilinged lobby. He passes an artificial Christmas tree and a wide-screen TV displaying a weather forecast. It's chillier than usual for north Texas in December, perhaps even dipping into the thirties overnight. But the Euro gamer couldn't care less. He'll barely step outside the hotel over the next three days. He's here on business.

The gamer takes an escalator down to the subterranean level of the hotel and steps over to double wooden doors labeled MARSALIS HALL. He reaches out for the shiny brass handle. It's go time.

Entering a professional videogame tournament is like walking into a good night at a bad casino, a big Saturday at one of those rundown Vegas joints halfway between the Strip and the airport. The place is ramshackle, tattered and cheap, with barely enough requisite whistles and bells. Once you're inside, there's no way to know if it's day or night. Yet somehow there's a buzz in the place, an electricity. For every one of the losers in here, someone is winning, too.

Instead of rows of video poker and slot machines spitting coins into metal baskets, CPL Winter has tables topped with computer monitors, keyboards, and mousepads. And pulled up to the tables on folding metal chairs are hundreds of hard-core gamers, man-boys mostly, between the ages of about eighteen and twenty-two hammering away on their keyboards and jabbing away furiously with computer mice.

"I got a head-shot!" one hollers.

"He's on the arch! He's on the arch! I've got him!"

"Yeah, baby. That's what I'm talking about."

About a third of the competitors in this madhouse aren't even shouting in English. Competitive gaming is very much global. Because of a greater fascination with tech culture there, it's far bigger in Asia and Europe, throughout Scandinavia especially, than it is in the United States. So at a major international gaming event like this one, for every rousing cry of "Come on!" from an American player, there's a Swedish scream of *"Comiendo!"* or a German howl of *"Gehen Sie!"*

The CPL Winter Championships are held in a double-wide basement conference room about eighty yards across and half that deep. It's dark and windowless in here, and the principal light source is the collective illumination from the computer monitors themselves. Gamers like it dark, so they can focus better on their screens.

Upon entering, the first thing you encounter is a shantytown of promotional booths where corporate sponsors push the latest games and accessories on all the teenagers passing in and out of the convention hall. The two most prominent booths are reserved for the two companies who've poured the most money into pro gaming to date, the microchip giant Intel and the graphics-card maker NVIDIA. They're underwriting this CPL Winter, so they get the choice spots by the door and the steady pedestrian traffic.

Behind them there's a booth pushing the Razer Copperhead precision laser mouse, sleekly contoured to fit the hand and with extra buttons. Apparently an ordinary ball mouse, like the kind you'd find at the office, would be as useful here as a smoothbore Civil War musket in modern warfare. Even the mousepads here are cutting edge. One, called SteelSeries, features a smooth-glide "IceMat" surface.

Wandering around the sponsor tables are "booth babes" in teensy skirts, trying to lure passersby with free samples of Jolt energy gum. Caffeinated gum is better for gamers than coffee or energy drinks because with gum, there's no need to take a hand off the mouse and reach for a can. Plus there's nothing to spill and no need for a bathroom break.

Past the sponsor village, Marsalis Hall is divided in half by a partition wall. On the near side is the competition area, a chaotic expanse of tables where the multilingual battle cries hover in the air like gun smoke. Across the partition is the pitch-black BYOC area. That's BYOC as in "bring your own computer."

A major gaming event like CPL Winter always consists of two separate attractions. There's the tournament for competitors, and there's the BYOC for the masses. The BYOC is the cyber-Woodstock, the commune, the meeting place for a global gaming subculture that otherwise exists anonymously on the Internet.

This is the gathering. This is where, for an entry fee of $75, anyone can drop by and plug in their laptop or PC for the weekend and play games around the clock on a lightning-quick server without Internet delays. The BYOC at the Hyatt looks like a giant sleepover. Backpacks and pillows are strewn about, and empty pizza boxes and plastic soda bottles pile up underneath the tables.

The BYOC and tournament together are what's known as a LAN party, with LAN being an acronym for "local area network." Acronyms are big in gaming. It's not the Cyberathlete Professional League, it's the CPL. With the acronym LAN, though, the letters aren't enunciated. It's not L-A-N, like C-P-L or B-Y-O-C. It's pronounced "lan," like "man." Year round, gaming lives and breathes with online play. Any time of day or night, if you want a game, all it takes is an Internet connection, preferably one that's high-speed. But the hard-core gaming action is at these LAN parties.

In gaming, there's a huge difference between winning online and winning at a LAN. In online play, there are too many variables to distort the action.

First, everyone has a different quality computer at home, which affects results. Second, there are discrepancies in "ping," or lag time, between a player executing an action—like pulling the trigger—and that information bouncing over the Internet to a game server and bouncing back updated. But most important, there's cheating. At home, it's easy to use one of the common cheat downloads like "Speed Hack" for extra foot speed, "Aimbot" to lock your shot on target, or "ESP" to let you see through walls.

Because of these discrepancies, no gamer gets any real respect until they perform at a LAN, especially a major one like CPL with the added pressure of big cash on the line. Until then, they're not "LAN-proven."

CPL is the ultimate in LANs. Since its early days in 1997, the CPL has hosted two major tournaments a year, CPL Winter and CPL Summer. For the gaming elite, these are the two LANs that truly matter.

In the BYOC at this CPL Winter, there are two distinct camps. There's the "death match" crowd, revolving around first-person-shooter games, and there's the MMORPG crowd, which stands for Massive Multiplayer Online Role-Playing Games.

The MMORPG scene revolves around World of Warcraft, a Tolkienesque fantasy world of gnomes, trolls, and orcs. It's the modern incarnation of the fantasy realm of Dungeons & Dragons. In Warcraft, you gather spells, accrue weapons, and embark on quests to explore Silverpine Forest or liberate the druids of Kalmidor.

With an MMORPG game like World of Warcraft, you don't win, and you don't lose. You just keep playing, which is why the game is considered obsessive. It never ends. The Warcraft gamers at CPL will play in the BYOC for three days straight without truly resolving a damn thing.

The other half of gaming's societal delineation is the first-person-shooter crowd, which plays games like Doom, Quake, and Halo 2, and the most popular action computer game in the world today: Counter-Strike.

Counter-Strike is played five-on-five. It's a team game, and it's tribal. The driving force behind major LAN events like CPL Winter, it's at the frontier of competitive gaming.

Sixty-four Counter-Strike teams, called "clans," are here at the Hyatt, battling for a piece of the $60,000 in prize money. The team that wins the tournament will earn $18,000. Split among the five guys on a clan, that's more than $3,500 a player. Not a bad weekend of work.

Each of the sixty-four clans here at CPL have put down stakes somewhere in the sprawling BYOC. Each has taken over a row of chairs and set up a base camp, but right now those chairs are empty. The tribes are gathered across the partition at the tournament tables. The battle has begun.

# Chapter 2

I'S HIGH NOON AT CPL WINTER. THE COUNTER-STRIKE quarterfinals are under way.

In the tournament area, ten of fourteen long cafeteria tables sit empty. Sixty-four teams entered this competition yesterday, filling the tables and eliminating one another from the brackets. Now only eight unbeatens remain. Over the next hour, four more will be sent packing.

Along both sides of the tables are five metal chairs, and in front of each chair is a corresponding computer monitor. The CPU towers are tucked away under the tables and hidden by black cloth bunting. The five-man teams face off across the tables, all working their keyboards and mice and hollering like pinned-down Marines.

"They're coming in! Flash that fucker!"

"Two in Ramp Room. There's two. Shit!"

"They're splitting! Cover flank!"

Amid the chaos is the German team Mousesports, with their spiky hairdos and sponsor-splattered white jerseys. The Mousesports gamers cast unblinking glares into their screens. They are all business, an efficient, precise machine. Totally German.

At the next table there's Lunatic-Hai, a clan of South Korean pretty-boy hipsters dressed in gray and gold patterned jerseys with their own gelled-up haircuts. Between matches, the Lunatic-Hai guys mug and posture for Korean TV crews like teenage pop stars, which is how they're treated in gaming-crazy Seoul.

Other clans in contention include Evil Geniuses from Canada, a Swedish squad called Begrip, and a couple of U.S. teams, JaX Money Crew and CompLexity.

But the showdown match that everyone's here to see is between the last two teams to dominate the globe: former world champions SK Gaming from Sweden and the current number one, Team 3D from the United States.

Team 3D (short for "Desire, Discipline, Dedication") is fresh off a win two months ago at the World Cyber Games in Singapore. They're the top-ranked clan on the planet. In a Counter-Strike world of stealth assassins lurking around every corner, Team 3D are the ones in the crosshairs.

A crowd of about thirty rubberneckers are hovering behind Team 3D's table, crowding in behind the players' chairs to get a peek at what's happening on their monitors. Being the top Counter-Strike clan in the world means you're in the spotlight. And at CPL Winter, being the global powerhouse Team 3D means your many admirers are lurking and crowding and watching your every move.

One of 3D's players turns around from his computer with a look of irritation. This is crunch time, with $18,000 on the line. It's not the time to put on a show for a bunch of starstruck fanboys.

"Not to be a dick, but could you guys back up?" says Ronald Kim, sternly. "We're trying to win a tournament here."

Ronald Kim is Team 3D's leader. But here, in this world, he's not Ronald. He's Rambo. In gaming, aliases are an identity and a mystique. What began in the arcade days with three-letter tags for high scores like RAY or JIM has evolved to modern blood-soaked gaming aliases like DestruKshun or Lawenforcer, or Rambo.

So while Ronald Kim is a brainy, twenty-one-year-old Korean American kid who still lives at home and lugs trash out to the curb for his mom, Rambo is a commando who can take your ass out with a sniper rifle from two hundred yards through the sliver of a gap between two railroad cars.

Rambo is Team 3D's leader, their quarterback. He sits in the middle of five players, all wearing the black team jersey bearing the logos of their many sponsors. The five 3D players are all pitched forward, anchored in with feet wrapped around chair legs, all with unblinking eyes scanning their monitors for enemy.

"Okay, let's go Warsong," Rambo barks into his headset, using a code name for the play, "and take Ramp Room slow!"

Rambo calls the strats for 3D. Strats, short for strategies, are like plays you'd draw up in a backyard game of football. With five players on a team, Counter-Strike attacks are coordinated. One strat may be to send three players attacking left and the other two to the right. Another might be to send all five in a bull rush up the middle.

Onscreen Rambo and his teammates sneak around with weapons drawn through a maze of half-lit hallways. Some players peek forward, scouting for the enemy, while others hang back and crouch behind stacks of crates for cover.

"Two in Lower," says the team's sniper, Kyle "Ksharp" Miller, into his headset. He's scoped out two opponents hiding across a courtyard.

"Okay," Rambo tells the team. "Flash and smoke and go. Now!"

Team 3D charges with grenades flying and guns blazing.

With their left hands, these guys work the keyboard faster than any accountant punching a ten-key in the second week of April. In Counter-Strike, each of a dozen keys initiates a different action onscreen. Pressing the *W* key moves you forward. *S* is to backpedal. The *R* key is reload. It's the *Ctrl* key to duck, and if you're in an opponent's crosshairs, you'd better be hasty about it.

Meanwhile, the mouse hand is for aiming and firing a weapon. And if a player is holding an M4 Colt assault rifle, for example, a left-click can unload an entire clip of thirty rounds in four seconds flat.

A Counter-Strike game is contained mayhem. There's machine-gun burst fire and exploding flash grenades that turn screens a blinding white. Players climb ladders, jump off ledges, and boost each other up onto crates. But mostly they "frag." To frag is to kill.

"Shit," says Josh "Dominator" Sievers of Team 3D. "There's another one in Pit."

"I've got him," says Rambo, calmly. "I'm rotating around to flash."

There's a war going on inside those video screens, and the first time you stand around as a spectator, you feel about as lost as a Martian who landed outside a farmhouse, wandered inside and attempted to watch *Monday Night Football* on the TV set.

What's happening onscreen is somewhat baffling. One guy shooting another guy is self-explanatory. But beyond that, these Counter-Strike fraggers are circling the map, buying weapons, laying down smoke screens, shouting about "Ramp Room" and "rotate to B" and "another one in Pit." Trying to take it all in is about as flabbergasting as an NFL football newcomer attempting to sort out "second and six" and "weak-side linebackers" and "three-four blitz packages."

So at first glance, watching a Counter-Strike match is not all that interesting. But gradually, the connection emerges between what's happening onscreen and the players sitting at the tables. For a first-time onlooker, it's not what's going on inside the monitors that's immediately absorbing—that's just a videogame, even if it is a cool one with blood and guts and smoke grenades. What's more compelling is the synchronization of the teammates and the hours of practice that obviously went into planning and perfecting their attack strategies.

This is not about getting high scores on Missile Command or low times on a Grand Prix racing game. Each of these players has a job, an assignment in the game. Counter-Strike is five teammates inhabiting an alternate world, bringing not just their skills, but more bizarrely, their own personalities to another guise. Some lead, others follow. Some call out for help, others rush over to watch their backs. There's an interpersonal dynamic here, bridging the real world and what's going on in the monitors. Players win each other's respect and let each other down, inside the game.

And just as it does in real combat, or in real sports, you've got to wonder if those in-game heroics and failures affect relationships outside of the game as well.

Thankfully for a newcomer, despite the mysteries of watching a match for the first time, the basics of Counter-Strike are fairly simple.

Each match is played on a particular "map," which is more of a maze than a battlefield, per se. Nobody's crossing a river or charging a hill. There are no tanks to commandeer or helicopters to fly. There are no extraneous civilians getting caught in a crossfire. It's a simplified urban-combat scenario in a desolate and abandoned setting, something not dissimilar to a computerized game of Capture the Flag.

A match is played in rounds lasting up to one minute, forty-five seconds each. Winning a round gets you one point. That's it. No gimmicky bonus scoring. The first team to win sixteen rounds wins the match—unless it goes into overtime, where you must win by two.

Each round begins with both teams at full strength, five on five, and ends one of three ways. Most commonly, a team wins a round after fragging all five guys on the other side. That's self-evident. More rare, but still a big part of the game, is the bomb objective. The team on offense wins a round by planting and detonating a bomb in one of two places defended by the other team, Bomb Site A or Bomb Site B. If a bomb is not detonated, defense wins the round. In every match to sixteen, each team plays both offense, known as Terrorist (or "T"), and defense, known as Counter-Terrorist ("CT").

A typical round of Counter-Strike goes like this: The Terrorists attack with a strat designed to blow up a bomb site. The defensive team reacts. All hell breaks loose, bullets fly, bodies drop one at a time and whoever's left standing wins the round.

In today's quarterfinal showdown, Team 3D, starting the first half on T-side and attacking the bomb sites, has jumped ahead of SK Gaming 6–0. Rambo is leaning forward, his face just a foot away from the monitor. Through big-rimmed glasses, his eyes are constantly darting, gathering information, watching as his team's tactics unfold.

Between rounds, there's a fifteen-second break. As his teammates crack their knuckles or blow warm air into their hands, Rambo decides on a strat for the next round. He looks down at his mousepad and picks away minuscule specks of lint and dust, in deep concentration. It calls to mind a backyard quarterback, ripping up blades of grass in the huddle while brainstorming the next play.

Once decided, Rambo calls out the strat through his headset. "War-song two-one-two" comes the command, or maybe "Bumble Bee" or "Crush." Then Rambo throws in something like "C'mon, guys, hit it hard from both sides" for good measure, and again, Team 3D charges into the fray.

Standing there among these pretend commandos, looking over their shoulders as they wage virtual war, one of the most commonly held misconceptions about gamers—that they are mentally tuned out and antisocial—is quickly debunked. This is the furthest thing from antisocial. Not only are these players strategizing and operating together as a fighting unit, but there is also a community that watches them play and discusses their various strats. An actual fan base with a rooting interest exists, both here at CPL and spread out worldwide across the Internet.

The fact that three dozen spectators are gathered behind Team 3D is telling. People care about this match, beyond those actually playing in it. They're standing here, straining to get a look at the monitors, glued to the action and dissecting the minutiae of the match in a gamer language all their own.

"If 3D can 9–6 or even 8–7 this half, it's all over," says one onlooker, sounding every bit like an armchair quarterback. "Nuke is such a CT-sided map. There are only three choke points. If they shut those down, SK is screwed."

A friend rebuts, "No, there's four choke points if you count defensive entry. It's not that hard to take Upper."

"Well, yeah," concedes the first kid. "But it's not like Dust 2. I mean, it's so easy to spam the Rafters and force the action to Ramp. I mean, if you get bad spawns, forget about taking B Site."

Clearly, there was much about this game to learn.

Judging by the team jerseys in the crowd, the one hundred or so spectators scattered around all eight of the teams in the quarterfinals are almost entirely fellow gamers whose clans were eliminated in earlier rounds. It seems nobody comes to a CPL just to watch. This is the interactive Internet generation. Nobody buys a ticket to a LAN event, grabs a seat in the audience, and orders a hot dog. If they're there, they're there to play, either in the tournament or in the BYOC.

But a marquee Counter-Strike match like SK-3D does draw a crowd, both real and virtual. Aside from the fraggers here at Marsalis Hall from clans eliminated earlier, thousands of subelite gamers worldwide are also watching along on the Internet.

As strange as it is to see five nearly grown men compete together in a team videogame like Counter-Strike, the most unexpected sight at CPL is the "shoutcasters"—two sportscasters calling the action on an elevated platform beside the tournament tables. This is TSN, or Team Sportscast Network, which streams Counter-Strike matches live over the Internet, complete with play-by-play.

These are the wannabe John Madden and Al Michaels of e-sports, the guys in the booth. As 3D and SK run and gun, one shoutcaster follows with rapid-fire verbiage: "Here comes Dominator with an M4 on an open approach to Bomb Site A, but *ooooooh*, out of nowhere he's blindsided with a Glock rush from the catwalk. That had to hurt."

"I bet it did, Corey," says his partner. "You've always got to keep an eye out for the backside flash and rotation when you're in Z-Hall. I mean, that's just common sense."

As counterintuitive as it is to think a videogame could ever be a spectator sport, the very existence of this TSN broadcasting crew reveals there already is some demand for it.

Just as in any other competition, "e-sport" or otherwise, gamers are willing to stop playing for an hour or two to watch more talented players compete. Odd as it sounds, Counter-Strike is *already* a specialized spectator sport, one whose reach extends through cyberspace far beyond the walls of this hotel. Someone out there is watching. Who knows how many hundreds of thousands around the world?

Being a Counter-Strike spectator, in fact, has many advantages over following traditional sports simply because of advances in software.

As TSN's shoutcasters call the match, they're not just watching the players' screens. They're maneuvering around inside the game itself, invisible and unnoticed by the competitors. It's an aspect of Counter-Strike, unique in the world of videogames even, that allows the broadcast duo to actually be their own cameramen. The software that enables this omniscient third-person viewing is called HLTV, for Half-Life TV, and was developed by the game's maker, Valve Software, to further serve Counter-Strike's massive fan base.

For its online stream, TSN is not just airing the screen images from a player's perspective. They can invisibly follow a player around the map, then swing around to show his opponent, then pan up to an overhead bird's-eye view of the gunfight. With features like that, what gamer *wouldn't* want to spectate?

HLTV also allows viewers at home to download previously recorded matches—or "demos" in gamer-speak—and choose their own perspective as well. So let's say Rambo has a great match today. By tonight, once it's uploaded, his admirers can follow Rambo's every move on the demo, learn all his tricks, and—best of all for future opponents—even scout out where his favorite hiding spots are.

The enormously user-friendly HLTV is enough to make you *want* to love the game in the same way that sports fans love basketball or hockey. Imagine watching an NBA or NHL game from the court or the ice itself while maneuvering around the players like a phantom. That's the total sensory immersion that Counter-Strike fans enjoy, and the fact that such an infrastructure exists reveals the depths of devotion toward the game.

The crowds gathered behind the tournament tables aren't waiting for a demo. They're watching the matches live, getting a similar experience by keeping an eye on all five of a team's monitors.

At the SK-3D showdown, the American team has finished the first half ahead of the Swedes 10–5. Now they'll switch sides, with SK going on offense, or T-side, and 3D switching to CT and playing defense.

As they refit their headphones and pull their chairs back up close to the table for the second half, 3D needs only six rounds to reach sixteen and win the match. Rambo tells his mates, "Come on, they're playing scared. Let's do it. Let's close this out."

At the next table, SK isn't giving up, encouraging each other with fist pumps and shouts of *"Comiendo!"*

It's then that another voice comes from the far end of the tournament. Above the multilingual clamor of rallying cries and gamer chatter, this voice is utterly misplaced yet strangely familiar. It's not some twenty-year-old warning a teammate about a lurking sniper. It isn't a shoutcaster calling the action. It is something else altogether.

It's a voice that belongs on a muddy ball field on a drizzly afternoon or echoing off the walls of a high-school gymnasium.

It is the voice of a coach.

"Okay, boys. Let's light the fires and kick the tires! It's time to go to work now."

Beyond where Team 3D and SK and Lunatic-Hai and the other teams sit, at the very last table in the tournament area, pacing back and forth behind a row of kids is exactly that—a *videogame coach*.

"Yeah! Yeah! Nice, Tyler. Nice!" shouts the coach as he whacks the back of one of his players' chairs with an open palm. "Good communication, guys."

This guy can't be for real. Pacing behind five players in maroon jerseys, he looks like a manic varsity basketball coach in the final two minutes of a state-championship game, or maybe Bobby Knight right before he threw a chair on the court at Indiana.

"That's the way to play, Danny!" he bellows to another of his kids. "Intensity. Intensity. Let's get it done."

The videogame coach is unlike anyone else at the tournament. He's in his mid-thirties, while aside from a few CPL organizers and marketing reps, no one else here is much older than twenty-one or twenty-two. He's dressed in a white shirt and red tie, with black pants and shiny dress shoes. He's a big guy, an ex-jock from the looks of it, about six-foot-two and 260 pounds.

"That's Jason Lake," says one of the spectators behind the 3D table. "He manages team CompLexity."

Lake stands behind one of his players' chairs. He puts his hands on his hips and quickly scans left and right, eyeing all five of his players' screens. First one, then another, back to the first. Always analyzing. Left, then right. Then left again quickly. Then a furrowed brow, a wince, a look of anguish, and again he begins to pace.

Apparently his team, CompLexity, just dropped the round.

"Put it behind you. Come on, now," Lake says, as his kids get ready to go again. Lake kicks a hind leg on one of his players' metal chairs after CompLexity drops another round. "No more," he shouts, red in the face. "This ends right now!"

Other than Lake, there's nobody else at CPL whose behavior comes close to that of a coach, although many of the top clans do have managers, whose duties include things like soliciting sponsorships, covering salaries and travel expenses, arranging transportation to the airport, and setting up media interviews. The seven other elite teams still vying for the CPL title all have managers, but they "manage" in the sense of managing a rock band, not managing a ball club, like Lake.

Alex Garfield is manager of the Canadian clan Evil Geniuses. He fits the gamer mold of brainy slacker. A college junior, Garfield wears a tan ski cap, T-shirt, and tattered jeans with a messenger bag slung over his shoulder. He stands with the other onlookers behind his team and offers a few claps or some occasional verbal encouragement. "Good round, guys," he says now and again.

SK Gaming from Sweden is a top European team with multiple sponsors. Their manager, Andreas Thorstensson, has an air of professionalism. He's a bit older than his players, pushing thirty perhaps, but even he's unshaven and wearing a hooded sweatshirt.

And mixed in among the throng behind Team 3D is their manager, Craig Levine. He looks to be in his thirties, judging by a receded hairline. He's tall, about six-foot-three, but otherwise utterly inconspicuous, wearing a black sweatshirt, faded jeans, and well-worn gray running shoes. No collared shirt. No tie. Levine isn't even wearing anything that says Team 3D..

His clan is locked in battle against SK Gaming for a shot in the semifinals, but Levine doesn't even seem particularly engrossed in the match. Team 3D is one of very few teams with a sixth player on their roster, an alternate, and it's the sub who's standing close behind the chairs and keeping up team spirit.

Levine, meanwhile, stands well back and off to the side and says little besides an occasional "Play smart, guys," without raising his voice.

They're a study in contrasts. Across the room, CompLexity's Jason Lake is pacing and stomping his foot over his team's struggles. "Come on, Danny! Lock it down, Danny! Lock it down!"

And here's Team 3D boss Craig Levine, who looks about as absorbed in the competition as a half-bored spectator standing along a marathon route. Even Levine's occasional "Be smart, guys" comes across as almost obligatory, like a parent at a playground whose thoughts are drifting but who scolds every so often to reestablish authority.

Lake and Levine. Two managers with opposite methods, yet both with elite teams. At the edge of the tournament area, near the shoutcasters, a video screen displays the current Counter-Strike world rankings. Atop the list is number-one-ranked Team 3D, and right below them is CompLexity at number two. Sounds like a rivalry. Ohio State and Michigan. Duke and North Carolina. Yankees and Red Sox. Team 3D and CompLexity.

Right now, though, number-two CompLexity is on the ropes against another U.S. clan called JaX Money Crew, which needs just one more round to win the match and advance to the semis.

CompLexity's players are dropping out one by one. When one falls, Lake steps over to stand behind another's chair. Then another, and another. Finally the coach is at the end of the row, staring desperately over the shoulder of his last remaining player. The four other CompLexity players have pulled their chairs back and are likewise peering down at their sole surviving teammate's monitor.

"Come on, Tyler," Lake says, softly. "Come on, Tyler. You can do this."

After a tense moment, the coach bows his head. The game is over. CompLexity has been eliminated from the tournament.

Lake musters a stoical front and tells his kids, "Go shake their hands. Go shake their hands." Team CompLexity shuffles dejectedly over to where JaX Money Crew is celebrating their 16–11 upset, and like two Little League baseball teams, the squads pass each other and slap hands. "Good game. Good game. Good game, man. Good game."

CompLexity grabs their gear, wrapping up their keyboards, mice, and headsets inside floppy mousepads, then wordlessly head for the door. One by one they exit the room, followed out finally by the crest-fallen Lake, who reaches into his pocket for a pack of smokes.

Back at the other table, Team 3D is locked in its own battle. Tied 15–15 with SK at the end of regulation, their slugfest spilled into triple overtime. SK pushed back ahead 24–21, meaning 3D must now win the next three rounds to force a fourth overtime.

"Staircase your way in," Rambo commands. "I'm cutting across. Don't flash me."

His teammate Dominator makes a mad dash into an open courtyard. Halfway across, he's cut down in a torrent of enemy gunfire. Dominator falls to his knees and pitches forward, dropping to the cobblestones. It's a dying-breath POV. A pair of boots run across in front of his eyes, those belonging to his killer, and then his screen fades to black.

One by one, so do the others. It's lights out for Team 3D.

The SK players all yank off their headphones and leap up in celebration. Rambo pushes his chair away from the 3D table. "That's such bullshit," he says. Dominator slams his mouse onto the table, cracking it into pieces. "Fuck!"

Craig Levine steps forward, emerging from the crowd of onlookers. "Hey," the manager says sharply, restoring order and pointing a disciplinary finger. "This is not the end of the world," he scolds. "This is when you act like professionals."

# Chapter 3

**N**IGHT HAS FALLEN ON CPL WINTER, AND THE SWIRL OF activity has moved upstairs to Monduel's bar on the Hyatt's Atrium Level. Across the lobby, two glass elevators give riders a view of the manmade waterfalls and ponds below. Through the atrium's glass ceiling, the Reunion Tower sparkles.

Jason Lake is due here any minute. An hour earlier he'd been upstairs in his hotel suite, lying back on a couch still fully dressed in shirt and tie, shoes included, with his right arm draped across his face. The suite was otherwise empty, aside from a couple of suitcases and three laptops flipped open on a table and plugged into wall jacks. This was the CompLexity team command center, where Lake posts updates on the clan's Web site. Laid out on the couch, the coach looked in need of a therapist to unburden himself of today's heartbreak.

The hotel is buzzing this Saturday night. Heavily bejeweled Dallas women swathed in fur coats are flittering into the bar for a quick Cosmo before heading downstairs for the Innovage Corporation Christmas banquet. But tonight the Hyatt belongs to the gaming crowd, just as it has once or twice a year since 1997, with the birth of the CPL, when videogame fanatics from around the country started showing up at the hotel to compete for prize money. But whose idea was it to start paying kids who played videogames? And who was signing the checks?

The story begins with Angel Munoz, the founder of the CPL and father of professional cybergaming. Now forty-six, Munoz goes by the gaming alias Prometheus. It's a tag that's as appropriate as it is egotistical. It was Munoz who first brought the underground gaming subculture into the light.

A Dallas stockbroker who grew up in Puerto Rico, the enterprising Munoz walked away from a successful career in investment banking in 1995 and set about founding the first-ever organized and fully sponsored videogaming tournaments. At the time, Dallas was already well known as the capital of the first-person-shooter movement in videogames, ever since pioneering software programmers John Carmack and John Romero established iD Software here in 1991 and began publishing spellbindingly realistic shooters like Wolfenstein 3D, Doom, and Quake. Munoz, like many, was awed by the realism of those early PC shooter games and wasn't in the least bit bothered by their violent, blood-splattered content.

A subculture was forming in Dallas, which at first meant three or four kids lugging their computers to each other's homes and playing Doom head-to-head until the sun came up. By the mid-1990s, Munoz was witnessing firsthand the earliest LAN parties, held in warehouses, storage spaces, or in the backs of electronics stores where techs would link up a network for fifteen or twenty gamers to compete.

Munoz also saw dollar signs, so in 1997 he took the LAN party above ground, launching the Cyberathlete Professional League as the first-ever pro gaming organization with a standardized set of rules. In June 1997, the inaugural CPL Summer event drew roughly three hundred attendees.

There is some dispute about Munoz's claim of hosting the first "organized" LAN event, as about a hundred kids had showed up the previous year at a La Quinta Inn in suburban Garland for an event called QuakeCon, which also exists to this day. But regardless of who came first and which was the first "legitimate" organization, the CPL indisputably provided the foundation for professional gaming.

Munoz, the man who poured the concrete, is equal parts intelligent, odd, and intense. He walks fast, talks fast, and at this CPL event at the Hyatt, he roams the hotel like an uneasy and distrustful monarch. Inside gaming, everyone knows who Angel is, but nobody seems to really know Angel.

Munoz dresses in solids—blacks and silvers mostly—and he complements a completely bald, round head with square glass frames. The aesthetic is intentional. It's always circles and squares with Munoz, and the imagery is echoed in everything he does.

His company's logo is a tight bundle of the three letters C-P-L compressed into a single icon that incorporates the curves of the $C$ and $P$ and the straight edges of the $L$. Even his home, which he designed himself and which sits in a quiet neighborhood off the LBJ Freeway in northern Dallas, reflects the aesthetic. The left side of Munoz's house is curved, the right side angular. Same with the swimming pool in the backyard, a black and silver carpet in the living room, and his kitchen countertops as well.

It's more than a design motif, this disharmony of squares and circles. It's an unintentionally apt symbol of Munoz's decade-long attempt to push professional videogaming into the mainstream. It's been a forced fit, like square pegs and round holes.

Financially, Munoz has done well for himself. In 1997, the CPL began as a tidy little in-the-black business model: charging kids to plug in their computers for a fun weekend of gaming. It has grown to attract six-figure sponsorships from Intel and NVIDIA, companies for whom Munoz now helps push merchandise on the gamers coming through the door.

A small slice of revenues goes back to the winning gamers as prize money, but still, after eight years of profiting off teenagers, you've got to wonder if anyone besides Munoz and perhaps his sponsors has made any real money in the niche industry.

For years, as sales of recreational videogames and systems have surpassed even Hollywood box-office grosses, Munoz has trumpeted his pro gamers in the media as the superstars of the future.

The CPL has gotten a few write-ups in tech magazines like *PC Gamer* and *Wired* and gets occasional ink as a curiosity item in the business section of the *Dallas Morning News*. Meanwhile, his attempts at getting CPL scores onto the agate page of newspaper sports sections have been laughed off.

Hoping to expand the audience for pro gaming, Munoz has pitched the drama of CPL's head-to-head competition to networks like ESPN and MTV, hoping they'd agree to shoot a tournament for broadcast. Thus far, though, he's gotten little but uninterested yawns from TV executives who aren't sold on gaming as the sport of the twenty-first century.

Despite the popularity of TSN's online broadcasts, few spectators show up at CPL events to watch the elite players compete. And unlike the X Games and the World Series of Poker, which are crossover hits on ESPN, or obscure competitions like billiards, cheerleading, aerobics, paintball, and even dominoes on ESPN2—competitive gaming hasn't made the leap onto the airwaves despite Munoz's repeated attempts to reach out to TV networks.

To date, Munoz's "cyberathlete" and "e-sports" concepts have gained little footing with anyone outside his world.

Given the popularity of recreational gaming, it seems only a matter of time before someone cracks the code to putting tournaments on television and taking gaming to the next level.

Some speculate the CPL's inability to expand is due to the reluctance of advertisers and networks to associate themselves with games such as Counter-Strike and Quake that contain violent content. Admittedly, it is a little gory seeing a commando take a sniper bullet in the head, drop to the cobblestones, and leave a pink mist in the air.

It's a little eerie, too, that the epicenter for first-person-shooter competitions is just a quarter-mile from Dealy Plaza, where John F. Kennedy was assassinated in November 1963. In fact, half of the Hyatt's rooms upstairs face eastward with a clear view of the Book Depository, the Grassy Knoll, and the hairpin turn at the corner of Houston and

Elm. The DART trains that run in front of the Hyatt cross the bridge that forms the underpass through which Kennedy's motorcade sped moments after the shooting. Is it macabre that this hotel is where gamers gather to peer through computerized crosshairs and aim for headshots with make-believe sniper rifles?

That's likely reading too much into it. Seeing these clans of kids horsing around in the hallways or hanging out in the lobby and laughing, it's apparent that elite gamers are nothing like their stereotypes, meaning they're not nerds and they're not psychos.

Granted, the Warcraft crowd is a little geeky, what with their alliances of gnomes and dwarves on quests to the dungeons of Blackwing Lair. But the Counter-Strike crowd, at least, is different. There's an aggressiveness, an attitude to the first-person-shooter scene. They talk smack at opponents. They curse in frustration. They slam down their equipment after losses. And nowhere in the Counter-Strike crowd do you find the moody Trenchcoat Mafia types of schoolyard killers of tomorrow. Those brooding loners, feared by critics of the violent content in videogames, sadly may be lurking somewhere out across the Internet, but they're not on the pro circuit.

"Total myth," says one gamer here at Monduel's. "I've been playing Counter-Strike for years, and I haven't heard of one violent incident like that. Maybe if a guy talks shit about you online and then you see him at a LAN, you might get into it. But that's not a videogame thing, or a Columbine thing. That's just twenty-year-olds being twenty-year-olds."

Sitting at the bar and waiting for Jason Lake is a good opportunity to eavesdrop on the scene. A few guys from the gaming Web site Gotfrag.com are here talking shop. Along with the shoutcasts, Gotfrag is the best source of gaming info for the hard-core community. It's the ESPN.com of e-sports, the place for news, scores, stats, and schedules. It's Gotfrag that decides the worldwide team rankings.

The Web site has a large presence at LAN events. Here at CPL, Gotfrag has a staff of eighteen writers and editors posting tournament results, updating stats, and looking for scoops. These are the Woodwards and Bernsteins of gaming, the intrepid e-journos who at the moment are pursuing three salacious rumors at the Hyatt: One, a young Asian girl named Dani, last seen in a pink tank top and glittery sunglasses, is seducing gamers and detailing her sexual exploits on a blog; two, a group of Norwegian gamers are up in the penthouse suite bingeing on cocaine and smoking up "a QP of bad-ass hydro"; and three, an American clan called United 5 was kicked out of the tournament after being implicated in a laptop theft this afternoon in the BYOC.

Who would have thought CPL Winter could be so scandalous?

One of the Counter-Strike team managers, Alex Garfield of Evil Geniuses, is at the bar talking with the Gotfrag reporters about the competitive imbalance of pro gaming. It turns out Counter-Strike is nowhere close to an even playing field, and the reason is financial. There are hundreds of clans in North America, but only two have the resources to pay their players salaries—Craig Levine's Team 3D and Jason Lake's CompLexity.

So here these two managers are again. Not only do they have the highest-ranked teams, but apparently they've also got the deepest pockets.

"It makes it a challenge," says Garfield, "because paying salaries means those two guys grab up all of the best players."

Salaried players make about $1,000 a month plus prize money, and their travel expenses are covered. In addition to the U.S. squads 3D and CompLexity, four European teams are also fully salaried: SK Gaming and Ninjas in Pyjamas from Sweden, Mousesports from Germany, and 4 Kings from England. Players on salaried teams in a good year of gaming can clear $25,000 or $30,000. Not a bad way to make a living doing what many would consider goofing off. But for the hundreds of unsalaried have-not clans, their only real income is tournament prize winnings, which they generally lose to one of the big boys, anyway.

Garfield, a student at Pomona College in California, is a manager because he likes being around the scene. He used to play Counter-Strike but couldn't cut it at the top level. So now he's exploring the business side of the industry, which mostly means trying to solicit sponsorships for his clan. As the top team in Canada, EG gets about a thousand bucks a month from Intel. It helps offset costs like flights to Dallas, but it's nowhere near enough for Garfield to pay his players salaries.

He motions to the far end of the bar, where Team 3D's manager Levine is shooting a game of pool. "If you're looking for the big-money guy in North America, that's Craig," says Garfield.

According to Garfield, Levine's two major sponsorship deals with Intel and NVIDIA bring in over $150,000 a year, compared to the modest $12,000 a year that Garfield is happy to get from Intel. That explains why Levine can field a squad of six elite-caliber players. Even after covering flights and hotels and paying out six annual salaries totaling about $70,000, the 3D boss is still pocketing a nice profit.

Craig Levine hardly looks like the "big-money guy in North America." He's wearing a Gloucester Rugby Club sweatshirt and holding a pool cue. But with Levine, all is not as it appears. For starters, with his thinning hair, he looks at least thirty but is only twenty-one. So, in landing six figures in sponsorships and turning a profit from gaming, Levine impressively is making money off his own peer group.

"Craig runs his team like a business," Garfield says. "He cuts players. He poaches players off other teams. It's easy for him, too. He could grab any player off my team tomorrow. Who's gonna turn down a salary? Craig does anything it takes to win."

Levine is beginning to sound like some kind of George Steinbrenner of Counter-Strike. He's got funding. He's got an all-star team. He's ruthless. After one kid smashed a mouse today after losing, he scolded his team and ordered them to act like professionals. For all his seeming lack of interest during the match, the guy is a cutthroat one-man front office.

"Craig was literally ready to cut his entire team halfway through last season," Garfield adds, explaining that Levine threatened to fire them and sign everyone on CompLexity because they were playing better than 3D at the time. "I mean, what does that say about this business?" he asks.

It says that pro gaming, like any other sport or business or pastime, can get ugly when big dollars are involved. And it also says that Levine is a monopolist operating in a competitive environment without institutional restraint. A funding gap of $150,000 to the $12,000 a year Garfield gets for Team EG? That's not Steinbrenner discrepancy. That's robber-baron territory. No wonder he's got the number-one team in Counter-Strike.

Jason Lake arrives and takes an open seat at the bar. "Grey Goose and grapefruit," he tells the bartender.

The CompLexity coach has straightened up since an hour ago, when he was laid out on a couch upstairs. He's showered and changed into a freshly ironed shirt.

"Yeah," says Lake, shaking his head and stirring his drink. "I was pretty devastated before. This tournament has been a total disaster."

Lake speaks like a chagrined losing coach in a postgame press conference. You can almost see him replaying today's loss in his head, isolating exactly when things spun out of control. When he speaks in disappointment, he begins each sentence with a lamenting "yeah," which with his slight drawl is more like a two-syllable "yea-uh."

The country drawl is a mix of Lake's upbringing in Iowa and living in Atlanta the past ten years after moving there to attend Emory Law School. Jason Lake is more than just a tightly wound videogame coach. At thirty-four, he's also a successful real-estate lawyer with his own practice, a two-year-old daughter, and a pregnant wife at home. "No," he admits, "I'm not the typical person you run into at a gaming tournament."

It's baffling that a real-estate lawyer pushing middle age is also the sideline-pacing coach of the number-two Counter-Strike team in the world. Lake's father was the high-school baseball coach in Lemars, Iowa, and some of Jason's earliest childhood memories were picking up equipment on the field as a bat boy. So that's bound to be part of his desire to be a coach. But why videogames?

Lake says his obsession began by chance, when he got hooked on Counter-Strike in 1998 while living in an Atlanta high-rise. He befriended a young engineer in the building who had recently moved in from Dallas, where Counter-Strike was already popular. One night, Lake stopped by with a six-pack and the friend was on his computer.

"We were supposed to go out clubbing that night," he recalls, "and when I walk in, he's playing this game. It was all over after that." That night, Lake and his buddy never made it out to the clubs.

Lake formed his own clan and called it CompLexity. "I was never as good as these guys are," he admits, motioning to the gamers milling around the Hyatt. "I knew I'd never be elite caliber, but I did take it seriously."

It would be six years, though, before CompLexity became professional and started paying salaries. In 2004, Lake began signing top gamers to the team and benched himself to be full-time owner and manager.

"Now," he says, of running the gaming organization, "I'm putting in anywhere from five to seven hours a day working on this thing."

During matches, Lake is fire-and-brimstone, a Knute Rockne kind of coach. But away from the tables, Lake is also a businessman heavily invested in gaming—both financially and emotionally—who, like Angel Munoz, will tirelessly push the notion of e-sports as the next big thing to anyone who'll listen.

Tonight there's no time to dwell on the loss. A tournament this size is too good an opportunity to work the room and network with potential team sponsors. Lake scans the bar and checks his watch. A marketing rep from Verizon Wireless is supposed to meet him here to bounce around ideas for streaming gaming scores on cellphones.

"If you want to reach this demographic, you've got to do it through alternate means," Lake says. "These kids aren't watching TV anymore, and major American corporations need to be in this market. That's what I'm banking on. I'm betting the farm they're gonna figure that out."

When a guy from western Iowa tells you he's betting the farm, you get the idea he's speaking more literally than most.

"What we're all doing here is planting the seeds for the future," he says.

Of course, EG's Alex Garfield and a dozen other managers are also here on business, hoping to push gaming across to corporate America. But they weren't stamping their feet and kicking chairs earlier at the tournament tables. They also weren't encouraging their players so vocally and instructing them to be good sports and shake hands after a loss. This isn't just business for Lake. This goes deeper. Gaming fulfills some kind of head-to-head competitive yearning for Lake, a former all-state high-school linebacker.

Two kids from his team pass by the bar and say hello. They call him Jake, a mash-up of Jason and Lake. "Hey, Jake." "What's happening, Jake." His players are headed to a Texas hold 'em poker game in one of the rooms upstairs. Gamers are competitive kids, whether it's Counter-Strike or hold 'em with a $100 buy-in.

A few minutes later, rival player Josh Sievers stops by to say hello. He's Dominator from Team 3D, the kid who smashed his mouse into pieces after today's loss. Dominator is a junior at Iowa State University, where Lake went as an undergrad. They joke about an ISU bar called People's, where Lake spent too many nights back in his old college days.

"They still got that pool table with the ratty red felt?" Lake asks, smiling.

"Oh yeah," says Dominator, with a laugh, "and Pabst Blue Ribbon for a buck on Trailer Trash Night."

When he's not in class or playing Counter-Strike online, Dominator hunts deer with a bow and arrow in the woods around the Ames campus. He equates first-person shooters to hunting. It's the thrill of the one-on-one moment, the duel, that's so addictive.

"When you spot the target, that's the ultimate adrenaline rush," says Dominator, who's wearing a T-shirt that says FAST FOOD above a picture of a deer. "You start shaking, and you can't think straight. You have to calm yourself down and control your endorphins. It's the same thrill in a one-on-one situation at a big Counter-Strike match. First you try and ambush. Then it's about staying calm under fire."

After Dominator heads off to the poker game, Lake begins to talk about sponsorships. "Yeah," says Lake, again in a lamenting drawl. He signals the bartender for another round, as if this topic might take awhile.

"I am personally funding the whole team out of pocket," he says, finishing off his first Grey Goose and grapefruit. "And it isn't cheap."

That's got to be some kind of joke. Jason Lake is funding CompLexity out of pocket? Of all the hundreds of Counter-Strike clans in the world, five others besides CompLexity pay player salaries—and they do so because they have corporate sponsors. It's the sponsors who ante up for salaries and plane tickets and hotel rooms. That's the whole point of sponsorships. Who the hell pays out of pocket? Lake does, apparently.

He pays $60,000 a year in salaries for his five players, plus he's got a couple of part-time staffers who shoot photos and videos for the clan's Web site. The whole crew travels to a dozen tournaments a year in places like Dallas, L.A., New York, and Las Vegas. Over the past two years, they've also been to France, Spain, and China. And everywhere they fly, Lake is also picking up the tab on hotels, taxis, and most of the meals, too.

"This month alone I'm probably pushing ten grand in travel expenses," he says. "We don't have any sponsors yet. I've done it all myself."

The bottom line: CompLexity has been a fully salaried clan for a year and a half, and in that time Lake has dropped about $200,000. It's a staggering amount, especially considering that over the same time, the other elite U.S. squad, Team 3D, has brought in at least $250,000 from their sponsors. "The pie's only so big right now," Lake says, "and Craig's got both of the big boys."

By "big boys," he means that Levine has sponsorship deals with the two major sponsors of e-sports, Intel and NVIDIA. A handful of other clans, like EG and United 5, have modest deals with Intel for about

$10,000 a year. Others work deals with companies like SteelSeries mousepads or Sennheiser headphones for free gear, but no cash.

It's only Levine who has struck gold in North America, raking in $150,000 a year combined from Intel and NVIDIA. Meanwhile, here's Lake going into the hole $200,000 and counting. What is he thinking?

"I'm targeting other companies outside of gaming," he says, "trying to get them interested in the demographic. But, yeah, it's taking longer than I'd planned."

Lake stirs his drink. He looks a little bothered now. Clearly this is unpleasant territory. "Sometimes my wife," he says, "well, she hasn't figured it out yet. She gets pissed off. She doesn't understand why I'm so passionate about this. You know, I'm thirty-four years old and…"

Lake takes a sip and wills himself back to a place where he's more in control, where he's more assured. He goes back to being a coach.

"But you've gotta win," he says with renewed gusto, sitting up on his bar stool. "You can't go five tournaments in a row pulling that shit we did today."

The competitor inside Lake tells him that beating Team 3D means taking their sponsors and stanching the fiscal bleeding. "You win, and the rest takes care of itself," he says. "You win, and the rewards follow."

Beyond that, Lake is banking on e-sports breaking through to the mainstream this year, hoping some forward-thinking network executive finally recognizes its merits as a legitimate competition and puts Counter-Strike on the air.

"This is the year that gaming will cross over," he says. "This is when these gamers start becoming household names and their pictures go on the sides of Taco Bell cups. And when people finally start paying attention to us, I plan on having the Counter-Strike team that's number one in the world."

A hand touches Lake's shoulder. "Hey, Jason." It's Craig Levine, the 3D boss and Lake's biggest rival, who leans into the bar. "Not exactly the best tournament, huh?"

"Not at all," agrees Lake, swiveling in his stool to face Levine. "Not at all."

Lake offers to buy him a beer. It's a show of generosity, but the tension in the air makes it obvious this is a screw-you kind of beer buy. There's a palpable distrust between Lake and Levine, and about the only thing taking the edge off the tension is the humility of both of their losses today. For their disappointing finishes, Team 3D and CompLexity each get a paltry $900, so neither manager is throwing around much attitude.

"Nope," says Lake. "There have been better days."

Lake feels a slap on his other shoulder. "Great fucking tournament," says another manager with a clearly different opinion of the earlier events. He's Alex Conroy, or JaX as he's known in gaming circles. He's the JaX behind JaX Money Crew, the U.S. team that eliminated CompLexity this afternoon. At the moment, he's not someone Lake particularly wants to deal with.

"Yeah, man," says JaX. "What a fucking tournament. Unbelievable."

JaX has spiky hair and a goatee, and he's dressed in a mustard-yellow suit with a lilac tie. It's a suit as brash as his personality. JaX is only nineteen, but he's a New York City rich-kid nineteen, so he's got the attitude and apparently the fake ID to order a drink at the bar.

"The top U.S. finisher here," he says, self-referentially, to the bartender, "will have a Jack and Coke."

With today's win, JaX Money Crew can finish no worse than fourth overall, worth $5,400. And, as JaX is happy to rub in, regardless of tomorrow's semifinal results, his team will finish tops among U.S. clans.

"I've got to congratulate you," Lake tells him, begrudgingly. "You guys were prepared, you scouted us and you had a good strategy. But you're not an international powerhouse. Not after one win."

"Okay, okay, live in the past," JaX says to Lake and Levine, circling a finger. "Just make some room for three of us in your little Counter-Strike club."

Right now, Lake would give anything to be somewhere else. He's stuck at the bar between Levine, the guy he's pursuing, and JaX,

the guy who's on his heels. "Jesus," Lake says irritably, again looking at his watch and scanning the room. "Where the hell's that Verizon guy?"

A football game is playing on the TV behind the bar. On the screen,
Atlanta Falcons quarterback Michael Vick scrambles and throws an
incompletion. Desperate for any excuse to ignore Levine and JaX, Lake
asks a man sitting two bar stools down for the score. The man doesn't
fit neatly into any of the groups at the Hyatt tonight. He's just some
tumbleweed who blew in off the plains.

"Falcons are losin'," says the man in a very thick Texas drawl. "But
what do you expect? Can't win with a *niggra* quarterback."

It's a conversation stopper. Everyone's conversation.

"What did you just say?" responds Lake, after a few seconds of
stunned disbelief.

"You'll have to 'scuse me. I'm from south Texas," the man says,
emphasizing "south," as if that makes his comment acceptable. "Take
it from me, you just can't win with a niggra quarterback. Coon can't
play dropback."

This time there's no delay. Lake fires back at the bigot, "You're an
idiot, do you know that? You don't know me, who my friends are,
what color my friends are, what color my wife is."

Now the bigot, his face bright red, is staring straight ahead at the
TV, with an evil smolder in his eyes, like some sadistic prison guard in
a chain-gang movie.

"You know what, pal," says Lake, his temper rising. "Do yourself a
favor and take a walk. As in, now."

The bigot finally gets the message, and with a defiant tip of an
imaginary cowboy hat, he decides it's time to mosey. But before he
even reaches the escalators across the lobby, he's on his cell phone calling in backup. There's trouble brewing.

Levine and JaX reason with Lake to head upstairs to his room
before something regrettable happens. The old linebacker in Lake's
head isn't buying it, but the lawyer in there agrees.

Ten minutes later, Lake is upstairs in his hotel suite. He's trying to cool down, but his blood is still up. He reaches into the minibar and grabs a bottle of beer.

"You know," he says, pacing angrily in the room and jerking off his tie, "after we lost today, I almost packed my bags and went to the airport. I thought, this is fucked. This is insane. I'm risking my financial security, my *family's* financial security for some goddamn videogame?"

He throws his tie onto the coffee table.

"I've got a wife at home who might be about to leave me. I've got a two-year-old daughter that I just want to see and put to bed. What the hell am I doing here? Really. If I was smart, I'd walk away from this goddamn mess right now."

Lake is starting to crack. The near-fight at the bar lit the fuse, but the dispiriting loss today and then taking shit about it from JaX, plus his frustration over being number two and failing to beat Team 3D and Levine either at the Counter-Strike tables or in the financial game has clearly pushed Lake all the way to the edge.

"I've got Craig Levine trying to steal away my players," he rants, still pacing. "I hear about it all secondhand. I know. He's going to their hotel rooms when I'm not there, badmouthing me, trying to get them to jump ship.

"And now he's apparently badmouthing me to sponsors. 'He's a hothead' or 'He's a loose cannon' or 'You don't want him representing your company. He'll say the wrong thing at the wrong time.'"

"It's Levine," Lake says, shaking his head and taking a draw off his beer. "It's all Levine. The guy has been trying to drive me out of gaming since day one."

Pushing heavy turquoise drapes to the side, he slides open a window and lights a cigarette, inhaling deeply and exhaling a cloud of smoke through the screen.

It was a dubious venture from the start, paying kids out of pocket to play videogames. Nobody's done that. Even in the early days, Angel

Munoz only paid out a part of the door gate. Craig Levine doesn't spend his own money. Nobody's ever truly invested in these gamer kids, except Lake.

He believed in this game. He believed it was sport, it was cool, it was worth taking a chance on. Now he's down $200,000 because nobody else cares as much as he does. Nobody else is willing to take a chance on these kids.

Lake can't attract anyone outside gaming to invest in his team, and he can't pry loose the only money that exists in this little world. Gaming must get bigger, but Lake can't figure out how. He's stuck, and the only sure escape from this mess is to catch a flight back to Atlanta tonight, return to real-estate law and forget about e-sports forever.

"You know, I wanted to walk away, but I didn't," he says a little more calmly after another drag on his Marlboro Light. "I took a nap instead. I didn't go because I can't leave good people hanging in the wind.

"I can't do it. I made promises to all of my guys. I've got these kids on the team depending on me, looking to me for guidance, paying their college tuition from CompLexity. I have responsibilities to all these people...all these people that believe in me."

Lake stubs out his cigarette and sits down at the table, rocking back on the legs of a wooden chair and clasping his hands behind his head.

"I can't let them down," he says, staring up at the ceiling in search of faith.

It had been an eventful day at the Hyatt Regency in Dallas. And even as Jason Lake sat there in his hotel room searching for his own answers, many more questions remained.

Would these cyberathletes ever be seen as anything resembling regular athletes, and would gaming ever be respected and regarded at all like traditional sports? Did e-sports have any hope of making it out of the underground, from the Hyatt basement to the big time? The gaming community hoped to make the improbable leap, like X Games and hold 'em poker before them, to find success on TV and bring fame and fortune to its stars. But who would be the pioneer to take it there?

At this point, there was reason to be skeptical, but sport or not, breakthrough or not, there was nonetheless real drama here in Dallas. There were egos, anxieties, ambitions, ulterior motives, vested interests, desires to belong, chips on shoulders, and scores to settle. Most curious of all, there was a group of seemingly otherwise normal people who were experiencing life's highs and lows, its joys and heartbreaks, through a puzzling videogame called Counter-Strike.

Last, there was Team 3D and CompLexity, a true American rivalry that practically nobody outside e-sports even knows exists. And because those two teams both wanted something so passionately—to be number one—there was one more question that needed an answer: Who would win?

# PART II

## Lanwar Is Declared

# Chapter 4

**F**RANK NUCCIO IS A DIMINUTIVE ITALIAN MAN WITH jet-black hair and a Brooklyn attitude who runs a family pizza restaurant called Pizza by Marco in Dallas. Nuccio's old man ran a watering hole called the Carroll Lounge in the 1950s in this city, just down the street from Jack Ruby's nudie bar. The two were friends. Ruby would swing by the Carroll Lounge before work for a drink and a slice of the Sicilian pizza made with the family tomato-sauce recipe from the old country.

Everyone loved the pizza at the Carroll Lounge, so much so that after a few years, they scaled back on the liquor and renamed it Marco Polo Pizza Bar. Eventually the Nuccios scrapped the barroom idea altogether and called it Pizza by Marco. Today on the walls of the pizzeria are paintings of Venice and a framed article from *D* magazine naming it "Best Pizza in Dallas 2004," ahead of local joints Piggie Pies and I Fratello.

These days Nuccio is happy running the family pizza joint, and he almost never says a word to his many young employees about his pioneering past in videogames. What they don't know is that their boss, Frank, is the man most responsible for making Counter-Strike what it is today: the most popular action computer game in the world.

In 1998, the Counter-Strike phenomenon began inconspicuously with the release of a game called Half-Life. By the late nineties, Internet speed had advanced to the point where online leagues existed for the most popular first-person-shooter games, like Doom and Quake. Half-Life was something of a poor man's Quake, a decent one-on-one shooter but on the surface nothing revolutionary. What was revolutionary was the prescience of its developer, Valve Software, in allowing players to "mod" the game.

A mod is short for modification, and what Valve did was make available much of the programming code to allow users with a fair amount of programming know-how to customize the game to their liking. A user could change the look of the characters, the number of players in the game, the scoring and objectives, the background, almost anything if they had the brains to figure out how. It was nerd heaven.

Hundreds of Half-Life mods were born. Some were fairly good adaptations, and through word of mouth, gamers would download the most popular mods through the Internet and give them a try. It was free file sharing and nobody made any money off mods—except, of course, Valve Software. That was the brilliance of it. You couldn't play any of the mods without owning the original Half-Life software first. In that way, not only would mods widen the appeal of the software, but they could also elongate the shelf life of Half-Life indefinitely, or at least until the "engine" at the heart of the game became obsolete.

Truthfully, most of the Half-Life mods were lousy. Other than introducing a multiplayer element, few even matched the enjoyment of the original Half-Life itself. That all changed in the summer of 1999, when two college whiz kids named Jess Cliffe at Virginia Tech and Minh Le at Simon Fraser University in British Columbia put their two programming brains together and designed a Half-Life mod they could play simultaneously with all their buddies. They named their new team-oriented game Counter-Strike.

Even their "beta," or early test version, gained an underground following. Students would hang around the computer labs at Virginia

Tech and Simon Fraser into the wee hours playing this new shooter game their classmates Jess and Minh dreamed up. Word had spread even before the game was officially launched, and when Counter-Strike version 1.0 was made available for download on November 8, 2000, it was an instant cult smash.

Enter Nuccio, a then-thirty-year-old gamer who downloaded Counter-Strike the day it was released. By nightfall, he and four friends were LANning in Nuccio's living room. They played on original maps called Mansion and Weapon Depot, and despite numerous bugs and glitches in the program, there had never been anything quite like it. It was lifelike. It was head-to-head. It felt right. To Nuccio, it felt like hockey.

"It was the same kind of excitement," Nuccio says, sitting outside Pizza by Marco and recalling that day in 2000. "In hockey, you use speed and a synchronized offense. You rush the opponent and you overwhelm them, take it to 'em. Counter-Strike is the exact same sensation."

Angel Munoz's "cyberathlete" notion that videogames are equivalent to sports simply because they require steely nerves, long hours of training, and exceptional hand-eye coordination, in truth, has really never been convincing. When you think of it, good chefs have all of those attributes, too. So do air-traffic controllers and game-show contestants.

Playing a Formula 1 driving game is nothing like racing a real car. Playing a FIFA soccer game is nothing like running around a soccer field. It's ridiculous to suggest that kind of correlation exists.

But there's something different about a team game like Counter-Strike that makes the "e-sports" label less of a stretch. It has X's and O's, offense and defense, skill players and role players. There's a simplicity to it, despite its various maps and machine guns and strats and smoke grenades. Its appeal is not fantastical escapism, like most videogames. It's not otherworldly. On the contrary, it has a kind of backyard football or YMCA hoops appeal.

Counter-Strike is akin to sport not because anything on screen resembles sport or because it requires any real form of athleticism. It's like sport in that it creates the same sensation for the participant.

It gives the same adrenaline rush as a coordinated give-and-go in basketball or a power-play rush at the net in hockey.

There's another parallel between hockey and Counter-Strike, a truly unique aspect to this specific videogame that makes it so addictive. In Counter-Strike, players are killed off one at a time and must spend the remaining time in each one-minute, forty-five-second round watching while "dead." In Counter-Strike's system of attrition, unless you're the last player alive, you're stuck in what's tantamount to a penalty box for some part of each round. In effect, you're being punished for screwing up and watching enviously as other players run around having fun.

It's in that time, while gamers are pining to get back in the action, that the craving builds. It's that jonesing to play, that feeling of being benched—the punishment and ultimately the reward of being released—that makes Counter-Strike more addictive than any other videogame. It's what keeps players anchored at their computers for hours, either playing or aching to get back in on the action.

Nuccio had played hockey as a kid and later coached a Bantam team of teenagers. He also owned a small videogame store in Dallas in the 1980s and '90s, where he hooked up two computers in the back so kids could play Doom. It was, in essence, an early mini-LAN for two. Even the millionaire programmers who founded iD Software, John Carmack and John Romero, would swing in occasionally to watch.

After the NHL's Minnesota North Stars moved to Dallas, Nuccio anticipated a surge in local interest in hockey, and Dallas being a city that's ice-challenged, he opted to devote half of his videogame store to selling roller-hockey equipment. Years later, when Nuccio played his first game of Counter-Strike, it struck the same balance—half videogame and half hockey.

Nuccio believed in this new team videogame. He started an online league called Domain of Games, with sixteen teams divided by geography into western and eastern conferences. The standings were based on a hockey point system. A win was worth two, a tie was one, and a loss zero.

The kids ate it up. Domain of Games was the biggest thing since the joystick, and Nuccio was hailed around gaming as a genius.

"It wasn't anything brilliant," he says, true to form downplaying his role as a pioneer. "The average videogame player in America knew jack shit about sports because they were social outcasts. All I'd done was copy the NHL."

Other copycat leagues followed, some with rule variations. One was called RITD, for Rumble in the Desert, but their version of the game was seven-on-seven. Nuccio wasn't buying that. "Way too crowded. It's ridiculous. It slows down the game."

To him, it was simple. There are five offensive hockey players, five guys on a basketball team, so there should be five per side in Counter-Strike. End of discussion. "After a year, everyone knew that my rules were the way to go," he says, triumphantly.

A friend of Nuccio's named Monty Fontaneau was working for Angel Munoz at the time. One day he swung by the store and suggested Nuccio stage a Counter-Strike side tourney at the next CPL event. He could run it behind a curtain in the back, past the popular Doom and Quake tourneys.

Munoz really didn't think much of Counter-Strike at the time. He was a computer guy. He was no ex-jock, like Nuccio. To wit, Munoz has a basketball in his office he sometimes tosses in the air while talking on speaker phone. That basketball is painted silver. Enough said.

It took an ex-athlete and sports fan like Nuccio to recognize the appeal of a five-on-five game of offense versus defense like Counter-Strike. He knew the head-to-head thrill and team strategy would appeal not just to nerdy escapist gamer types. This game would also translate to all those other kids—the ones who loved to lace up skates or high-top sneakers, the cool kids who played sports after school and talked smack and occasionally got in scraps. Counter-Strike was the game that could cross over, and Nuccio knew it.

Angel Munoz may have started pro gaming, but it was Nuccio who expanded the circle. At his first Counter-Strike side tournament at CPL in 2000, two long tables were set up in the back with twenty computers. Few at the Hyatt even knew it was going on, until they began hearing shouts and hoots coming from behind the curtain. Gradually spectators around the Doom and Quake matches began wandering back to see what all the excitement was about.

What they found wasn't another 1-v-1 shooter with two kids sitting and staring silently into their monitors. This was five kids on each side of the table, shouting to teammates, high-fiving after wins and cursing a blue streak when they got fragged. This game wasn't just inside the computers. Counter-Strike was a spectacle in the living, breathing world.

The following CPL, more teams showed up for the Counter-Strike sideshow. At its third event, CPL Winter 2001, the mouse company Razer sponsored Nuccio's tourney with $10,000 in prize money, and Counter-Strike came out from behind the curtain forever. From this point forward, the team game would occupy the majority of floor space at CPL and Quake was pushed off to the side.

Attendance at CPLs jumped from about 250 in 1998 to over a thousand in 2001, thanks mostly to Counter-Strike and its five-man teams. Prize money jumped as well. The Internet voiceover firm Speakeasy put up $20,000 in prize money for the next Counter-Strike tournament and $30,000 for the one after that.

Nuccio was named commissioner of the CPL in 2001, and for three years set about perfecting Counter-Strike as the virtual sport that he'd envisioned. He worked with mapmakers to ensure all battle layouts had competitive balance and no gimmickry.

Teams should win or lose because of skill and strategy, not because of a disappearing space portal or something. Counter-Strike wasn't about force fields and superboosts in powers. It wasn't Mario Bros. It was schoolyard, stripped down and basic, like roller hockey.

As CPL commissioner, Nuccio implemented the first no-ghosting rule forbidding "dead" players from talking to their still-playing teammates. Counter-Strike is a battle of attrition. Once you're out of the game, you're out for the rest of the round.

Beyond that, if any other deficiency or glitch in the game needed changing or patching, Nuccio had the ears of Counter-Strike's designers, Cliffe and Le, who by now were out of college and working at Valve, having sold their mod to the software maker.

Thanks to Nuccio, Counter-Strike was now the biggest thing in gaming, and by far the main draw at LAN events. Sponsors took notice, upping their funding of CPLs and eventually sponsoring top clans like SK Gaming and Team 3D.

Nuccio's online league Domain of Games was officially absorbed by the CPL in 2001 and renamed CAL, for Cyberathlete Amateur League. When he'd started Domain of Games almost two years earlier as the original online Counter-Strike league, sixteen teams took the field with eighty kids playing. By the time Nuccio left the CPL in 2004 and went back to the pizza biz, CAL had over 200,000 players in the Counter-Strike section alone.

Nuccio eventually parted ways with Munoz and the CPL over philosophical differences on how best to advance the industry. Nuccio pushed to reinvest profits into a national league based on geography in which teams would compete in various cities at local LAN centers to earn a spot in a national championship tournament.

Munoz, he was dismayed to learn, never seemed to want to spend the money to oversee that kind of expansion. Munoz was the boss, and he opted to stick with the CPL's safe and profitable two-a-year tournament plan. It was an acrimonious split, and in large part the reason Nuccio is now so dismissive of his past in gaming. He was denied the chance to take Counter-Strike to the next level.

So now Nuccio is back twirling pizza dough in a north Dallas strip mall, and there isn't a single videogame in his pizzeria—not even a stand-up Birdie King or Tetris—to suggest his past as a gaming pioneer.

Nuccio never brings it up. "I don't like talking about myself much," he says. "The way I figure it, Counter-Strike would've been popular no matter what."

When pressed, though, for a brief moment Nuccio drops the dismissive façade.

"I don't know, maybe I am responsible for a lot of its success," he says, allowing himself a bit of credit. "You know what. That's the first time I've ever said that. I guess I am proud of it."

# Chapter 5

T HE MUG N MOUSE INTERNET CAFÉ IS TUCKED AWAY almost unnoticeably in a strip mall near the Royal Street exit off I-35 in north Dallas. It's about fifteen miles upcountry from the city's skyscrapers, in an area of Dallas known unofficially as Korea Town.

Comparatively speaking, there aren't a great number of Koreans living in Dallas, so Korea Town isn't so much a neighborhood as it is a strip mall. Even right across the parking lot by North Stemmons Street, the city's massive Mexican American community takes over dusty Crown Park nightly to blast salsa music out of their car trunks, kick around soccer balls, and improperly dispose of Tecate cans. But here in this row of stores pressed up against southbound I-35 is a self-sufficient Korean American community unto itself.

The storefronts are marked with signs bearing circles and stick-figure Korean letters that look like upside-down *L*'s on top of *T*'s. About the only English you'll read is smaller-print translations, like "ID cards" or "karaoke." In the center of the strip mall is the Mug N Mouse café, the "mug" part implying hot coffee and the "mouse" referring to the type you plug into a computer.

It's mid-May in north Texas, and the chilly nights of December's CPL Winter have given way to a demanding ninety-degree sun offset by an omnipresent wind off the flat, encircling range.

Inside the air-conditioned Internet café, chairs and couches are mixed in among twenty-two ready-to-play PCs. This is the LAN center, the modern version of a video arcade, where gamers play on computers with the best keyboard-and-mouse peripherals, sharpest monitors, and fastest broadband Internet connections. Rarely anymore do kids drop quarters into stand-up arcade games. Now they pay $2.50 an hour at LAN centers.

Mug N Mouse is owned by Jim Lee, a forty-year-old immigrant from Seoul who moved to the States in the eighties to attend West Texas A&M in Amarillo. He runs the café with his thirty-six-year-old wife, Sonae Kim, whom he met in school through the Korean student association. Sonae was getting her bachelor's in graphic design and at the time worked in a campus coffee shop called The Stomping Grounds.

"So," says the affable Jim in choppy English, pointing out the logic of this eventual business venture, "we combine computer and coffee shop."

Jim shuffles around the café in sandals with white socks, fixing frozen computers and helping out at the register. Sonae works behind the counter blending mango and honeydew "Asian bubble tea" smoothies with gelatin beads to be sucked up through extra-wide straws. In the evenings when it's slow, Sonae sits at a piano in the corner of the café, pushes up the sleeves on her frilly black blouse and plays to sheet music.

Mug N Mouse is a family business, from Jim and Sonae to her mom Kim, who makes sandwiches in the kitchen, and their black Pomeranian named Preto, who does tricks for customers. "Preto, high-five and roll over," says Jim, and when she obliges, his ever-present smile grows wider.

In the back of the café, a smaller, noise-proof room with eight computers is devoted entirely to hard-core gaming. This back room is where Team 3D has come for its annual preseason "boot camp."

In gaming, a boot camp is a weeklong X's and O's practice binge with all five players gathered in one location. Ordinarily, throughout the year, Counter-Strike teams practice five or six nights a week, spread out nationwide across the Internet. It's at boot camps where teams can sit down, brainstorm new strategies together, and practice without distractions. This boot camp in Dallas is the equivalent of a preseason training camp for Team 3D, as they prepare for a slate of upcoming summer tournaments. The first major LAN of the season, Lanwar in Kentucky, looms just three weeks away.

It's been a tumultuous five months for 3D since their disappointing quarterfinals finish at CPL Winter. After which, they immediately lost their number-one worldwide ranking to SK Gaming, which won the event.

In January, another bombshell hit when 3D's biggest star, sniper Kyle "Ksharp" Miller, retired at the ripe old gamer age of twenty-one, walking away from Counter-Strike for a nine-to-five job at an IT company in Virginia.

After a few lackluster performances online and at small LAN events, Team 3D slipped all the way to number eight. What really stung, though, was getting leapfrogged by CompLexity, which was now ranked number three in the world and tops among clans in North America.

Word on the street, reflected by the Gotfrag rankings, was that 3D was on the fade. After two frustrating years pursuing 3D, was 2006 to be the year Jason Lake's team finally broke through and supplanted their nemesis as world champions?

In 3D's defense, those new rankings were largely speculative. The fact remained that in two years of challenging for their throne in U.S. gaming, CompLexity still had never beaten 3D when it mattered—at a major LAN under the bright lights with a big payday on the line—and with the summer season fast approaching, 3D intended to restore order.

"The first thing you guys have to understand about CompLexity is that the moment you fear them, the moment you hesitate, you're done," says Dave Geffon, sitting smack in the middle of Team 3D's practice room in the back of Mug N Mouse café. "CompLexity is nothing but a bunch of smoke-and-mirror tricks. They have one or two guys that are good, and the rest are totally average. They win because they partner up and they run their shit to a T, and it all comes together."

Dave Geffon is the new leader of Team 3D, the guy manager Craig Levine has chosen to provide the kick to his team's suddenly under-achieving ass.

Geffon, known in gaming as Moto, is a twenty-three-year-old with good facial features and short black hair gelled up in a tilted faux hawk. In addressing the team, he doesn't stir emotions with the bombast of a coach. Instead he comes across as reasonable and assured, but with the slightest hint of oversell. He's like a trial lawyer in final arguments who's sufficiently made his case but whose fate still rests on getting a jury to agree.

It's a fitting analogy. Moto comes from a family of trial lawyers, and he knows full well that in getting others to comply with your agenda, it's just as important to be convincing as it is to actually be right.

"You want to beat CompLexity?" Moto tells the team, "You play aggressive, you play organized, and you play fast. You take away spots on the map so they *can't* run those strats they've practiced a thousand times before. And then they'll fall apart. Trust me."

This is Moto's second go-round with Team 3D. His first run with the team was from 2002 until his "retirement" in the summer of 2005. A natural leader and a bright tactician, both times he was chosen by Levine to whip an out-of-sync collection of all-stars into a winner.

It worked in 2002, when Team 3D ascended to the top of the U.S. gaming scene, where they have remained until this season. Now, after their quick exit at CPL Winter and the resulting slide in the polls, the veteran gamer is back in boot camp, cracking the whip and trying to spur 3D back ahead of a CompLexity squad that's suddenly running with them neck-and-neck.

Manager Craig Levine is not at boot camp. He's back at home in New York, overseeing the clan's business operations. Levine is not a coach. He's an owner who motivates players largely through the fear of being fired, not with pep talks. Here in Dallas, it's Moto's job to run practice. Yet halfway through day one, he's mostly earning his pay-check as team babysitter.

As Moto speaks, Griffin "ShaGuar" Benger swivels around in his chair with one leg tucked up under the other, resting his chin on the palm of an open hand like a bored kid in detention. The twenty-year-old from Toronto is easily distracted—he has four windows open on his monitor and is listening to rap through one ear of his headphones.

At the next seat is Mikey "Method" So, a droopy-eyed, twenty-two-year-old Korean American from L.A. Method is a gamer by trade but a skate punk in attitude, wearing baggy jeans and an olive-green Burton snowboard shirt. Instead of a dinged-up skateboard, it's Method's keyboard that's held together with strips of hockey tape.

He's also ignoring Moto, instead watching a downloaded video of Shaun White, the X Games skater and snowboarding star who vaulted from obscurity to the cover of *Rolling Stone* magazine after winning gold in halfpipe at the 2006 Winter Olympics. In the video download, the grinning White tells a CNN interviewer that female flight attendants were showering him with attention on the way home from the Games in Torino, Italy, and styling him with free drinks. When the interviewer notes that White is only nineteen, the snowboarder wise-cracks, "I'm talkin' about Mountain Dews, baby."

The parallels between extreme sports and pro gaming aren't lost on this group. It wasn't long ago that the mainstream refused to accept extreme sports like skateboarding or surfing as legitimate competition, and snowboarding was still banned at top ski resorts. Team 3D's players know if gaming could ever get any real TV exposure, they would be the Shaun Whites of e-sports. They're the best, the most talented and accomplished competitors among millions worldwide who play Counter-Strike.

Their ability to run, jump, and hit a moving target with a computerized bullet is every bit as challenging—meaning, just as often attempted and failed by less-talented competitors—as any "backside air" or "front-side heel flip" pulled off by White. Team 3D's players are elite among their peers, and they know it. The lesser clans they trounce at LANs know it. The e-sports enthusiasts at TSN and Gotfrag know it. It's the people outside gaming who don't have a clue.

The two other players sitting here are Sal "Volcano" Garozzo, a quiet computer-science major at Manhattan College in New York, and

Rambo, the former team leader who's only half-listening to Moto's pep talk while scrolling through an online thread comparing NBA old-timer Kareem Abdul-Jabbar to Shaquille O'Neal.

Rambo isn't exactly holding up practice, but he's not helping start it either. It was Rambo whom Moto supplanted as team leader a few weeks ago, and he's clearly not thrilled with manager Levine's decision. Inside the game, Rambo is known as "the ninja," because he stalks from the shadows, observing and patiently awaiting his opportunity to strike. Here at boot camp, it seems he's doing the same.

Team 3D are a competitive group of guys. They don't like losing. Of course, as the only fully sponsored and salaried team in North America, that hasn't happened much since their formation in 2002. Until recently, 3D had never faced a challenge on their home soil.

Now, because of Jason Lake's willingness to pay top players out of pocket and assemble a worthy rival, 3D's reign faces its first real threat. And it's more than just pride that's on the line.

First there's prize money. Winning a major LAN is typically worth around $30,000 or $40,000 to split. Second, and of greater financial impact, is the risk of losing their golden-goose sponsorships.

Companies like Intel and NVIDIA sponsor 3D for one reason: to push their products to the core market of hard-core gamers. The concept is, if you want to beat the best, you'd better have the same heavyweight processors and lightning-quick graphics cards they do. And those companies may lose interest if 3D slips to number two in the United States. To 3D's players, losing their sponsors to CompLexity could mean the unthinkable: getting a real job.

Few hard-core gamers have ever held full-time employment. ShaGuar, Method, and Volcano have never worked a day in their lives outside gaming. Rambo has literally worked *a* day in his life. He spent one afternoon at a Sonic fast-food restaurant near his home in Dallas, where he poured frozen slushie drinks for seven hours and then quit.

Pro gamers aren't much for an honest day's work. Even the ones who don't pull salaries, as a rule, would rather stay at home until they're twenty-two or twenty-three and live off whatever prize money they pull in at LANs. Making $20,000 to $30,000 a year is great, as long as you're still mooching off your parents.

Beyond salary and prize money, Counter-Strike stars also pad their wallets giving private lessons online. For about $25 a half-hour or $40 an hour, they'll teach beginners shooting techniques or show them hiding spots on maps. It's tedious work, but a week of lessons can bring in as much as $400.

ShaGuar has given about fifty lessons over the years but quit recently after a student turned on him in the middle of a tutorial and shot him dead. "The whole lesson," ShaGuar says, "I'm asking if there's anything he'd like to learn, and he never answers. I'm like, 'Hey, what's your name?' And then he just runs up and shoots me in the head. And I hear him yelling, 'Whaa-haaa, I just killed ShaGuar!'

"That's as retarded as seeing Mike Tyson walking down the street and trying to punch him out. I called the guy a fucking loser and left."

The career arcs of pro gamers are fairly standard. Until about seventeen years old, they play solely because it's fun. Between seventeen and about twenty, they play to win money and possibly make a salaried clan like 3D or CompLexity. If they're still playing from twenty-one to twenty-three, it's probably because they're making a few bucks, seeing the world at the expense of a sponsor, and content to hold off the nine-to-five as long as possible.

Truly elite players like those on Team 3D have still one more motivation. They're not here because they love the game. They're not here because they're friends. They're ultraskilled mercenaries waiting it out to see if gaming ever takes the next step so they can cash in on their talents.

Guys like Method and Rambo all have the dream of being the Counter-Strike equivalent of Shaun White, or better still Tony Hawk, the skateboarder who parlayed a two-and-a-half-rotation "900" trick at the 1999 X Games into household-name celebrity. Beyond lucrative endorsements, Hawk even has his own series of videogames in which players compete against a computerized likeness of him.

No doubt Rambo has dreamed of some kind of "Rumble vs. Rambo" videogame where players could go pistol-to-pistol against a virtual version of the 3D star. But that won't happen unless gaming gets more exposure, the way extreme sports did when ESPN began airing the X Games in 1995. That's when these guys could start making some serious cash, instead of stretching $30,000 a year by living at home rent-free with their parents. In the meantime, gaming is just a way to avoid pouring icy drinks at Sonic.

Moto is the exception to the lazy-gamer rule. He had plenty of jobs growing up, toiling at a hockey rink, a Burger King, and a movie theater. One summer he worked at a pet store lugging eighty-pound bags of horse feed out to the parking lot. "It sucked," he says.

For the past year, during his retirement from Team 3D, Moto worked for an escrow company, researching homeowner records at Virginia courthouses. "If someone was trying to refinance their house, I'd check for judgments or undisclosed loans," he says. "God, that was depressing."

Mostly, though, he drove around bored, dwelling on how good he'd had it while getting a paycheck for playing Counter-Strike.

"Nothing beats playing videogames for a living," he says.

In his year away, Moto lived in Charlottesville, Virginia, with gamer friends not associated with Team 3D. In the first six months away, he played just fifteen minutes of Counter-Strike. Yet because of his value in public relations, Moto remained partially on Craig Levine's payroll to make promotional appearances as a Team 3D member "on hiatus." Moto is good with the media, which is rarely the case with gamers. On camera, he's well spoken, extroverted, and able to give concise sound bites. To Levine, Moto is a guy who can sell gaming to the masses. In short, he helps dispel the stigma that gamers are dorks.

As 3D's leader, he's done interviews for CNN, CNBC, ESPN, *The New York Times*, and *The Wall Street Journal*. In the summer of 2003, he appeared on ABC's *World News Tonight with Peter Jennings*. His sound bite provided perfect exposition to the segment: "This is our full-time job, as opposed to a lot of people our age who are flipping burgers."

Unlike most gamers, Moto doesn't speak in "ums" and he doesn't end sentences with "...and stuff." He doesn't talk too "inside gaming," dropping unusable references to maps or strats in TV interviews for audiences on whom the lingo would be lost anyway.

To the media, Moto is engaging and appealing. Off camera, his personality is subtly off-putting, perhaps because he's so conscious of his on-camera appeal. Ask where he's from, and instead of answering Westlake Village, which is a planned suburban community on the edge of Ventura County, he'll answer "Los Angeles, California," with a little too much self-satisfaction. Especially since anyone really from L.A., like his teammate Method, for example, just says they're from L.A. Still, it's the kind of confidence that plays well on camera.

"It's always been a given since day one that I'd be handling all the media stuff," he says, adding of teammate Rambo, "I mean, you can stick Ronald in front of a camera and he can say something, but I'll just be better at it."

Right now, though, Moto's responsibilities aren't promotional. His job at present is to motivate his teammates and come up with new strategies to hold back the challenge posed by CompLexity.

"All right, you guys," he says, trying to start practice, "let's go over strats."

ShaGuar is ignoring him, watching a YouTube video clip of Britney Spears almost dropping her baby.

"Seriously, Griffin," Moto says sharply. "We've got to practice."

"Yes, Dad."

Next to Moto's computer is an open playbook full of strats. It's a thick black binder full of pages with screen grabs and assignments written in Counter-Strike lingo for each of the five players, like "First breach man takes Tower" or "Third man smokes Mid."

Each on-screen character in a game of Counter-Strike has the same basic attributes. Basically they're all six-foot, 200-pound army commandos. One side may be wearing green and the other blue, but all the characters are built to run, jump, and duck with the same speed and agility. What separates the characters on screen—aside from the comparative skills of the gamers controlling them, of course—are the weapons they employ. And this particular first-person-shooter game contains a virtual armory of homicidal hardware, including AK-47s, M4 machine guns, Desert Eagle pistols, Arctic Warfare sniper rifles, and smoke, flash, and HE explosive grenades.

The firepower a player carries determines his role on the team. Or, in sports terms, his "position." So, for example, when Moto devises a strat, much like an offensive coordinator drawing up a play in football, he may send two guys ahead first with spray-fire AK-47s to breach the defense—almost as if they're blocking on the play—while keeping a sniper back in a high perch to scope out the scene and await a counterattack.

Strats are all about synchronization and teamwork. Judging by the thickness of his binder, Moto has at least fifty in there, each designed specifically for the four maps used in competition—Nuke, Dust 2, Train, and Inferno.

"Don't make it obvious what you're doing," he says, running the team through one of the fourteen T-side strats in his binder for Train. 3D is signed on to a private game server, so there are no opponents. It's just the five of them running around and drilling on the map alone.

First they run Inner Push, and then its variant Delay Inner Push. Then there's Normal Delay Inner and Stage Move, and Stage Move Fake. Next comes 3-1-1 Slow and, naturally, 3-1-1 Fast. Then it's T-Mid Z Push, Outer Fake, Delay T Mid, Bomb Train Hold, and on and on and on.

The point of having so many new strats is to mix up their attacks and keep a well-prepared team like CompLexity confused. Right now, though, Moto is mostly just confusing—and increasingly aggravating—his own teammates.

"Let's do it again from the top," Moto commands, after they botch the Delay T Mid strat for what seems like the twentieth time. "Still too fast. You guys came out before they were blinded by the smoke. Come on. This really isn't that hard."

Begrudgingly his teammates again run through the strat, and again they fail.

"Nope," Moto says impatiently. "Do it again."

In front of Mug N Mouse, chairs are set up at a circular iron table for gamers to take a smoke break. Every ten minutes or so, a plane roars loudly overhead, coming in for a landing at Love Field to the south and stopping all conversations until it's quiet enough to resume speaking.

Occupying the table at the moment are three guys with strong opinions on all things Counter-Strike. It's a roundtable akin to *Meet the Press* or *Hardball with Chris Matthews*, except instead of politics, these pundits are discussing 3D and CompLexity.

These are the types of gaming diehards who jump on and off Gotfrag all day long, checking scores from tournaments half a world away and joining threads to debate Counter-Strike in the same way sports fans argue about the NBA. The only difference is, on a Gotfrag thread, an opinion might be supported by a stat like frags per round instead of points per game.

"3D has lost a step," says one eighteen-year-old gamer with the alias Crutch. "Why do you think they're boot-camping right now? They're panicking."

His friend, Corey Dunn, agrees. "3D is beatable."

The third member of the discussion is Mason Dickens, whose alias is simply Mason, and who plays on the Mug N Mouse house team, also simply called Mug N Mouse. Mason is a nineteen-year-old from Houston whose older brother Matt plays for CompLexity.

"They used to just run over people," Mason says of 3D. "Now they can't just rush in blind, not against teams that scout them. And especially not against CompLexity."

All three are in agreement that 3D needs new tactics to regain its dominance. With many of their past matches available to download as demos, other teams now spend much of their preparation time memorizing 3D's attack tendencies. That's where Moto comes in. His job is to draw up new strats to conceal their tactics.

"They're not going to beat CompLexity," says Mason, "if CompLexity knows which way they're coming at 'em."

Before he retired, Moto was never known as a top fragger. Even then, he pulled his weight with leadership and tactical prescience. A good strat caller is viewed like a catcher in baseball whose ability to call pitches behind the plate offsets his limited offensive skills. It's an acceptable tradeoff.

The consensus here is that Moto's smarts will help 3D, but not if he's so rusty that he's a liability in battle. At twenty-three, Moto is about a year or two beyond the usual burnout age for gamers. And he did take a year off.

Also an issue is his at-times officious personality. A twenty-three-year-old cracking the whip on his peers is not always appreciated. When Moto retired a year ago, the official line from 3D was that he was burned out after two and a half seasons with the team. The real story is he was forced out after a power struggle with the team's star player, Ksharp, who blanched at Moto's authoritarian tone and grew resentful of his micromanagement.

For Ksharp, the whole point of playing Counter-Strike had always been to have fun, to outgun your enemy. Moto's heavily choreographed strats were making the game joyless. At times, his elaborate schemes would have players so busy cloaking attacks by running decoy routes or laying down smoke screens, they'd get picked off before even firing a shot. Then they'd sit for the remainder of the round and stew.

"Team chemistry is complicated," Dunn says. "You want someone to bring discipline, but if you're not friends, then you won't communicate about each other's weaknesses. You'll point fingers."

Crutch adds: "With 3D, you've got these amazingly skilled players, all-star U.S. players put together to win. But I don't know, do they have the chemistry?"

Another jumbo jet roars overhead for a landing at Love Field, suspending the conversation and leaving the rhetorical question hanging in the air.

Into the parking lot swings a silver VW Jetta. The driver steps out, standing six-foot-six. He's dressed in a black T-shirt, baggy khaki shorts, and black low-top Converse All-Stars with no socks. He's got a white bandana over his head and two thick, fourteen-gauge silver hoops pierced through his lower lip.

He's also wearing tinted red sunglasses and a shit-eating grin the size of Texas. This is Josh Dacus, known around these parts as Punkville.

"What's up," he asks Mason, stepping up onto the sidewalk with a swagger. "We playing or what?"

It takes about two seconds to deduce that Punkville is a badass, the alpha gamer on the Mug N Mouse team. But there's also a comedy to the guy, the way he stands duck-toed in those sockless black Chucks. Or maybe it's his red shades and shit-eating grin, which tell you he's obviously baked off his ass.

The Mug N Mouse clan is hoping to scrimmage, or "scrim," against 3D sometime today. Having a top team boot-camping in town gives Mug N Mouse a perfect opportunity as sparring partner to see how they measure up.

"They're in there going over strats," Mason says, shifting uncomfortably in his seat. "So, I guess in a while."

Another teammate, sitting in the Jetta, pops his head out. "What's the deal?"

"Half-hour probably," says Punkville. "Let's cheef up."

Punkville jumps back into his car and goes fishing for a plastic bag full of marijuana in the compartment under his arm rest. He started smoking pot a year ago on the suggestion of his anger-management counselor while on probation for pummeling a guy who hit on his girlfriend. "I just lost it on the dude," Punkville says. "We were best friends, even. He pressed charges. I stepped on his neck I think was the main thing."

Now the twenty-one-year-old gets out his aggression through Counter-Strike and mixed martial arts. His goal is to compete in Pride Fighting, a Japan-based brawler circuit that's so brutal it airs in the United States on pay-per-view only. Six mornings a week, Punkville hits the gym to body-slam lacquered, 250-pound logs and practice "toe holds, finger holds, front chokes, back chokes, arm bars, reverse arm bars, rakes, cross-face, one-handed chokes, and half Nelsons."

"Only things you can't do in Pride Fighting," he says, "is elbow on top of the head, knee on top of the head, or kick in the nuts."

Every other Friday night, Punkville also fights in "illegals," which are underground fight clubs in hush-hush locations around Dallas. One was in the parking lot at American Airlines Arena, where the Mavericks play. Another was in an alley behind a Starbucks in the seedy neighborhood of Deep Ellum, where about forty people showed up.

"A lot of bikers," he remembers. "A few older men, which was a little weird. A lot of Mexicans, but they don't fight. They just bet. And a few babes. Girls eat that shit up. They get so horny off that stuff."

Punkville flicks a lighter and hits his bowl of weed. "Dude, illegals are beast," he says in a croaky voice, handing the glass pipe to teammate Brian "Gosu" Longhofer.

Gosu wears a Texas Rangers ball cap backwards and has the words STRENGTH and PRIDE tattooed on his forearms. The only book the nineteen-year-old high-school dropout says he ever read was It by Stephen King, and that was only to kill time while stuck in detention for a school-record sixty-six consecutive days. "Yeah, but that shit was like a thousand pages," Gosu says proudly, passing the pipe to a third teammate in the backseat, Kevin "Bzrk" Russell.

Bzrk, as in "berserk," is back in Texas for the summer, on break from a government-contract job on the atoll of Diego Garcia in the Indian Ocean. He does IT work at an airstrip used by U.S. warplanes to bomb Iraq. As a network troubleshooter, basically Bzrk is the guy the Air Force calls when *Ctrl-Alt-Delete* won't unfreeze their computers.

Despite his alias, Bzrk has a constant nonexpression, like one of the Moai head statues on Easter Island, except more burned out. Like his teammates on Mug & Mouse, it's mostly that Bzrk is just a little numb from getting smacked around by life.

If 3D are the privileged all-stars, then Mug N Mouse are the fuck-ups, the cyberdelinquents, orphans brought together by a videogame.

His junior year of high school, Bzrk's mother died from breast cancer and his dad remarried and moved to Colorado. "That's when my life started going downhill," he says in a flat monotone. "That's when I started hanging around Mug and Mouse," he says. "Jim let me sleep here when I had nowhere else to go."

Mug N Mouse clan is ranked number eight in North America. They're no 3D or CompLexity. They're the everyteam, back in the same chase pack with the likes of JaX Money Crew, United 5, Evil Geniuses, and a few other clans. Mug N Mouse has no sponsors, no team manager like Jason Lake or Craig Levine, no guidance at all, really. Three of them don't even have computers at home. The café owner Jim gives them a place to practice, free sodas and sandwiches, and a place to sleep in a pinch. But Jim is running a business, not funding a team out of pocket.

Heading into the summer season, Mug N Mouse's goal is the same as the hundreds of other aspiring clans in America: pull off a major upset and maybe land a small sponsorship. Even a one-off merchandise-only deal could translate into a little spending cash. If they could work a deal for, say, twenty gaming mice from Razer, for example, they could use five and sell the rest on eBay for $50 a pop.

That might give them the funds to fly to a LAN, the way the salaried clans do, instead of piling into a van for fourteen-hour cross-country drives. Maybe they could afford two hotel rooms at a tournament, instead of all five cramming in together and taking turns crashing on a pile of comforters on the floor.

"My motivation isn't necessarily to make enough money in Counter-Strike to live, have my own house or anything," says Gosu. "Just making enough to get by would make me happy. I'm addicted to this game. Ask anyone who's ever been decent at Counter-Strike, and they'll tell you the same thing: they'll never give it up."

Punkville sends the bowl around again, and Gosu takes a hit.

"I ever tell you about the time I fired off an AK-47 in Cambodia?" Bzrk asks in monotone non sequitur. Before starting his government job, while backpacking in Southeast Asia, Bzrk happened upon a ramshackle gun range in the jungle outside Phnom Penh. For a buck a bullet, he fired a real-life AK-47 to see if it was anything similar to the one he'd been pretending to use for years in Counter-Strike.

"That thing was inaccurate as fuck," Bzrk says. "I burst-fired at a target on a tree twenty yards away and hit it once. After I emptied the clip, the Cambodians said I could fire an RPG at a cow, but it was like two hundred bucks."

Punkville's cell phone buzzes. It's a text message from his girlfriend, Bianca.

"I've gotta split," he says, irritated. "Be back in a minute."

Punkville sounds pissed off. Something's not right. These guys know Bianca. She drops by practice to bring him food, usually enchiladas or tamales. Bianca is half Mexican and half Argentinean, cute with black hair and big eyes. When she calls his cell during a LAN, he'll pick up quickly, even letting go of his mouse in the middle of a match, and quickly say, "I'm at a tournament. Love you, bye."

Gosu and Bzrk step out of the car. Punkville backs out of the parking space, throws the Jetta in gear and speeds out of the lot.

Inside the café, 3D is drilling on Inferno, a map set in a town reminiscent of Florence, Italy, with maroon corrugated rooftops, winding cobblestone streets, and arched passageways.

"Okay, this strat is to take Banana," says Moto. Banana is the code name of a curved alley in Inferno. All maps have strategically important areas with code names, such as Mid, Jungle, or House. It's the shorthand through which these guys communicate, as in, "Look out, two shooters in Mid. Stay in Jungle. I'm circling around to House."

In Moto's new Inferno strat, the team rushes up Banana alley after throwing flash and smoke grenades to blind any defenders who might be lying there in wait. The trick is the timing. Rush in too fast after you've thrown a flash or smoke grenade, and you'll be blinded by it, too.

3D practices the new strat, with Moto standing at the far end of Banana alley in the place a defender would likely be positioned.

"It's not working, I can still see you. And if I can see you, I can shoot you," says Moto after the fourth consecutive failed attempt. "Run it again. And Griffin," he lectures ShaGuar, "get in position before you start throwing shit."

It's been a half-hour on this strat, and short-attention ShaGuar is about to lose it. All he wants to do is jump online and play the goddamn game for real against an actual opponent. They're Team 3D. They can outgun anybody, right? Why do they have to rehearse this overly choreographed Moto bullshit a hundred times?

After ShaGuar throws his smoke grenade, the strat calls for him to move forward a few steps so Rambo will have room to throw his own grenade without bouncing it off the back of ShaGuar's head. But every time ShaGuar steps forward, he's exposed to the defender—in this case Moto, who's standing in for the opponent.

"You can't peek like that," scolds Moto again. "I could shoot you."

"Well, do it," ShaGuar snaps back. "Shoot me if you think you can."

Mastering Inferno is a point of pride for Moto. It was on this map that he built his legend, at the 2003 World Cyber Games.

Every map has crates to hide behind. In the back of Bomb Site A on Inferno, there's one crate that's so close to a wall corner that if you jump down into the space behind it, you're basically stuck. You're pinched in by two walls, and you can't get out unless a teammate gives you a boost.

Basically, it's a dead-duck spot, which is why nobody ever hides there...which is exactly why Moto did just that. 3D was playing SK Gaming, and Moto knew they'd never look for him there. The problem was, soon after dropping behind the crate, his teammates all got fragged. So Moto was stuck behind the crate, at a one-on-four disadvantage. The one thing he had going for him was that SK had no idea he was there. Why the hell would anyone be behind that box?

SK came into the site to plant the bomb, and Moto popped up and started firing. Bobbing and weaving from side to side, he took out all four SK players in seconds. It was a miracle moment, and within days the match became the most downloaded demo in history. In Counter-Strike lore, it was the equivalent of the Willie Mays basket catch or

Doug Flutie's Hail Mary pass. Beyond legendary, it also made Moto eponymous. Now, in the same way that players refer to areas on a map with code words like Banana or House or Rafters, gamers worldwide universally refer to that particular crate on Inferno as Moto Box.

"Nope," Moto scolds his teammates after 3D's eighth failed attempt at the new strat. "It's gotta be quicker. Run it again."

"It's not working," says Rambo.

"It *will*," argues Moto. "This isn't difficult. Come on."

"I think we need to find our bread and butter," says ShaGuar in dissent. "Ronald, do you think we should find our bread and butter?"

Rambo flashes him a look. The seditious subtext of the comment is lost on Moto. "Bread and butter" was Rambo's favorite expression when he was strat caller. It defined his whole approach, finding a strat or two that worked, that the team was comfortable with, and sticking with it.

ShaGuar's "bread and butter" quip was more than a wisecrack. It was a thinly veiled vote of no confidence for Moto as new team leader. It was the seed of mutiny.

Moto's tactical approach and Rambo's are philosophically diametrical. Moto favors deception. His ego trip is to outsmart foes, to corner them into checkmate, and his own teammates are his pawns.

Rambo's approach is the opposite: Don't overcomplicate it. Just get in there and gun. It always worked in the past. For three years, Team 3D's players cleaned up on the U.S. scene. And now that CompLexity is posing a challenge, Rambo still would rather face them man-to-man than rely on subterfuge. Let them beat us at a major LAN under the bright lights, he figures, before we change the whole program.

Finally, on the twelfth attempt at the new Inferno strat, 3D's barrage of grenades detonates in sync and Moto is satisfied. "Okay, good," he says, leaning back in his chair. "We'll call that one Banana Peel."

Moto steps outside the café, where the Mug N Mouse clan is hanging out and smoking cigarettes, to see if they want to scrim.

"Yeah, but I don't know when," answers Mason. "We're waiting on Punkville. He should be back any minute. I think he went to Bianca's."

It's after eight o'clock and business has slowed. Sonae steps out from behind the counter and takes a seat at the piano in the corner. She opens sheet music and begins to play "Over the Rainbow" from *The Wizard of Oz*.

In front of the café, Preto the Pomeranian hunts down a dragonfly on the sidewalk, then begins devouring his kill.

Punkville's car pulls back into the lot, swinging up right in front of the café. Everyone stubs out their smokes and heads inside to scrim.

Punkville steps through the door in a typically cavalier manner. "Okay, let's play," he says, leaning over the counter. "Hey, Jim, you got a bag of ice back there? Like, a baggie with ice cubes in it or something?"

"Sure, why?" says Jim.

"Oh, I just fucking rocked a guy," says Punkville, glancing down at his swollen right hand. His teammates come over for a look. "You know that douchebag from the tattoo shop that's always hitting on Bianca?" Punkville says. "He told her today he'd give her a free piercing for a blowjob. Fuck that, dude. I went over there and jacked the guy, right in the middle of the store. Just walked in, floored him and walked out."

Punkville is still wearing his sunglasses. It's doubtful he even took them off for the punch-out. "Shit," he says, replaying the episode in his head. "You think they got that on the store camera?"

Across the street from the café, the sun has set beyond the dusty soccer fields. In north Texas, the land is so flat that twilight lasts for hours.

Rambo pulls Moto aside. There's something he wants to discuss. "Listen," Rambo says, "me and Griffin were talking it over. And the other guys, well, they don't really care either way. But I guess we all pretty much agree that I should go back to being team leader."

Moto shakes his head in disbelief.

At the piano, Sonae brings home her rendition of "Over the Rainbow" with the final drawn-out notes of "why oh why can't…" and then a long sustain on "…I…"

She finishes and looks around to see if any customers need help.

At this hour, the place is nearly empty. Rambo and Moto are gesturing and bickering over control of Team 3D, the other gamers are setting up in the back to scrim, and Punkville is leaning casually on the counter with a bag of ice on his hand.

In other words, just another normal night at Mug N Mouse café.

Sonae turns the sheet music back to the beginning, lays her fingers down meticulously on the piano keys and begins to play again.

# Chapter 6

"SUSA FREDA MEKA," SAYS A DETERMINED LITTLE TWO-year-old named Allie, wide-eyed and pointing her tiny index finger. Then, since she didn't get her message across, she says it again with feeling. *"Susa freda mekaaaa!"*

"She wants a doughnut," says her dad without looking up from his laptop. He cradles the Sony VAIO in his left arm like a baby, his eyes still glued to the screen, and walks with it from the living room into the kitchen.

Dad fishes around in a box of Hostess mini-doughnuts on the counter and gives one to the little girl in the terrycloth Winnie the Pooh jersey. Little Allie clutches the doughnut and smiles, then asks, *"Where gaboo?"*

"I don't know, honey," says her dad, and Allie runs back into the living room to eat her doughnut, play with her toys, and get powdered sugar all over the carpet.

"She has her own language," says Dad, who grabs a doughnut for himself. "I know *manoo* is candy. Don't know about *gaboo*. Watch this. Allie, what's your name?"

Allie's bored with this one.

"Allie, what's your name?"

*"Shee-Shee,"* she says.

"See what I mean," says Dad.

This is life at home with the coach. This is where Jason Lake prepares to take his Counter-Strike team into battle. It's the War Room meets *Romper Room*. And with the first big LAN of the season in two weeks, there's little time for playing around.

The CompLexity coach sits on the couch and pushes aside a *Jungle Book* and three pink elastic bracelets to make more room on the coffee table for his laptop. A black lab named Lexie runs in, followed by golden retriever Hayley, who stops long enough to lick Lake's leg before moving on.

It's 5:30 on a warm Georgia evening in late May, and Lake has been home from his law office barely long enough to greet his daughter and loosen his tie. Team practice is in half an hour, and the coach is hoping to first squeeze in a quick demo from 3D's most recent online match.

To prepare for CompLexity's anticipated—no, make that inevitable—showdown with Team 3D at the upcoming Lanwar tournament in Kentucky, Lake is, in essence, watching game film. He's scouting 3D by studying their highlights. And because these are videogames he's watching, it's far more interactive than a traditional game film. With Counter-Strike demos, Lake can maneuver around inside the game itself, watching everything that transpired from whatever point of view he chooses.

So, he's viewing this month-old match between 3D and United 5 from 3D's own perspectives. He's noting where ShaGuar perches to snipe, where Rambo lurks, and how often 3D chooses to attack Bomb Site A versus Bomb Site B on any given map.

"When I'm watching a Counter-Strike match," Lake says, "I'm seeing fifty things the average person isn't noticing. Just like if a coach watches a basketball game, he's seeing offside pick-and-rolls and stuff the average fan doesn't notice."

If the average hard-core gamer has watched thirty demos, the coach has watched three hundred while sitting here five nights a week. Online practice for CompLexity is 6 to 10 P.M., Sundays through Thursdays. It's not all drilling. Mostly they scrim against other elite teams—never 3D, though, for fear of giving away strat secrets—and often they're competing in online leagues like CAL or another called CEVO.

Lake doesn't overlord at practice. He's not orchestrating the attacks. That responsibility belongs to one of his players. But he does sign on each night in spectator mode. "I can watch the whole team," he says. "I can watch any one player. If I want to—which I never do—I can go in their voice program and hear them all talking to each other," Lake says, "just to see if they're communicating."

Most nights, he's only half paying attention. But even when he's roaming around the house or looking after Allie, what's important is that the team sees he's signed on.

"They practice harder if they know—or even think—that I'm watching," he says with a little smile. "They won't half-ass it."

As animated as Lake gets during matches, comparisons to hotheaded coaches aren't entirely fair. Unlike, say, Bobby Knight, Lake has never berated and certainly never laid a hand on any of his players. But that doesn't mean he won't get in a kid's face if he's dogging it—if it's possible to get in someone's face via e-mail or instant messenger, that is.

"I'll tell him, 'Put in two or three hours extra a day on your own in pickup games. Send me the demos. Show me what you've been doing.' It's like shooting foul shots in the gym before basketball practice."

Lake corroborates Frank Nuccio's theory that Counter-Strike, far more than any other videogame, replicates the sensations of sports, if not the physical activity. For Nuccio and the millions of other gamers who've played the team game, the adrenaline rush of a coordinated attack on a bomb site is reminiscent of a fast break.

And just as playing Counter-Strike recreates the visceral thrill of team sports, coaching the game for Lake replicates the gratification of running a team from the sideline. Odd, yes. But is coaching videogames ultimately any more preposterous than a grown man teaching teenagers how to correctly bounce a basketball?

So Lake sits here in his living room five days a week, watching practice and trying to balance his biological family with his boys online.

The coach is at one end of the coffee table, eyes on his computer. And at the other end sits Allie's make-believe Barbie laptop.

The Lake house, as it were, is in the upscale Atlanta suburb of Marietta. It's a mini-mansion influenced by classic southern architecture, pale yellow with a stone chimney and white columns on the front porch. In front, purple petunias grow beside trimmed hedges.

It's the perfect place to raise children, a leafy cul-de-sac with no through traffic and plenty of well-off young families. There's a Lincoln Navigator or BMW in practically every driveway, and adjustable-height basketball rims in half.

Lake's house is the largest in the neighborhood by a small margin, just as it's slightly highest above the street. A newly paved driveway winds up to the home, and at the top is a black Mercedes S600 parked next to a Big Wheel.

Inside Lake's front door is a music room with a piano that his wife, Danielle, used to play before having children. In the back are the kitchen and living room where Allie and her thirty-four-year-old dad eat doughnuts and play on their laptops.

Across from the couch where Lake sits, framed family photos are spread out across the mantel. One is of Jason and his younger brother, Matt, wearing their yellow Little League uniforms while growing up in Lemars, Iowa. Matt Lake was a baseball star who went on to the University of Arizona and Cal State Fullerton and had a cup of coffee in the minors, once playing against future big-leaguer Darryl Strawberry. Now Matt and his family also live here in Marietta, less than a mile away from Jason and his.

Their dad was the high-school baseball coach in Lemars, but growing up Jason was more of a football player than his brother. He was always less gifted physically than Matt but made up for it with grit and determination. His senior year he made all-state at linebacker. As for scholarship offers, Kansas State football coach Bill Snyder had seen Jason play at a summer camp and recalled him being a tough-nosed kid. K-State expressed mild interest, but being only about six-foot-one and 210 pounds, Lake really wasn't cut out for Division I football.

Instead he signed on for the study/party hard college plan, enrolling in 1990 at Iowa State in Ames, where he hit the books and the bars with equal tenacity. Then, as now, everything was a competition.

One of his favorite movies back then was *Real Genius,* and he idolized the character played by Val Kilmer. "I wanted to party and have a hell of a time but also ace everything I did," says Lake, who joined the fraternity Beta Theta Pi. "I took great pride in the fact that I was going to the bar at night and still pulling better grades than anyone the next morning."

He finished with a 3.9 grade-point average, tops among his classmates in finance. After graduation came a handful of adventures. He backpacked around Europe, went scuba diving at the Great Barrier Reef, and spent one summer in Alaska waking each morning at 4 A.M. to catch halibut in the freezing waters near an Eskimo village called Savoonga. Later, Emory Law School brought him to Atlanta, where he stayed after graduation and the bar exam to hang a shingle.

It was shortly after law school, in 1998, while Lake was living in a high-rise in the yuppiefied Buckhead suburb, that he was turned on to Counter-Strike. That's when he swung by a buddy's apartment to go out clubbing but wound up playing the game all night instead.

A decade later, Lake no longer plays Counter-Strike. He watches it, studies it, scans it for weaknesses in opponents. "3D is vulnerable, they're beatable," he says, with his eyes still on his laptop. "No doubt about it."

The only drawback of this particular demo is that it's two months old, from before Moto took over 3D and tore up the old game plan. Whatever strats they're running on the demo won't be much help now. Still, he watches it start to finish. Lake genuinely loves Counter-Strike, and despite knowing how the match ends, still gets drawn in by an exciting moment. "Look, he's gonna get it. Here he comes up here. Oh, he defused it! Ha, ha! Right before he got killed, too."

There are few things that can pull Lake's attention away from a Counter-Strike match. One just entered the room in the arms of his wife, Danielle. It's his three-week-old baby boy, Jordan.

"There's my little angel," says Lake, rising from the couch to see his firstborn son, who's wearing a onesie that says DADDY'S LITTLE BUDDY.

Lake's wife, Danielle, is a statuesque, dark-haired beauty. She's visibly exhausted from too little sleep since Jordan arrived, but it's not the kind of weariness a weekend spa getaway wouldn't fix. It's highly doubtful, though, that a mud bath is in her immediate future. Between her kids, Allie and Jordan, and Jason's surrogate family online, the wants and needs of the thirty-three-year-old Danielle are on hold.

Originally from the San Fernando Valley, Danielle caught Jason's eye while they both were hanging around the pool at the Rio Hotel in Las Vegas. She was in town with girlfriends to see Pearl Jam, and Jason was there for a bachelor party, already getting raucous with buddies by the pool at ten o'clock in the morning.

After asking for her number, that night, while Danielle was at the concert, "He left, like, ten messages on my voice mail," she says, rolling her eyes. It was typical Lake, never say quit. After they dated long-distance for a year, she moved to Atlanta and found work as a surgical nurse. They married in 2003.

"She's an amazingly supportive wife," Lake says. "If she wasn't so understanding, I could never do this. She's put up with way more than most women would."

Danielle is supportive, or rather tolerant, of Jason's tireless passion for e-sports. But she's not exactly a cheerleader. That's clear just in the way he tones down the coach routine when she enters the room, half lowering his laptop screen and asking about her day.

Danielle appreciates Jason's determined side, the way he's striving to build a business from the ground up. It's also appealing to her that he's paternalistic with his team. She loves those positive qualities in her husband. But it's apparent that her patience is not without limits and that the clock is beginning to run down on "this whole videogame thing," as she puts it. That's especially true now that she has a second child to raise. Sharing her husband with five young guys spread across America is not part of Danielle's long-term plan.

"He does spend a *lot* of time on it," she vents, with him out of earshot. "He comes home from work and coaches online. And now he's traveling more. He's gone one week and then two weeks later, and then two weeks later again. He'll say, 'Oh, but this is the championship.' And I'll say, 'But the championship was last week.' And he'll say, 'Oh, that was just the regional championship,' or something."

Before Jordan was born, Danielle told Jason he had to help out more with the kids. "So the agreement is that he doesn't go on the Internet until Allie goes to bed. That's eight o'clock."

As she says this, Jason is watching a demo on his laptop. It's 5:46 P.M. As he admits privately, "The new baby is really bringing this situation to a head."

His cell phone rings. He checks the caller ID and flips it open. "Yeah?" he says, followed by a pause. "Uh-huh. Wait a second, I'll give you another one."

Danielle watches as he pulls a Visa card out of his wallet. "Three-six-four-six...two-one-nine-seven..." He's shelling out once again for airplane tickets, this time to the upcoming event in Louisville, Kentucky. Annoyed, Danielle grabs a cordless phone from the kitchen counter and takes the baby out to the back porch, putting her feet up on a round glass table and calling her sister in L.A.

Inside, Lake snaps shut his cell phone. "That was one of my guys, Warden. He's our unofficial travel agent on the team."

It's been five months since CPL Winter, when Lake was rocked back on the hind legs of a chair and teetering on the edge of an emotional breakdown, his hands clasped behind his head and staring up at the ceiling in search of faith. That was in December. Now it's May, and he still hasn't landed a major sponsor.

He did stanch the bleeding some in January by inking a small merchandise deal with SteelSeries. They offered to provide customized mousepads bearing the swirling crimson and silver CompLexity logo, which Lake sells on the team Web site for $50 a pop. So far, he's sold a few hundred. It's not big-time money, only a few grand in the team's coffers, but more than anything it's a vote of confidence. It's a sign to Lake that he's moving in the right direction.

Of late, Lake's law practice has suffered a downturn. Interest rates on loans are up, so the home-buying market is down. Real-estate law is in a yearlong slump. That's put even more pressure on Lake to make "this whole videogame thing" profitable.

"I'm reaching out to sixty-two companies right now," says Lake, who has spent the past six months calling, faxing, and e-mailing mainstream corporations like Adidas and Pepsi, hoping to secure sponsorship. "I only need one or two to ante up so I can keep this thing airborne."

Since December, Lake has gone upside-down another $50,000 in salaries and travel expenses. That pushes the tab on CompLexity to $250,000.

"It puts a toll on my family, especially when I'm gone every other weekend," he admits. "I'm maxing out my credit cards. I'm pulling strings. I'm trying everything to turn this thing around. It's a tough situation, but we're gonna see if we can pull it off."

Lake has two shots at escaping ruin on his investment in pro gaming. He can either topple Team 3D and take Craig Levine's sponsors. Or, better still, gaming can grow and attract new sponsors, making the pie big enough for all.

"I honestly feel this is a pivotal moment for e-sports," he says. "We're either gonna make it huge or we'll be this thing in the closet that no one knows about. I want to be one of the people that makes it huge."

Nobody has extended himself financially in pro gaming anywhere near as much as Lake. In two years running a professional team, beyond a few mousepads sold, Lake hasn't seen dime one in return. He has no cash sponsors and, unlike most clan managers, who typically get 15 percent of prize money, he takes no cut from his players.

It's hard not to root for a guy like Lake, who believes so strongly in the future of gaming. But with two kids and a wife to support, is it wise for him to continue throwing money into a dream when the industry at present can't even keep two U.S. teams in the black?

Even if Lake landed a six-figure sponsor now, it would take five or six years after expenses to climb even halfway out of his $250,000 hole. As a businessman, and especially as a husband and a father, it's obvious that the smart move is to walk away.

The odd thing is, Lake knows it.

"The longer I talk about how great this thing is without showing any kind of return," he says, "the more I look like some old man in a kid's game chasing after a fool's dream."

There's a knock on the front door. It's Jason's mother-in-law, in town from L.A. to help with the baby. She's with Jason's sister-in-law, Wendy, and her own baby boy, four-month-old Cooper. Allie runs to hug Grandma as Danielle hangs up the phone and comes in with Jordan from the backyard.

It's pretty much a daily occurrence for Wendy to stop by. The other Lakes live right around the corner. Tonight Danielle's mom will be making American chop suey for dinner while Wendy and Danielle play with the kids in the living room…in the War Room…where the coach is trying to oversee practice.

"Hey, Jason," says Wendy, trying to pull him away from the laptop, "can you get *Grey's Anatomy* on that thing?" Lake tries to ignore her. "Oh, he always tunes us out," she says.

Lake grimaces and tells his wife, "I'll be downstairs."

The basement of the Lake home is a frat boy's dream come true. He's got a full-sized pool table with gold mesh pockets. There's a big octagonal table topped with green felt specifically for poker and blackjack. He's got a dartboard, a wet bar, and a home theater with eight plush leather seats, a movie screen big enough for a Greenwich Village art-house theater, and surround sound worthy of the Air Cav chopper scenes in *Apocalypse Now.*

"Funny thing is, I hardly ever use any of this stuff," Lake says. "It's the playroom I've always dreamed of, and now that I've got it, who's gonna use it with me?"

As he racks a triangle of billiard balls without even asking if you want to play, it becomes clear why a former frat-house jock like Lake would be drawn to Counter-Strike. It's head-to-head. It's mano a mano. Even Lake himself acknowledges, "I really don't think of it much like a videogame. It's not Pac-Man. It's not Super Mario. It's not like you're playing against a computer, where you beat it and nobody's pissed off on the other end. Where's the fun in that?"

He breaks the rack loudly, sinking the ten. As he lines up another striped ball, the conversation veers to his two favorite topics: how he built CompLexity into an elite Counter-Strike squad and how that squad will finally overtake Team 3D this season.

"The irony," he says, "is that 3D might actually be stronger now than they've ever been in the past, when nobody challenged them. It's only since we started putting the pressure on, in the last couple years, that they've been reshuffling their lineup, bringing in new guys, getting panicky. They know we're coming. They hear our footsteps."

The story of Lake's rise in pro gaming is the story of the pursuer, and it only truly matters in relation to the pursued.

"Back when I was still playing, around 2002 before Allie was born," Lake says, "3D was actually my favorite team. They were unbeatable in America. They were the kind of team I wanted to be on."

Lake began playing online in 1998, and over the next few years found teammates as dedicated as he was to practicing regularly. The original pre-professional CompLexity clan was never top-level, but they were good enough to play online in the middle competitive tiers of the CAL league. Everything changed for Lake in 2002, when another sub-elite player, Craig Levine, forever altered gaming in North America by soliciting the first-ever cash sponsorships for a U.S. clan and forming Team 3D.

Lake observed the entrepreneurial blueprint provided by Levine, and with his law firm thriving, he began to ponder the business potential of gaming as well.

"I thought, what's to say this can't be the next big thing? What's to say a decade or two down the line, CompLexity can't be the Atlanta Braves of gaming?" he says. "How many branded computers can I sell?

How many mousepads can I sell? One day there could be CompLexity hats in every junior high. That's where I saw this going."

Lake was already a passionate Counter-Strike player. He never doubted that the game would capture the public's imagination if given the right exposure. If anything, he thought it was a golden opportunity to get in a year or two before gaming went big. It was a can't-miss, Lake figured.

So in the summer of 2003, he took his first baby steps toward making CompLexity the United States' second professional team, seeking out two elite players in Miami and throwing them a few grand apiece to quit their part-time jobs and practice every night. A few thousand more went to hiring a well-known Norwegian player living in L.A. named Knoxville, who provided them with their first strats.

Over the next year, CompLexity showed modest improvement in online play. But it wasn't until April 2004 that Lake truly took the plunge into pro gaming, and he did so with three bold moves.

First, knowing he was dragging the team down with his mediocre skills, he voluntarily benched himself forever. Second, he signed his first elite-caliber talent, Matt "Warden" Dickens from Houston. That's the same Warden who earlier was booking flights with Lake's credit card.

Last, Lake made a cannonball splash in the gaming world by doing the unthinkable: he signed a founding member of Team 3D, Sean "Bullseye" Morgan.

If that sounds devious, the truth is Bullseye had already told Levine that he was retiring. He was an aging gamer at the end of his run, being all of twenty-three years old, and he'd had enough. The opportunistic Lake stepped in and talked him out of it. Eight days after leaving 3D, Bullseye signed with CompLexity.

"If there was a Hall of Fame for gamers, this kid would be there," says Lake, who brought Bullseye on board for an unprecedented $1,400 a month, making him the highest-paid Counter-Strike player in history. Not even the top Swedish or German players were pulling in that kind of cash, and 3D's players at the time were only making $800 a month.

"It was the pickup that shook e-sports," Lake says earnestly, if a bit hyperbolically.

The move was designed to make CompLexity a name overnight and get the community talking, so Lake played the signing for all it was worth. Splashed across CompLexity's Web site was a photo of him and Bullseye shaking hands on the deal in Lake's law office.

From that point forward, Lake became more than just a competitor in Counter-Strike. Now, with his investment in gaming, he was also a pitchman. The two roles would prove difficult to harmonize for Lake, as his fiery and competitive nature would often be an obstacle in business. It's hard to make friends when you're making enemies.

The Bullseye deal was entirely aboveboard. It was no player poach. Not even Levine disputed that. Yet, because no official announcement had been posted on 3D's Web site regarding Bullseye's retirement, most in gaming assumed Lake had acted stealthily. Rumors grew quickly, fueled by unfounded speculation on Gotfrag chat-room threads. Bullseye faked retirement to ditch 3D and play for Lake, some said. Another rumor was that Lake gave Bullseye a 401(k). Still another was that Bullseye wouldn't sign so Lake sweetened the deal by throwing in a brand-new Ninja motorcycle.

The truth wasn't nearly as salacious.

"Look, I'm trying to top 3D and Bullseye retires from 3D," Lake says. "So I call him up and say, 'I'm a lawyer in Atlanta and a businessman, and I'm gonna build the best Counter-Strike team the world has ever seen. You want to come over and talk?'

"He was understandably a little wary," says Lake, "so I told him, 'Bring a couple of buddies so you know I'm not some kind of freak or pervert.' And I said I'd give him five-hundred bucks just for sitting down and speaking with me. If he didn't want to join the team, he could keep the five hundred and walk away."

As Lake talks, he caroms the thirteen-ball off a rail into a corner pocket. He motions to the door beside the pool table in his cellar.

"We stood right outside there and smoked cigarettes. We shot a game of pool in here and drank a couple beers, and I signed him. That's it. The only rumor with any validity was the one about the Ninja. I did buy him the motorcycle, but he had to pay me back in installments out of his salary."

As for the $500, he told Bullseye to keep it as a signing bonus. Lake had bought his way onto the elite tier. He now had a team designed to take CPL by storm. Still, few in gaming had ever heard of Lake or CompLexity until now.

"Nobody could figure out what my story was," says Lake, who decided the best way to clear the air was to sit down for an interview with the shoutcasters on TSN. Big mistake. That interview, in some ways, Lake is still living down today.

It was a brazen, off-putting, over-the-top performance that brought out both the competitor and pitchman in Lake. What was meant as an introduction to the new clan owner on the scene came across like a WWE pro wrestling bombast-a-thon.

"This organization is highly motivated, highly financed, and we are going to be corporately sponsored. Like it, hate it, agree with it, think I'm insane, it doesn't matter. CompLexity is the future of e-sports," Lake boasted on the air.

Later, during the half-hour live interview, he said, "Today you laugh, but someday you'll write about this: CompLexity will sign the first one-million-dollar contract in professional gaming."

Later, when TSN tried to wrap up the segment so they could shout-cast a match between Team 3D and a clan called Meepins, Lake was unrelenting. "Everyone that's listening already knows 3D is gonna win," he said. "3D can wait. They've had enough airtime."

Then Lake threw down the gauntlet before America's top team. "Look," he said. "I respect 3D for what they've done for the business and everything else. But they're washouts. They're washups. They're going down, period. I'll say it again: CompLexity is the future of Counter-Strike."

If Lake was looking to make waves, mission accomplished. It's true that at the time, Team 3D was struggling, having finished seventh at CPL Winter 2003. Regardless, Lake's words were viewed in gaming as arrogant bluster by some rich no-name whose pro team had never even competed at a CPL event. To the community, all that this new guy Lake had done was throw a ton of money at Bullseye.

"You know what," Lake says now, in reflection. "I admit, that interview was something of a publicity stunt. I was looking to make a splash, sure. But the thing was, at the time, I really did feel like 3D had seen better days. I didn't think they had any of those *D*'s left—desire, discipline, or dedication. So that's what I said.

"Do I regret it? I don't know. I've never taken more heat for anything in my entire life. But I will say this. Later on, a lot of people came up and told me I was right."

It didn't help Lake's case that just two months after the much-hyped Bullseye signing and the inflammatory TSN interview, CompLexity went to CPL Summer 2004 and flopped. 3D also failed to place. It was a bust for both clans, who never faced each other at the event.

That September, CompLexity squared off against 3D at a LAN for the first time. It was no CPL, just a smaller qualifying event in L.A. for the World Cyber Games, and Team 3D demolished CompLexity 13–1.

So much for Lake's claim that Team 3D were "washouts" and "wash-ups" and "going down, period." In the parlance of gaming, Lake got owned. That means trounced, badly. Round 1 to Team 3D.

It was time for a new plan. Lake consulted Warden, the elite player he'd signed even before Bullseye. At the time, Warden considered bailing on Lake and hooking up with a better clan. After tanking in their debut at CPL Summer and taking a 13–1 beating from 3D, CompLexity struck fear in the hearts of no one. He'd be walking away from a $1,200-a-month salary, but quick math told Warden if CompLexity continued to finish out of the money, the $7,200 in salary he'd make over the next six months could actually be less than he might earn in prize money with a better team.

Warden considered his options and chose to see it through. He pledged to help make CompLexity the best Counter-Strike squad in the world, but he told Lake he'd need help. He needed more guys who could frag.

"Looking back," says Lake, chalking up his pool cue and lining up another shot on the table, "the part of the story people forget is that when I assembled the team I have now, I was forced to do it with throwaways. It wasn't like people were knocking down my door to sign up. Most of the guys I picked up came over because their other clans fell apart."

In the fall of 2004, a clan named Team Stomping Grounds merged with United 5, meaning ten players were trimmed to five. Of the five others who were sent packing, for $750 a month Lake signed three: Corey "Tr1p" Dodd, Tyler "Storm" Wood, and Danny "fRoD" Montaner.

"Three kids who got left on the side of the road," says Lake, beaming with pride. "And if you know anything about sports, you know that nobody has more motivation than a scorned athlete."

Lake calls his players "scorned athletes," but it was Lake who felt scorned. Back in 1998, it was random luck that a guy like him got hooked on Counter-Strike. On a whim, with money to throw around from a thriving law practice, he took a shot at running a pro gaming team. Then he got smacked in the mouth 13–1 by Team 3D. He'd been embarrassed. Now Lake got serious. Now he had something to prove.

"After I put that team together, I worked the bejesus out of those guys," the coach says. In their first months together, the rebuilt CompLexity practiced seven hours a night. In their first season online at CAL's top level, CAL-Invite, CompLexity with Warden, Bullseye, and the three new guys went 17-1 to win the title.

Soon after, Bullseye again decided to retire. "He was twenty-four by then," says Lake, "and he mostly just wanted to hang out with his friends, ride his Ninja and pick up girls."

The parting was amicable. Lake even paid the last few months of his salary in full. To fill the vacancy, in the fall of 2004, CompLexity added Justin "Sunman" Summy to complete its lineup of today.

The reloaded CompLexity dominated the next CAL-Invite season without dropping a single match. The team was making a name for itself online. Still, few in Counter-Strike were ready to bow down to Lake just yet. With all the flaws of online play, nothing had been proven. CompLexity was not yet "LAN-tested," and so they entered CPL Winter 2004 with an almost insulting twenty-seventh seed.

Three days later, they left with a validating fifth-place finish. Team 3D, meanwhile, was a disappointing eighth. Again, the two clans never faced each other.

On Gotfrag's forum threads, fans were beginning to posit the previously unthinkable: Was CompLexity better than Team 3D? Hardly, scoffed the legions of 3D fanboys. CompLexity was nothing until they beat 3D head-to-head at a LAN.

Four months later, on July 25, 2005, they met at an event called ACon5 in L.A. Nobody was mistaking ACon5 for a major event like CPL. Still, excitement was high for the second-ever match between the two clans, and the first in which CompLexity was playing with its fully assembled pro squad.

The match didn't disappoint. When Sunman dramatically finished off a 22–20 overtime victory, CompLexity had its LAN win. "That changed everything," Lake says.

Now it was a rivalry. CompLexity had landed one squarely on 3D's chin. To paraphrase Lake himself, someone was pissed off on the other end.

The rest of 2005 grew uglier, as Team 3D came back throwing haymakers. First Levine tried to sign away Lake's players behind his back. Then 3D pummeled CompLexity at three straight LANs to end the year. The one-two-three punch was "earth-shattering," in Lake's own words.

Heading into CPL Winter 2005 at the Hyatt in Dallas, where this collision-course season began in December, Team 3D had silenced the uprising. They had beaten back CompLexity's challenge and again were number one in the world rankings.

Lake again chalks up his cue and looks over the pool table in his basement.

"I'll be honest, beating 3D is a big part of what drives me," he says. "Dispelling the myth that 3D is the best gaming organization in America, that's a big part of my motivation.

"Are we underappreciated because of 3D? Yes," he says. "Are we underrespected because of 3D? Yes. Do I have a chip on my shoulder about it? Absolutely."

To Lake, Team 3D is the white whale he's been obsessively pursuing for two years in futility. It's Craig Levine who still gets the face time on *SportsCenter* and the write-ups in *Sports Illustrated*. It's Levine who has Intel and NVIDIA covering his bills while Lake shells out for salaries and travel, giving out his credit-card number to book flights. It's Levine, a twenty-two-year-old, who's playing with house money, and it's Lake who's gambling—and losing—his family's financial security.

"To Craig, all this is a business, nothing more," he says. "His team is a bunch of all-stars. My team I picked up because they were guys who were never given the chance to prove themselves—guys like me, who are disrespected, have their backs against the wall, and want to prove the whole world wrong."

Lake is not a gamer at heart. He's from the world of football and frat houses and bachelor parties in Vegas. He's a jock who stumbled onto this world accidentally but now appreciates the parallels between athletics and gaming. He admires those elite players with the ability to do in Counter-Strike what he never could, and much of his back-to-the-wall, underdog rhetoric is Lake's way to stand behind all gamers, to recognize their exceptional talent and stick up for the social outcasts.

For the five kids who wear the maroon CompLexity jersey, it's also a coach's motivational tool. Lake wants to impress upon his players all of those clichés he learned from his baseball-coach dad back in Iowa. Concepts like commitment and discipline and loyalty. Lake wants to teach. He wants to have an effect. He wants to impart the lesson that a team working together, with trust and sacrifice and discipline, can attain something greater than the sum of its parts.

By some bizarre fluke of luck and design, Lake found this game that makes players feel like athletes and makes him feel like a coach. Now he wants them all to know what it feels like to become champions.

It's clear that Jason Lake will never walk away from pro gaming and abandon his clan of underdogs as long as Team 3D has the upper hand. That's the reason he's $250,000 in the hole with maxed-out credit cards and a wife who's fed up with his "videogame thing." That's why he's obsessively chasing after a dream that stopped making financial sense over a year ago.

It's Levine and his team of pampered all-stars. He can't let them win. He won't do it. He might go broke first, but he won't be broken. He won't let down his boys. Lake will take this thing all the way to the end, and it will finish one of two ways: triumph and absolution, or one catastrophic marital and financial shipwreck.

"When gaming gets big, I want CompLexity to be *the* American gaming team," he says. "I want to be at the store someday or walking down the street somewhere and overhear someone mention the name CompLexity without knowing I've got anything to do with it. That's when I'll know that my work is done."

Lake has a favorite expression, a credo really, that he picked up years ago from an old football coach. It encapsulates his attitude toward sports, school, business, maybe even leaving a dozen voice mails asking his future wife for a first date years ago in Vegas. It's the same philosophy that crystallizes his belief in CompLexity: "The saddest thing about giving up is never knowing how close you were to success."

The videogame coach circles around the pool table, leaning down low to the rail and scoping out the nine-ball in the side pocket. He knocks it across the table but misses. The ball comes back off the rail and drops in the near side pocket, falling to rest in the mesh.

# Chapter 7

**T**HE KENTUCKY DERBY IS THE PINNACLE OF HORSE RAC-
ing, famously held annually at Churchill Downs on the first Saturday in May. At that hallowed track in Louisville, Secretariat,
Seattle Slew, and Alydar each graced the paddock draped in a wreath
of victory flowers.

A mile down the road, at the intersections of interstates 264 and
65, sits the Kentucky Exposition Center. This is the home of Lanwar,
the debut event of the World Series of Video Games, or WSVG, a new
venture with ambitions to supplant the nine-year-old CPL atop the U.S.
gaming scene.

The WSVG launched in February 2006. It has no history of hosting LAN events and thus no track record. But given the number of
teams registered to compete here and the substantial prize money up
for grabs, Lanwar qualifies as the first major event in the summer gaming slate. First place is $12,500; second is $7,500 and third is $5,000.
That elevates it above lesser LANs like AmeriCup or ACon5. Bigger
events will follow later in the summer, so in gaming terms, Lanwar
is no Kentucky Derby. This is no first Saturday in May. It's the third
Friday in June.

Behind the green-tinted glass façade of the Expo Center, workers
have labored for three straight days to convert a massive hangar-sized

space into what might be described as a mini–amusement park. It's been a subcontractor symphony in there, with the beep-beep of forklifts harmonizing with the pounding of hammers and the pop of staple guns.

Forklifts shuttled around wooden flats of computers as workers with hand trucks followed behind with plastic tubs of extension cords and power strips.

The result is a cross between a CPL event and an indoor Coney Island. There's the usual sponsor village by the front door, a BYOC area to the side, and rows of tables for Counter-Strike and Quake tournaments in the rear. But unlike any CPL event, the WSVG also aims to lure in the kiddie crowd. To widen the audience, they're aiming younger.

There's a bouncy, inflated "Battle Pit" area that resembles a huge McDonald's PlayPlace, where tykes bash each other with dual-ended paddles that look like giant spongy Q-Tips. Nearby is an "Oxygen Bar" where passersby affix nose clips and inhale invigorating scents like peppermint and vanilla.

There are go-kart-sized Formula 1 cars for kids to sit in and play a racing game using the gas, brake, and steering wheel. Younger kids can play Dance Dance Revolution, jumping around on a sensor mat to duplicate dance moves, or Guitar Hero II to rock out to Mötley Crüe and Guns N' Roses on a plastic guitar.

Lanwar even has Simon Says, where participants can win gaming prizes, as well as a Lego-building competition.

Walking through the Expo Center, it's clear that the WSVG has added a few bells and whistles to the CPL template, but seeing twelve-year-olds touching their noses in Simon Says or rocking out with little toy guitars, you've got to wonder how this *Teletubbies* playland scene will go over with the hard-core gamer crowd.

Guys like Jason Lake have spent years trying to break down the nerdy stigma of gaming while pushing it to potential sponsors as a viable spectator sport. Are a bouncy play pit and Dance Dance Revolution really a step toward legitimizing e-sports?

"When you compare us with the CPL, keep in mind that we have a much broader marketing mandate in our DNA," says the man with the plan here, Matt Ringel, head of the World Series of Video Games.

A Yalie turned gaming promoter, Ringel launched the WSVG as an entertainment venture of the William Morris Agency. For the past four years, through his company Games Media Properties, Ringel has been staging small, peripheral videogame expos called GameRiot festivals at events like state fairs, carnivals, and concerts.

GameRiot consisted of a few games set up for demo play with window dressing to lure in passersby. It was an attraction about as sizable as the sponsor-booth village at a major LAN, nowhere near the scope of what the WSVG is attempting here with Lanwar.

Yet despite his inexperience, the quick-talking Ringel pulled the rug out from under Angel Munoz in February 2006 by signing away a dozen CPL staffers and commandeering its main sponsor, Intel. It was a seismic event in e-sports, as the company most heavily invested in pro gaming abandoned the man who started it all.

After years of waiting for the CPL to expand its audience, the microchip corporation was ready for new ideas. Ringel reeled them in, one can assume, by pointing at pie graphs and saying things like how the WSVG has a "broader marketing mandate" in its DNA.

Ringel insists GameRiot was sufficient on-the-job training for running a major LAN event. Seemingly always talking in corporate-speak, he trumpets a résumé that includes "mastery of crushing production logistics" and "orientation in the legacy of gaming competitions."

The WSVG, he boasts, is a "cross-fertilization of worlds" and "a package to move the whole space forward."

The plan is ambitious. In hosting both PC and console tournaments, the WSVG is competing on two fronts. First they're up against the CPL and its pioneering history in PC gaming. They're also competing against another recent gaming start-up called Major League Gaming, which hosts console-only events featuring Xbox games like Halo 2.

Ringel's big brainstorm is to lure in spectators with attractions like the kiddie park and a concert on Lanwar's final night by actor Jared

Leto and his band, 30 Seconds to Mars. The hope is that people who stop by for nongaming attractions will stick around long enough to get a look at the tournament. Or more to the point, they'll at least pass by the sponsor booths, which is how he sold Intel on the concept.

"What the CPL did in the past was market to the same fifteen hundred people that always go to the CPL events," sniffs Ringel, who also intends to expand gaming's appeal by getting it increased TV exposure. To that end, a camera crew will be circling around the gaming tables at Lanwar shooting footage for the GamePlay HD channel on the satellite provider Dish Network. "We plan on at least thirty hours of television in the U.S. alone this year," Ringel says optimistically.

Ringel is talking a big game in gaming. It's a little suspect, though, that despite that cross-fertilization and broad mandate, Ringel's supposedly revolutionary business model still includes charging every kid who walks through the door $85 for a seat in the BYOC.

A short walk across the parking lot from the Expo Center is a sprawling resort-style Tudor hotel called the Executive Inn. This weekend, the Exec is base camp for the teams competing at Lanwar.

Arrival day at a LAN event is like a family reunion. Players pass through the lobby, slapping hands. Laughter fills the halls. Out by the pool, Jason Lake is talking with shoutcasters from TSN and Gotfrag editors Lee Chen and Trevor Schmidt. It's an always-popular topic: the prospects of pro gaming breaking into the mainstream anytime soon.

Today the focus is on the WSVG and whether it's the right outfit to push gaming to the next level of recognition, as Ringel is promising.

Gaming insiders are a skeptical lot. For a decade, these guys have been waiting for the rest of America to get hooked on Counter-Strike and for the corporate advertising dollars that would follow. For a decade, they've been waiting for the outside world to take them as seriously as they take themselves.

None of them doubts Counter-Strike as a rootable sport or as viable spectator entertainment. It's a question of getting the message across, packaging it to appeal to a wider audience. And these guys have their doubts that Ringel will be any more successful getting the word out than Angel Munoz.

"To me," says one of the insiders talking with Lake, "the CPL and the WSVG are the same thing. It's a lot of the same people, the same prize money, the same sponsors."

Another says, "You're really not pushing the envelope with a Lego-building competition. That's a circus, a county fair. That's not what professional gaming needs. What gaming in the U.S. desperately needs is a mass-market validation that it's not some basement-dwelling activity for pasty-white nerds."

If that seems jaded, it's probably because the last time anyone talked this big about revolutionizing gaming, the results were disastrous.

In January 2004, a sports promoter with some NASCAR experience named Joe Hill held a glammed-up tournament at the Stardust Resort and Casino in Las Vegas that he dubbed the Cyber X Games, despite there being no actual affiliation with the well-known extreme-sports event.

The first-place prize for Counter-Strike alone was announced to be $100,000, a full $40,000 more than the CPL had ever offered. The problem was Hill had zero experience handling the technical end of a LAN, much like Ringel and the WSVG now, and his staff butchered even routine tasks like crimping network cable.

They also never arranged to have an on-site download source for gamers to activate Counter-Strike, which is standard procedure at any decent-sized LAN. Instead, the hundreds of competitors at Cyber X Games had to load the game through the Internet. Worse still, an old Vegas hotel like the aging Stardust was wired with an outdated DSL line. In seconds, the entire system crashed, and soon the Cyber X Games burned with it.

Despite all-night efforts to patch the network, glitches and delays remained rampant and sponsors pulled out. Facing a riot from gamers who'd paid entry fees and made the trip to Vegas, Hill tried to appease the crowd by announcing "show matches" between the top eight Counter-Strike teams for $10,000 apiece.

That only further enraged the dozens of teams who were left out of the show matches, and the scene turned uglier. Chairs were kicked over. Fights broke out. One gamer berated Hill in a torrent of profanity. It hardly mattered. Those four show matches were nothing but crowd control. Without sponsors, the winners would never see any prize money from Hill anyway.

The Cyber X Games fiasco in 2004 was gaming's darkest day and most deflating disappointment, and as WSVG kicked off its debut event in Louisville, its memory still lingered in the minds of those gathered here at the Executive Inn.

For nine years, the CPL had given gamers a home. Now the upstart WSVG had swiped the CPL's top sponsor and Ringel had the reins, and his grand plan to take gaming to the next level included...Simon Says?

CompLexity is crammed into their coach's room, number 511, for a team meeting, with all five players sitting on the two twin beds. One is fully dressed and actually in bed with the covers pulled up to his chest, despite its only being three o'clock in the afternoon. This is Matt "Warden" Dickens.

How to describe Warden physically? Let's just get it over with. Warden is the fat kid. He's five-foot-nine and weighs about 250.

Gaming isn't the kindest environment for tubby guys. Being an Internet culture, Warden is often the butt of malicious fat jokes posted on Web forum threads. "Vicious attacks from some kid hiding anonymously behind his computer in Podunk, USA," as Lake puts it. It's puerile stuff, like rhyming "fried chickens" with his last name or posting pictures with Warden's head superimposed on a picture of Godzilla.

"More than anyone I know in gaming," says his coach, "Matt has had to endure a lot of shit. And he's done it with dignity and class."

Like many heavyset kids, the twenty-one-year-old Warden fends off the insults mostly by cracking jokes. Warden gets all the big laughs in this crew. He's like the Eric Cartman of CompLexity, only not conniving. But he's no angel, either.

At the end of January, CompLexity canceled an entire week of practice because Warden went on a family vacation to Hawaii. As he

explained it—very regretfully—to his teammates at the time, the vacation had been planned for months and it was too late to get out of it. He
didn't even really want to go, he explained. You know, he'd really rather
stay and get ready for the season. It was just one of those unavoidable
things.

The one detail Warden left out about his family vacation to Hawaii
was the part about his family not going. They were in Houston, where
they live. Warden went to Honolulu to hook up with a girl named
Ashley he met on the Internet.

His teammates knew almost immediately his story was bullshit,
which wasn't difficult to deduce. Warden's brother Mason plays for
Mug N Mouse, so when he showed up for an online match that week—
instead of being on the white sandy beaches of Oahu—his brother's
cover was blown.

Warden's CompLexity teammates didn't appreciate being lied to,
but they promised to keep it quiet. Warden is the player who's been
with CompLexity from the beginning. No one doubts his dedication,
and it goes without saying that the shit will certainly hit the fan if
Lake finds out he cost the team a week of practice while chasing tail
all the way to Honolulu.

Mostly, though, these guys won't rat out Warden because it's just
not something you do to a friend.

"Okay," Lake says, to begin the meeting. He finishes a cigarette at
the window and stubs it out in an ashtray. "I want to focus on our CT
side. We could improve on terrorist, but that's not where we're soft.
My question is, why are we not working as a team on defense?"

Each of the five players no doubt has an opinion, but none vol-
unteers an answer. They know Lake isn't really looking for strategic
analysis anyway. It's the same before every big tournament. These
team meetings are really just an excuse for a pep talk.

The coach, by his own admission, was never all that good of a
Counter-Strike player. He doesn't second-guess or presume to know
more about in-game strategy than his players. Lake is a motivator. That's
what he does. That's why he's here. This is where his money goes, why

he'd never say he regrets getting into e-sports, even as he sinks deeper into debt.

Maybe a few years from now he'll be delivering riled-up pep talks on a Little League field at his son's T-ball games, but right now he's a Counter-Strike coach. For all the money he spends on CompLexity, he gets this opportunity to mold and motivate, to lead, to kick a little ass.

"Why are we not rotating?" he says, putting a foot up on a chair and slapping the back of one hand into the palm of the other. "Why don't we have team chemistry? What are we doing to fix CT-side?"

Warden, still half-tucked into a bed, assumes the role of spokesman. "Every single map is turning T-side, that's the bottom line. We're putting up 13–2 numbers on Nuke daily on T-side," he says.

Warden's counterpoint is that Nuke is a tough map on which to play defense, or counterterrorist. So in a match of fifteen rounds per half, getting 13–2 on offense (T) is enough to carry the day. Then you only need to steal three rounds while on defense (CT) to reach the sixteen needed to take the match.

Lake's not buying the argument. "I appreciate that our T is getting stronger," he says, "but why should we accept the fact that maps are going T and not adjust to make our CT revolutionary? What's to prevent us from doing some freaky shit, locking down Upper and making them go Lower, and then retaking Lower?"

Warden responds, "We can't give up Lower site. Then we're fucked. We can't come through the vents. That's not an option. Coming from Ramp, a possibility. But there's so many nooks and crannies they could hide in."

Lake backs off. This is a strategy issue, and he does defer to the team on strats. "Look, I don't mean to bust your balls, but we do have weaknesses," he says. "We have weaknesses going into the biggest summer in Counter-Strike history."

He leans against the windowsill, staring down to the pool outside. "I don't know." He sighs. "Maybe giving you guys that vacation time Warden asked for in January was a bad idea."

His teammates all look over at Warden. That "vacation time" was his rendezvous in Oahu. Warden slowly sinks down into the bed and pulls the covers up to his shoulders.

"No, I don't think so," concludes Lake, turning back from the window. "I say we're in pretty good shape even with that week off. But we're not perfect. We've still got room to improve."

Lake knows his team is entering the tournament as favorites. They've got the talent and teamwork to break through and become the top clan in the world. The point of this meeting is not to introduce doubt. It's to make his kids believe. The coach's secret agenda, though, is also to use the meeting to light a fire under the team's star player— Danny "fRoD" Montaner.

fRoD is a nineteen-year-old Cuban American from Miami, six-foot-two with a caramel complexion and dressed in a style that's hip-hop meets Little Havana—soft clog slippers, a white tank-tee and a pair of baggy green Hurricanes basketball trunks.

At present, fRoD is the consensus best Counter-Strike player in the world. With this kid, it's one shot, one kill. If he sees you through the scope of his AWP, you're dead.

An AWP is an Arctic Warfare (Police) sniper rifle, the single most effective killing weapon in Counter-Strike. AWP is another gaming acronym spoken as a word and not enunciated by letter. It's pronounced "op" as in "co-op," and it has numerous parts of speech. A player can AWP (verb), be a good AWPer (noun), and roam around the map AWP-ing (gerund).

Because the AWP is the weapon most capable of killing from long distance—delivering a bullet at up to six hundred yards—there is no player more important on a Counter-Strike team than a sniper. And the most lethal AWPer in the game today is fRoD. His proficiency with the sniper rifle is the single biggest reason that CompLexity is now ranked number one in North America.

How good is he? According to Gotfrag, in 4,186 rounds played in his career, which translates to about 150 matches, fRoD has 3,853 kills. That's a lot, obviously, but difficult to grasp. A better statistical measure of a player's dominance is +/–.

Counter-Strike matches are played in rounds, and no player survives every round. That's unrealistic. The goal in each round is to take out as many opponents as possible before you're eliminated. That's where +/– comes in. It's frags minus deaths. Each frag is +1 and each time you get fragged is –1.

Let's say CompLexity wins a match 16–9 and in those twenty-five total rounds, fRoD frags 22 guys while getting killed 13 times. That's 22 minus 13, so he'd be +9 for the match (which, by the way, is a solid performance).

Over time, all of fRoD's +9s and +7s and +12s have added up to a cumulative +1,384. To appreciate how gaudy that is, consider that among Team 3D's players, Volcano has the fourth-best career +/– in North America with a +661, followed at number five by Rambo (+657) and at six by Method (+592).

At +1,384 fRoD has *double* the +/– of anyone on Team 3D. To call fRoD the Michael Jordan of Counter-Strike is a disservice to fRoD. Jordan didn't double the career scoring numbers of Charles Barkley and Patrick Ewing. fRoD is in Babe Ruth territory, like in the 1919 season when Ruth was rewriting record books by swatting 29 homers when the player with the next-highest total had 12.

Unless fRoD takes his hand off the mouse to scratch his nose, he practically doesn't miss.

Not that fRoD is a one-man team. CompLexity also has the current number two and three guys in North America, Tyler "Storm" Wood at +995 and Warden at +661. Their strat caller, Corey "Tr1p" Dodd, is number seven at +586.

So, of the North American top ten, CompLexity has one, two, three, and seven and Team 3D has four, five, and six. That's why any real discussion of U.S. supremacy includes only those two teams. Paying salaries, of course, draws the top players, but the stats are also evidence that being paid to practice five nights a week further sharpens skills.

As closely matched as the top two U.S. teams are, the bottom line for CompLexity is that fRoD's prowess with the AWP is the key to success, and Lake knows it.

Unfortunately for him, fRoD knows it, too. It's that "good problem to have" for a coach: how do you keep a star player buying into the team concept as his ego begins to balloon along with his success and celebrity?

"What do you think, Danny?" asks Lake.

"What do I think about what?" answers fRoD, leaning back on the bed.

Over the last few weeks, his teammates have been grumbling about fRoD's attitude. Nobody here has gone to Lake with a complaint, but he has overheard griping about fRoD showing up late to practice or half-assing it during scrims. Why should he practice as hard, fRoD figures, if he's so much better than his teammates?

What fRoD is overlooking is that CompLexity designs strats around him, setting him up for shots and watching his back. That's what makes them a team, and not just a collection of elite players.

Lake is the only real coach in Counter-Strike, an authority figure who can step into personality conflicts and defuse tensions. Other clans, without that guiding force, often break down the same way. They point fingers and argue after losses, eroding team morale. They cease to communicate during matches, not warning one another of approaching enemies. Players skip practice, bicker, and eventually the clan falls apart altogether. Even Team 3D, with its manager Levine away from boot camp in Dallas, devolved into a power struggle.

Lake won't let that happen here. This meeting is about more than discussing T-side and CT-side. The coach also intends to send a message to everyone gathered in the room that, regardless of his talent, fRoD would get no preferential treatment.

"Danny," says Lake, "what was the problem last time we played on Nuke?"

"Well, for one thing," fRoD answers, "I was playing on eight by six."

Lake begins to simmer. When fRoD complains about an "eight by six," he's talking about the LCD monitors at their last event. It's true that every elite player has preferred equipment and settings for particulars like screen resolution, brightness, mouse sensitivity. But really, none of it makes all that much of a difference. Complaining about comparatively low "eight by six" resolution is like a golfer blaming a bogey on his putter.

Lake has his opening. This isn't about tactics and strats now. This is about attitude and fortitude, and all those other life lessons the coach is here to deliver.

"Your thing, Danny, and I'm going to say this in front of everybody," Lake begins. "You're one of the best Counter-Strike players in the world, but you have what I call a mental flaw. You think, 'If you don't have a certain hertz, a certain something, I can't play.'

"My LCD is eight by blah, blah, blah so I can't hit my AWP shots. And you know what, maybe there's a smidgen of truth to that, but you take that smidgen and you make it this big." He holds his hands out wide. "You go into a match with a shit monitor. Your keyboard doesn't quite fit on the table. Your chair isn't comfortable. These are all things to give you an excuse in your own mind why you can't perform."

Lake's blood is up now. He stands with his hands on his hips and flashes back twenty years earlier to some football field under the lights in the farmlands of Iowa. Then and now, he's in his glory.

"Let's say, okay, I'm an outside linebacker and it's raining like hell. I could say, I'm not gonna have a good game because I'm gonna be slipping and sliding, and I can't catch a running back. Or I could say, I'm Jason fucking Lake. I'm the best outside linebacker Iowa has ever seen. I'm the meanest, I'm the baddest. You can put me on ice. You can put me on snow. You can put me on a mud field, and because we're all on the same field, I'm gonna beat you.

"*That* is mental toughness," he tells fRoD, pausing to let the words sink in.

fRoD unwisely tries to clarify his complaint. "I didn't mean it like that. I don't care about the monitors. That's not a big deal. Chairs, tables. Nothing bothers me except resolution. I can't get 100 hertz on

1024. I don't mind playing 1024 on a fifteen-inch monitor, I don't care. As long as I get my hertz."

fRoD has a point. He can't shoot what he can't clearly see. He had a lousy monitor and missed his shots. It's a *videogame*. Yet here's Lake rallying the troops with talk of grit and heart and toughness. This is way past videogame to him now.

"You're Danny *fucking* Montaner," Lake says, his voice rising.

"Yeah, but…"

"There's no but. You're Danny *fucking* Montaner. I don't care if you're on eight by six. I don't give a shit if you're looking through a spyglass. You can frag."

"I do frag," says Danny, defensively.

"It's mental attitude, all you guys," says the coach, easing off his star and addressing the whole team. "The point I'm trying to hammer home is that adversity is going to happen. It's sports."

When Lake makes this point, that Counter-Strike is sports, there is no discernible response from the team. This is Lake's message, his purpose. His goal is to instill in these kids the belief and confidence that they're every bit the athletes that he and his football buddies were back in Iowa. The funny thing is, the players aren't in need of convincing. They know. They get it. They've never bought into the whole "gamers are outcasts" stereotype in the first place. That's an obsolete concept from Lake's generation, not theirs. They don't have anything to prove. They don't have chips on their shoulders.

These guys like Lake, and they appreciate that he cares so much about their futures. Plus he's paying them a grand a month to be here. So nobody's rolling their eyes during his impassioned pep talk, although nobody's obsequiously nodding their heads either. Mostly they're just staring at the wall or the window, patiently waiting for Lake to exhaust himself.

"Through your whole life, your brain is constantly making excuses why you can't perform to your best. The people who succeed are the people who can train themselves, convince themselves they can still outperform anyone else on a level playing field, no matter how bad that playing field is.

"Bad monitors, bad keyboards, bad chairs," Lake continues. "When shit sucks, convince yourself you can do better on it than the guy across from you, period. No matter what the obstacle is, well beyond Counter-Strike, what's important is that you can mentally adjust to it. Are we clear on that?"

Everyone nods, including fRoD. The lesson is over.

"Okay, I think you get the message," Lake says, and his players rise and mill toward the door. "And listen, the next couple days I want everybody to get some sunshine. I don't want you guys sitting in your rooms playing poker all day," Lake says. "Get outside. Go for a jog. Go sit by the pool and check out the lifeguard. Whatever."

"The lifeguard's a guy," cracks Warden.

"Get some sun," reiterates Lake. "And tonight, be smart. You want to have a couple of beers, fine. You're all adults. I don't want to see any rum.

"And hey," he says, stopping them at the door. "Everyone in their rooms by midnight."

# Chapter 8

THE FIRST DAY OF REAL COMPETITION BEGINS AT WSVG's Lanwar with twenty-nine teams vying for the Counter-Strike title. There is little international representation because the event is being held the same weekend as a major LAN in Sweden called DreamHack, which draws all of the top European teams.

A Gotfrag readers' poll has named CompLexity the team to beat here in Louisville, with 45 percent picking Jason Lake's clan to 36 percent for Team 3D. Behind those prohibitive favorites, JaX Money Crew had 7 percent of the vote; United 5 and Mug N Mouse each had 2 percent; and a clan named Pandemic made the list with 1 percent.

Inside the Kentucky Expo Center, all the top teams are cruising early. At the Mug N Mouse table, Punkville wears his red shades and a black bandana over his head. A cell phone, pack of Marlboro Lights, and a purple Bic lighter lie on the table a few inches from his mouse-pad. In the next seat, Gosu is wearing a black hoodie and sipping on a Monster energy drink. Mug N Mouse start out hot, blanking a nobody team named KwM in their opener, 16–0. Apparently they're not too groggy from their fourteen-hour van ride from Dallas.

Across the way, the young manager JaX is keeping an eye on his team, JaX Money Crew. The nineteen-year-old rich kid wears a baby blue oxford with a white collar, his cuffs undone and tie loosened like a fraternity brother after an overnight pledge haze.

By personally financing the team, and in wearing a suit at LAN tourneys, JaX is considered something of a Jason Lake imitator in gaming. The difference is that JaX is paying his clan's way with a six-figure trust fund, and for him being a part of e-sports is less about fielding a top squad than it is about having guys to party with.

With their high finish at CPL Winter, JaX Money Crew, or JMC, is the number-three-ranked team in North America. They cruise in their opener 16–0, slowed only by a time-out so one player could run to the bathroom and vomit. "Food poisoning," says JaX with a wink. It's safe to assume JMC had no curfew last night. At midnight they could well have been piled into a rental car driven by JaX himself, hanging U-turns across Louisville traffic into strip-club parking lots.

At the 3D table, Moto is edgy in his first tournament back from retirement. The table is too low for his liking. "I can't get used to this. It sucks," he gripes. It's not Moto who sits in the middle seat of the row of five, the place normally reserved for strat caller. Rambo is there, although officially Moto remains 3D's strat caller. That was the ruling by manager Craig Levine following the power struggle at boot camp. It's a tenuous cease-fire, despite Levine's appeasing Rambo with the promise he could "advise on in-game decisions and give primary input."

In its opener, Team 3D obliterates a cupcake clan called Violence 16–4 on Inferno, dominating with the new Banana Peel strat from boot camp. In 3D's first few matches, Moto is rusty and inconsistent. In one match, he posts a lousy −6 in +/− despite 3D cruising 16–5. Later he's +15 in a 16–1 victory. His up-and-down play has his teammates concerned, but their manager Levine hardly seems to care. He's barely even watching their matches.

Levine isn't much for hands-on leadership. Thus far at Lanwar, he's spent most of his time in the WSVG administration area helping the inexperienced crew work out bugs in their scorekeeping software. Even at the young age of twenty-three, Levine has been around gaming longer than most and has plenty of experience troubleshooting at

LANs. In their debut event, the WSVG is grateful he's here to help. Still, it's a little conspicuous seeing a team manager with a vested interest in the outcome of the tournament sitting in the admin area working hand-in-hand with WSVG officials.

Conspiracy theorists are murmuring that Levine is using it to his team's advantage, that he's rearranged the order of maps in upcoming rounds to give 3D the easiest possible path to the championship. Punkville, for one, is positive that shady doings are afoot.

Barring upsets in the brackets, Mug & Mouse is scheduled to meet 3D in the semifinals. Initially the map chosen for that round was Train. Now, with no explanation besides "software issue," it's been switched to Inferno, the map on which 3D dominates with the Banana Peel strat.

"This is bullshit," fumes Punkville, turning away from a posting of the revised brackets. "What, they just randomly push 3D's worst map up earlier? And now we get them on their best one? That's just a coincidence? Levine is so busted, dude."

At boot camp in Dallas a month ago, Mug N Mouse beat 3D on Train, albeit against new, unpolished strats. So now Punkville is certain that Levine manipulated the Lanwar brackets so 3D would play on Train earlier against a weaker opponent.

The conspiracy theory is far from airtight, but it may be more than unfounded paranoia. In their next match on Train, 3D barely wins 19–17 in overtime over a so-so clan called Check-Six. Although it turns out, after all the suspicion, they won't face Mug N Mouse after all, because Punkville's clan was upset by a team called Shockwave.

With the loss, Mug N Mouse is down but not out. Lanwar is double-elimination, so a first defeat merely drops a team into the tournament's "lower bracket" with the other one-time losers. It's a second loss that sends you packing.

In the afternoon, the tourney goes dark for lunch and the gamers kick back in the BYOC, with its usual grid of World of Warcraft junkies and Counter-Strike base camps. Today, the BYOC is the scene of a theft investigation. Call it "CSI: BYOC."

A middle-aged man in thick glasses and a Pittsburgh Steelers ROETHLISBERGER jersey steps onto a podium to address the concerned crowd. He taps the mike, sending a *mmmph, mmmph* over the loudspeakers.

His name is Troy Schwartz, but he goes by the alias Burden, which is also what it says in small letters on his orange ball cap. The thirty-seven-year-old Burden has been running LANs in Louisville for eight years, most with a modest turnout of around a hundred kids. Once a year, he hosts the "Million Man LAN," which has an attendance of about two hundred. In the Kentucky gaming scene, Burden is a big deal. Even if he's only about five-foot-five.

"Could I have your attention, please. This is Burden," he says into the microphone. "We've got an asshole in here who's running around stealing backpacks and girls' purses. If you see anyone around the bags that you don't recognize, come and get me immediately and I *will* remedy this problem."

Burden then goes all lawdog on the mystery outlaw.

"We've got a hundred people in here hunting you down," he says, "and if you're listening, I suggest you leave now before I personally kick your ass. Thanks very much for your attention."

You might assume there could be no weirder sight at a LAN than a minuscule man in a Steelers jersey threatening to pummel a teen-age kleptomaniac over the PA system. But you'd be wrong. It gets much weirder, right outside the doors of the Expo Center, in the parking lot, where a C-list movie actor is playing air guitar in the back of a Ryder truck.

Actually, he's playing air bass, to be exact. A stand-up air bass, no less. Stephen Baldwin, the guy from *The Usual Suspects* and youngest brother of Alec Baldwin, is rocking out in the open bay of a moving truck, pantomime-plucking away with his right hand as his left hand walks up and down an imaginary fretless neck. Huge speakers inside the truck are pumping out Johnny Cash's "I Walk the Line," and Baldwin is feeling it.

A born-again Christian on a mission, Baldwin rolled up to Lanwar at the last minute today, adding it to a promotional tour for his book,

*The Breakthrough Is Coming.* He's here to deliver the "Jesus is rad" message to the X Games generation with both the book and a religious skateboarding magazine called *Livin It.* Stacks of both are set on the tailgate of the Ryder truck.

"I'm here on a semi-kinda-kooky book tour," Baldwin says after finishing the lip sync. Five days ago the actor began his semi-kinda-kooky pilgrimage at the Icthus Music Festival up the highway in Wellmore. Swinging by Lanwar today was impromptu. "This was not by my hand," Baldwin says, in straight-faced piety. "We just happened to be nearby. For me, coming here is just bonus bucks for the kingdom of Heaven.

"So far, I've had probably a hundred kids come through the line for books."

As he talks, zero people approach the truck.

A few gamers are sitting nearby on the front steps of the Expo Center, either smoking cigarettes or spitting. Mostly both. Minister Baldwin tries laying the oratory charms on a cute ponytailed girl in a pink tank top. "You want an autographed copy? Free for you," he says to the girl, who might be all of sixteen.

She answers with a long, uninterested drag on her cigarette and an exhale of smoke. "Maybe in a little while," she says, then resumes talking to the guy next to her on the steps.

Baldwin figures he'll have a go at the teenage boy.

"Hey, bro, is this your girlfriend or your wife?"

The kid answers, "She's my sister." Then he nudges her, and they flick their butts and head back inside.

Baldwin looks around the empty parking lot. "So, yeah," he says nodding, "It's been pretty radical so far."

Inside, the tournament is back in full swing and Team 3D is facing the only other unbeaten, Pandemic, for a spot in tomorrow's final. CompLexity dropped a match earlier to United 5, so they're now in the lower bracket, battling JaX Money Crew in a loser-go-home showdown. A CompLexity win would return the favor from CPL Winter, when JMC ended their tournament. It was enough for Jason Lake to take shit from JaX that night in December at the Hyatt. He doesn't need to hear it again tonight over at the Executive Inn.

Lake likes his chances. At CPL Winter, JMC beat them on Comp-Lexity's worst map, its Achilles' heel, Nuke. CompLexity struggles on Nuke because it's a compressed battleground arranged vertically, in three floors. It's not spread out horizontally like the other three maps, Inferno, Train, and Dust 2.

Because of Nuke's tight spaces and close-up combat, a long-range AWP sniper rifle is almost useless. There's never enough space for it to be effective. And since CompLexity is built around the AWPing ability of fRoD, Nuke is a terrible fit. It's the one map out of four in which the fRoD factor is neutralized.

Right now, though, CompLexity is playing JaX Money Crew on Train. That map is the antithesis of Nuke. On Train, the bomb sites are located in wide-open rail yards with parked cargo trains the only major obstructions to sniping. The map is plenty spread out with long shooting lanes, and without effective flash and smoke concealment, attackers are exposed the second they enter the battlefield.

fRoD dominates on Train, spotting from one end of the rail yard to the other, and so JMC can do little to stop CompLexity. Lake's team wins easily, 16–6. In the match, fRoD is +12. In two rounds, he killed four of the five JMC players by himself.

That's uncommon in Counter-Strike. Taking out two or three in a round is good. Four is exceptional. An "ace," or fragging all five opponents in a single round, is nearly unheard of at an elite tournament.

At a nearby table, Mug N Mouse loses a 19–17 heartbreaker to Check Six and is eliminated from the tournament. A few players migrate over to shake hands, but Punkville turns his back. He angrily wraps up his mouse, keyboard, and headset and strides out of the tournament area, head tipped back and eyes locked straight ahead. He looks like he might walk all the way back to Dallas.

"Punkville's pissed," says one spectator, as he passes. For the tournament, he finished a cumulative +26. Gosu was +19 and Mason, the younger brother of Warden of CompLexity, was +18. Those are solid individual performances, but because of a lack of team synchronization, Mug N Mouse exits with a disappointing seventh-place finish.

Back at the tables, CompLexity beats Check Six to advance. They will play the loser of the last two unbeatens, 3D and Pandemic, who are battling on Nuke. It's assumed that 3D will mop up against these relative unknowns, especially after they push ahead 14–11. Then, without warning, Pandemic runs off five straight rounds for a 16–14 win.

It's a shocker, a fluke most likely. Late in the match, 3D got overconfident and began coasting. Other than the jubilant Pandemic players, nobody here is reading much into the outcome. That's why it's a double-elimination event. Every team gets one to throw away.

But now, instead of a head-to-head battle in the championship match as everyone had expected, Team 3D drops to the lower bracket and will face CompLexity in the morning. The loser is out, and the winner moves on to play Pandemic in the finals. That final is really just a formality, though. Everyone knows the 3D-CompLexity showdown will determine the champion. And bad news for CompLexity: it will be played on the one map they were hoping to avoid, Nuke.

It's nighttime at the Executive Inn, and Warden and Tr1p are running a Texas hold 'em poker game in the JaX Money Crew suite. Both CompLexity players are up big, sitting behind tall stacks of chips. These two are serious about their hold 'em.

Warden lives with his parents, brothers, and grandfather in the Deer Park suburb of Houston. It's a comfortable brick home with an oblong pool out back framed by a wooden deck so spotless it belongs in an ad for oil soap. Above the pool is Warden's second-floor bedroom, with a separate computer area and a private bathroom. On the floor of that bathroom is a stack of three soft-cover books: *Super System: A Course in Poker Power; Hold 'Em Poker for Advanced Players;* and *Harrington on Hold 'Em,* written by World Series of Poker legend Dan Harrington.

Hold 'em poker is about the only thing that bridges the double generation gap between Warden and his seventy-five-year-old grand-father, Bill, whom he either calls "Bapa" or simply addresses with "sir." They sit around the living room playing cards, and his granddad gives him tips from seven decades of life experience. Poker is the common ground for the Greatest Generation and the Point-and-Click Generation.

Warden's granddad joined the Army at nineteen and was shipped off to Germany at the end of World War II. After his discharge, he worked the docks in Galveston for thirty-four years with the International Longshoreman's Association, unloading 100-pound drums and 200-pound sacks of sulfur. "We used to haul that stuff by hand," says Bapa Dickens, whose massive forearms are tattooed with topless Tahitian hula girls. "And boy, I'll tell you one thing, you needed good gloves and a lot of muscles."

Warden's dad, Michael, also worked the Galveston docks and climbed through the ranks to become union vice president. Michael Dickens is the kind of guy who's never in his entire life given the weaker half of a handshake. His kids call him "sir," too.

Warden and his gamer brother Mason respect the older generations, but that doesn't mean they're interested in working as hard as they did. Warden rarely gets out of bed before noon, except on Tuesdays and Fridays, when the cleaning women wake him to take the sheets for laundry.

The only dock work he's ever done was two summers ago, driving brand-new Volkswagens off ships arriving from Germany. He'd wheel the cars an eighth of a mile down onto the docks, then stand around for a half-hour with other workers waiting for a bus ride back onto the cargo ship. All day long like that. He got $18 an hour.

"My dad gives me shit because I don't know how to change a car tire," Warden says, "but I'll give him shit because he doesn't know what a hard drive is. I can strip down a computer and fully rebuild it. And really, isn't that a more useful skill today?"

To Warden, lazy is a relative term. His skills are more technical, more cerebral. His effort is with his mind. His grandfather's and father's generations built the nation. It doesn't need to be built again.

Warden's generation is applying their skills to an online world still under construction.

Corey "Tr1p" Dodd is CompLexity's team captain and strat caller. He lives in Fargo, North Dakota, in an apartment four miles from his parents' home, but rent is so cheap in Fargo, Tr1p figures it's worth $450 a month for the privacy.

It's a typical twenty-one-year-old's pad, sparsely decorated with the same floor lamp with the martini-glass top that every guy has in his first apartment. On the wall is a faux oil painting of Kramer from *Seinfeld*. Tr1p has no instructional poker books lying around the apartment, just a Victoria's Secret catalogue and a copy of *The Hockey News*.

As the first of his Fargo friends with an apartment, Tr1p's place has become the default hangout on weekends. It's got everything his buddies need: a refrigerator, gas grill on the porch, and a $2,000 high-def Sony Trinitron XBR flat-screen for watching NHL games and broadcasts of the World Series of Poker.

Every so often, while watching poker, they'll spot an old Fargo gaming buddy named Tom "Crazyfox" Koral on TV. Crazyfox is an idol to these guys, practically a folk legend. He's the ultimate success story for the Internet generation, a guy who made it big without ever working for the man. The only jobs Crazyfox had were online: pro gaming and poker.

Tr1p may not be far behind. He cleared $25,000 last year in Counter-Strike, but every penny went into the bank. He pays for the apartment, TV, grill, steaks, and whatever else he desires with his online poker winnings. Last year, Tr1p made more money on PartyPoker.com than he did with CompLexity. At twenty-one years old, living in dirt-cheap Fargo, he cleared $50,000 through gaming and poker, neither of which has anything to do with the sluggish North Dakota economy.

"You know how people take a year off before going to college and build up some money?" says Tr1p. "That's what I did. Then I started making good money. So now it's like, if poker doesn't work out, I can fall back on Counter-Strike. Or vice versa. Either way, I don't see any reason to go to school now."

The common assumption about gamers is they're socially awkward, no-girlfriend nerds who spend all day holed up in their basements or bedrooms geeking out in front of computer screens. That stereotype is debunked after hanging out for a couple hours with Punkville and the other delinquents at Mug N Mouse café. Granted, gamers do spend an inordinate amount of time in front of computers. That's no misconception.

Still, what's revelatory about guys like Warden and Tr1p is that they're more than just *not nerds*. They're hustlers, scoring salaries and flights around the world, flipping merchandise on eBay, sleeping late and making more money than friends who work nine-to-five. And that's regardless of whether gaming ever makes the next step to mainstream acceptance.

"The thing about e-sports, and this may sound strange, but I never really thought it would get big," says Tr1p. "I've never been that optimistic about it. Even now, with WSVG and everything, it could get big, but I'm not relying on it. For me, this is about making an extra buck."

Tr1p's dad worked for the city of Fargo from the age of eighteen and drove a taxi on the side. Tr1p remembers growing up in a house filled with stacks of $20 bills—almost everyone pays for a cab with a $20. Now his dad owns the cab company and has thirty cars on call. So that's Tr1p's fallback: going into the family taxi biz. For now, though, he'll take his chances on cards and Counter-Strike.

"Gaming might be the next big thing, it might not be," says Tr1p. "But either way, I've got the money in the bank already."

Of course, it's not entirely about the hustle. Even for shrewd guys like Tr1p and Warden, Counter-Strike is also a competitive outlet. True, at twenty-one or twenty-two, they wouldn't still be competing at LANs if it weren't for the paychecks. But once the headphones go on and they're at the tables, they do want to win. For pride as well as paydays.

Tr1p was an exceptional defenseman in youth hockey who unfortunately never grew above five-foot-nine. At North Dakota high schools, which also play road games in hockey-crazy Minnesota, five-nine didn't cut it. At age fifteen, Tr1p grew tired of getting wrecked against the boards by guys who were six-three, 220 pounds.

So he messed around with in-line skating awhile, grinding rails and spinning off jumps. ("Jeez, dat's a bitchin' toe grab, yah.") Then he got into gaming. It's a typical backstory for the kids who find their way to Counter-Strike.

These are the followers of Frank Nuccio, who viewed the game through the prism of team sports and structured it to appeal as much to the inner jock as to the inner child. Most elite-caliber Counter-Strike players are the kinds of guys who once excelled in youth sports but washed out at higher levels of competition. Counter-Strike is for athletes too old for the JV team and not good enough to make varsity. So they get their competitive fix where they can, in e-sports.

Tr1p was too small for hockey, Warden too stocky for soccer. Punkville had a knee injury in football. Moto and Rambo both excelled in roller hockey, and ShaGuar was a skilled Little League pitcher who ruined his elbow throwing curveballs at too young an age. Now Counter-Strike is their substitute.

At the moment, Warden and Tr1p's competitive focus is on the Texas hold 'em game, where they're cleaning up on JaX Money Crew and a few guys from United 5.

This is like taking candy from a baby. A stoned baby. With their own teams already eliminated from Lanwar, these are high times for the JMC and United 5 players, who are much less interested in poker than they are in the Ziploc bag on the table stuffed with "purple northern Cali."

"This shit is Amsterdam Cannabis Cup quality," says the gamer who pulled it out of his sweatshirt pocket. "It's $175 an ounce. Check it out, bro. Crystally."

Sean "Hostile" Catron of JaX Money Crew jumps up from his seat. "Who needs a beer?" He's headed for the bathroom, where about twenty cans of Bud Light are floating in a tub full of ice. Hostile, a big kid whose goofball grin belies his alias, steps up onto a bed and tries bounding across the room. He drills his head on a low-hanging wooden ceiling beam and falls to the ground in pain. It's a *Jackass* moment. Hostile got owned by the beam. "Ow, that hurt so much," he groans.

"Dude, what did you do?"

"I hit my head on that fucking brown thing," he says, as everyone laughs at his expense.

Another gamer, Sean "Des1re" Khan, flips though channels on the TV. *America's Funniest Home Videos* goes over big, drawing big laughs with every slip-and-fall, konk on the head, or poodle on water skis.

Keith Olbermann's show *Countdown* comes on next and includes a segment about a "hard-core gamer" from Holland they're calling "Tim" who is entering rehab because he's hopelessly addicted to videogames. "I can't stop," says "Tim," a pimply-faced teen with a Dutch accent. "Videogames are taking over my life."

It's really just another weak attempt by the media to manufacture an angle on a subculture they know little about. But as laughable as the segment is, nobody in the room says a word. Most of them are too stoned to even process the sheer absurdity of this particular segment airing at this particular moment for this particular crowd.

Sitting here, passing around a joint, are a half-dozen guys who must have spent a cumulative eight thousand hours in the last year alone playing videogames. In their professional careers, they've probably attended five hundred LANs combined around the world, including many in Europe. And here's this Dutch whistleblower "Tim," smearing competitive gaming on TV by claiming it's dangerously addictive, yet none of these guys have so much as seen him at a single LAN event.

Finally, in a moment of clarity, one of the stoners says, "Who the fuck is this guy?" and the others snap out of their haze in unison: "Yeah, what a bunch of shit"… "Unbelievable"… "Give me a break"… "Who is this fucking loser?"

They laugh and Hostile bounces an empty, crumpled beer can off the TV screen.

Impatiently, Warden tries one last time to jump-start the poker game. "I'm raising here," he says. "Anyone care?" There's no response, and he tosses his cards on the table. This game's going nowhere.

He and Tr1p shouldn't even be here, hanging out with guys whose teams were eliminated. They should be gathered in Lake's room, watch-ing demos from today's 3D matches to formulate a game plan for tomor-row. The problem is, the only demos currently posted on Gotfrag are from 3D's early-round wins.

The demo that would really help, 3D's day-ending loss to Pandemic, isn't available online. What's especially frustrating is that the loss was on Nuke, the same map CompLexity will face them on in the morning.

"That's a pretty big deal," says Trıp, the strat caller. "Being able to watch a team lose on the exact same map the day before you play them, being able to watch POVs of each of their guys, that's huge."

It's more grist for Craig Levine conspiracy theorists. First came the Train map switcheroo and now there's a missing demo. From where Levine was working today in the tournament's operations center, his rivals figure he could've easily erased the file. The buried-demo "mys-tery" is extra suspicious because every other match played today was uploaded to Gotfrag. Granted, it was the last match of the day, but that was five hours ago. It's ten o'clock now. Most demos are available on the Web within an hour.

"Craig fucking cheats, bro," says Hostile, still rubbing his head where he hit it on the beam. "What can ya do?"

This isn't the first time Levine has been suspected of shady deal-ings to help his clan win, yet nobody has ever gone public with accusa-tions. It would be their word against Levine's, and he's the one with clout. He's also the one with sponsors, often the same sponsors who are financing the LANs, so any grievances against Levine would be brushed off by the admins, true or not.

"Plus, it's not like you can call him out," says Warden. "I mean, he's got the team that's established. What happens if Jake can't land any sponsors and has to shut down CompLexity? We might be asking Craig for a job some day."

Warden gets a call from his teammate Sunman, who's hanging out by the pool. Apparently, there's a poker tournament here in the hotel in some place called the Canterbury Room. Warden and Trıp figure it's worth a shot. This game's dead anyway. They kick away the rolled-up bath towel from the base of the door and exit, leaving the pothead gamers to their purple northern Cali.

On their way downstairs, Warden and Tr1p pass Gosu, who's heading up to the Mug N Mouse room with a cute girl on his arm. It's the same girl who gave Stephen Baldwin the brush-off this afternoon.

Warden and Tr1p pass the bar off the hotel's lobby. Jason Lake is sitting inside with an Internet entrepreneur named Andy Billing, who helps him sell CompLexity mousepads in Asia to spread the team's brand recognition. When Warden spots Lake at the bar, he jokingly tiptoes and gives Tr1p a *"shhhhhh."*

"Come on," he says. "We can't let Jake spot us."

"Why not?" asks Tr1p.

"We never got our sunshine."

At the bar, Lake is telling Billing about an interview he just gave to a couple of New York University film-school graduates here shooting a documentary about gaming.

The filmmakers asked if he felt pressure going into tomorrow's big match, to which Lake answered, "No, we're just gonna go out there, have fun and see what happens," claiming that the pressure was squarely on the shoulders of 3D.

"Which, of course, is total bullshit," he says now to Billing and reaches for his beer. "There's so much pressure on us—as a team, as a business, to attract sponsors so I can keep this thing airborne, to get this 3D monkey off our backs. It's like we're *this* close, and all we need is one little break."

Lake leans back on his barstool and gazes out across the lobby of the old Tudor inn. "Man, after a couple of days this place starts closing in on you," he says. "I feel like I'm stuck in that *Shining* hotel or something."

He swigs his beer.

"I feel like I'm in purgatory."

# Chapter 9

OR ALL OF WSVG BOSS MATT RINGEL'S CRITICISM OF Angel Munoz's inability to expand the appeal of e-sports, in 2005 the CPL founder did manage to land gaming's first-ever television exposure with a half-hour segment on MTV. It wasn't easy, either. The network only signed on after Munoz agreed to finance the entire project. The result was a half-hour piece during the videogame-focused *GameORZ Week* that spotlighted a one-on-one CPL match in the game Painkiller between Johnathan "Fatal1ty" Wendel and a Dutch gamer named Sander "Voo" Kaasjager.

The MTV producer assigned to the project was Salli Frattini, a veteran overseer of the Video Music Awards, for which her duties typically entailed things like orchestrating onstage liplocks between Britney Spears and Madonna. Suddenly, she had the job of making Fatal1ty and Voo look cool to the youth masses who watch MTV.

"The challenge of making videogames into television," Frattini says "is you need to find the most animated people to tell your story. It's definitely a challenge. Gamers are not movie stars. They're not on-air talent. Gamers have little experience being on camera. Their experience is looking at a screen."

The results of the CPL-MTV collaboration were disappointing. MTV added some glitz at the event, held at the Kodak Theater in New York, pumping up the house music and adding swirling spotlights. After his victory, the well-known American gamer Fatal1ty hoisted up an oversized $150,000 check for the cameras. The next day, he made an appearance on the show *TRL*, waving at the crowd outside in Times Square.

Fatal1ty is a twenty-five-year-old, sandy-blond kid from Kansas City. He's unthreatening and agreeable, if a bit vanilla in interviews. He also has a slight stutter. MTV had seen enough. They pulled the plug on future projects with the CPL.

The segments, says Frattini, "failed to connect" with MTV's viewers. Not enough attitude, not enough sex appeal. "If bigger personalities were created and publicized in the gaming world, it would work better for us," she says. "Introverted isn't our thing."

Munoz's failure to win over MTV or land any significant airtime with another network was a major reason his main sponsor, Intel, signed with the WSVG this year. Ringel knows that TV exposure is crucial for gaming's advancement, and he scoffs at Munoz's efforts. "Last year, the CPL tour did a total of a half-hour of television? They got a *half-hour* on MTV for the entire year. That's insane."

This weekend at Lanwar, two guys from the GamePlay channel have been wandering around the BYOC and tournament tables with a handheld camera and a boom mike. They're gathering footage for highlights segments on both the Dish Network and to stream on the WSVG's Web site. Off to the side of the BYOC, a makeshift greenroom has been set up for interviews with the winners of today's championship matches.

"Media is a big part of what we're doing," says Ringel. "That's really the next stage of evolution for this to become a big sport."

Having a camera crew here is a positive step, as is getting airtime on Dish Network, a satellite provider with twelve million subscribers in the United States, although it's not the first time gamers have seen cameras around the tables. In South Korea and Germany, cable TV channels are devoted entirely to competitive gaming.

Dish Network has a potentially wide reach, and the hope is that the segments will stand out in the glut of generally unpolished programming on GamePlay, which mostly runs a loop of product spotlights and game reviews. GamePlay is to television what a magazine title like *PC Gamer* is to newsstands—a veiled product catalogue under the guise of consumer report.

Ringel's real endgame with GamePlay is to repackage their footage to make another run at MTV and other networks, hoping to sell them on "life of a gamer" profiles with Fatal1ty and others who are perhaps more charismatic. That's if he can find them.

Predictably, many among the old guard here at Lanwar are skeptical that Ringel has found the pulse. The skeptics from Gotfrag and TSN consider what WSVG and GamePlay are attempting as far less than visionary. With its TV package, as with the whole event in general, the WSVG is half copying what CPL already tried with the MTV segment, and half guessing what will better draw in a mass audience.

"For three days now," remarks one Gotfrag writer, "all they're doing are panning shots, screen grabs off the monitors, and close-ups on gamers' faces. Who wants to watch that? They need to convey the appeal of the game, not just point a camera at the guys who are playing."

The TV crew has already spent significant time around the kiddie games Guitar Hero II and Dance Dance Revolution, while only occasionally passing through the Counter-Strike tournament. Now, as the final day of Lanwar gets under way, the GamePlay cameras are off shooting another sideshow: the Miss WSVG beauty pageant.

This is Ringel's coup de grâce: a parade of women strutting across a stage in evening wear. To the hard-core gamers at Lanwar, it's his most idiotic and desperate gimmick yet.

The Miss WSVG contest isn't even for girls competing here at Lanwar; Ringel hired models from around Louisville. So this will be the outside world's first peek into the gaming subculture—awkwardly forced sex appeal? And this will make the mainstream take e-sports seriously how?

For all that Angel Munoz failed to achieve in the marketplace, one of the insiders points out, at least he never compromised the integrity of gaming with a beauty contest.

"A beauty pageant? That's a con," says one of the Gotfrag reporters. "It's like, 'We've got a beauty pageant and oh, by the way, we also
have this gaming tournament.' That's not how it's done."

It's supposed to be about the competition, the rivalries, the one-
on-one showdowns. Yet here is this camera crew from the GamePlay
channel, and they're not even shooting the gameplay. Instead they're
shooting a beauty pageant.

For the thirty or so female gamers here, that's not only an insult
to anyone seeking to legitimize e-sports, it's also sexist. So the girl
gamers huddle and discuss a protest of the sideshow, but then come
up with a better idea: They'll enter one of their own, a gamer named
Shea "Paincakes" Brock.

As Paincakes scuffles across the stage in flip-flops, tattered jeans,
and a T-shirt, all the girl gamers go wild with applause, giving her the
win in a popular-vote landslide. "Did you see the girls I had to go up
against?" Paincakes gushes after her coronation, mostly in jest. "They
were hot. I'm talking, like, fake boobs and everything. And I won."

It's a successful send-up of the beauty contest, with an added
bonus: Paincakes gets a $500 check for winning.

In the tournament area, CompLexity and 3D are warming up. It's the
calm before the storm. The two teams are facing toward each other but
separated one table apart, the usual setup to prevent eavesdropping.

Onlookers fill in behind the players, and an admin brings Lake
and Levine together for an awkward pregame handshake. The admin
is the match's referee, and he'll circle around both teams so nobody is
tempted to alter their computer settings or whisper warnings to teammates after being fragged.

The mood at the CompLexity table is warily confident. Trip and
Warden are brainstorming last-minute ideas to free up fRoD for open
shots on such a tight map as Nuke. Really, though, there's no changing
the plan now. It's time to lock and load.

On 3D's side, Rambo is going through his usual fastidious prematch
routine of picking microscopic pieces of lint off his mousepad. Strat

caller Moto looks uneasy, but his mind is already in the game, visualizing battle scenarios in his head. This is his time, the reason he came out of retirement: to beat CompLexity.

A cameraman from GamePlay hovers behind Team 3D, shooting over the players' shoulders. The two filmmakers from NYU are here too, filming their documentary and trying unsuccessfully to stay out of the other crew's shot.

Levine gravitates off to the side of the action, as 3D's benched sixth player picks up the rah-rah duties. Josh "Dominator" Sievers has made the trip from Iowa, even though there was no chance he'd play at Lanwar.

"Come on, let's hear a battle cry!" shouts Dominator, slapping the backs of the chairs. "This is it, right here."

ShaGuar, the biggest mouth in Counter-Strike, can't resist a chance to talk shit. He shouts over at the CompLexity table, "It's LAN time, baby. You can't step up."

The first round in each half of a Counter-Strike match is known as a pistol round, since each player carries only a pistol. Later, by winning rounds, teams accrue enough money to stock up on grenades and machine guns and armor. But at the start of each half, all ten players have just a single pistol, and it's a scramble.

"Squeaky's open!" shouts ShaGuar. "One under Ladder!"

In a burst of gunfire, 3D wins pistol round and goes up 1–0. For that, they earn money to buy M4 machine guns, plus smoke and flash grenades.

CompLexity, since they lost the round, must also play the second round with just pistols. It's a mismatch weapons-wise, but CompLexity steals the round anyway. It's tied 1–1. The race to 16 is on.

"That's it!" shouts Lake, beginning to pace. "Take it to 'em now."

With fRoD unable to AWP effectively in Nuke's confined spaces and 3D spreading out in Moto's new defensive alignments, CompLexity falls behind 7–3.

Levine stands with arms crossed. "Give them nothing," he tells his 3D players.

Across the way, Lake looks uneasy. He tugs at his red tie and runs a couple of fingers under his collar to loosen it up. In their team meeting, Warden had said of the Nuke map, "Everyone dominates T-side now." Well, CompLexity is on T-side to start the match, and they're not dominating. They're losing.

"Come on, Danny," the coach says to his star player, fRoD. "Let's light a fire."

Late last night at the bar, Lake said all CompLexity needed was one little break. Halfway through the next round, they get it. A glitch in the software freezes 3D's Volcano against a wall. He's pinned, unable to dislodge himself. Flaws like this are not uncommon in Counter-Strike. Being one of the oldest games still used in competition, it's buggy.

If you look very closely at the screen, many of the walls are actually hovering nearly imperceptibly above the ground. It's a coding quirk that allows the program to run more quickly, but occasionally there's a glitch when someone throws a grenade or, like Volcano just did, steps into that tiny space. It's rare, but it happens.

That's no consolation to Volcano, who quickly asks for a time-out. "No time-out," says the ref. "Nothing I can do."

3D drops the round, making the score 7–4. "What a bunch of bullshit," gripes ShaGuar, standing and shouting across the tables at CompLexity. "We called time-out. Fucking bullshit!"

Levine steps forward. "Griffin, sit down," he scolds.

With 3D still fuming, CompLexity closes the half by winning three of four rounds to make it 8–7. Lake isn't ecstatic. Ideally, you want to be ahead after T-side, but it could have been a lot worse. "Good half, good half," he says. "Way to finish strong."

Halftime is less than a minute, only long enough for players to crack their knuckles or rub their eyes. CompLexity goes on CT-side for the second half, and wins the next round to tie the match 8–8. They're all even now. Perhaps the gods are finally smiling on CompLexity. Maybe Lake's luck has turned at last.

Or maybe it hasn't.

Before the start of the next round, Trıp has a problem with his keyboard. He's pounding down on a key over and over, trying to buy a bomb defuse kit, but it isn't registering. Trıp's key shortcuts—the "configs" that all players set up before a match—are gone, randomly erased.

"I need a time-out," he yells, trying to get a pause before the round begins. The ref starts to walk over, but Levine stops him to ask what the problem is. The ref shrugs and continues toward the CompLexity table, but now the round has commenced. The action is under way.

"No timeout," says the admin. "Nothing I can do."

"Goddamn it," says Trıp, who without his configs has to scroll down through a buying menu to get the defuse kit. He's about fifteen seconds late chasing after his teammates, and CompLexity gets overrun. 3D retakes the lead 9–8.

'Yeah," shouts ShaGuar. "That's what I'm talkin' about!"

Lake says nothing. He won't complain to the admin. The bottom line is each team lost one round on a glitch. Fair enough, but Lake knows his "one little break" just went bye-bye. 3D takes back the momentum and pushes ahead 11–8. Warden picks up a couple of key frags, and CompLexity battles back to tie it 11–11.

Volcano wins a 1-v-1 against Sunman, and it's 12–11 for 3D. fRoD gets picked off trying to hold a bomb site, but Trıp saves the round. Tie again at 12–12.

After a few rounds back and forth, 3D moves to 15–14. They're now one round away from the victory. A CompLexity win in the next round would force overtime.

"They're quiet, they're scared now," ShaGuar says, as they head into battle.

One by one, CompLexity's players all get picked off except for Trıp, who's pinned down in a metal hut by three 3D shooters. They storm the door and Trıp takes out ShaGuar, but Rambo finishes him off. Trıp falls dead to the floor.

3D wins, 16–14.

"Yeah!" shouts Rambo, jumping out of his seat. ShaGuar pulls off his headphones and yells at CompLexity, "That's what happens on LAN, baby. L-A-N!"

CompLexity can't even move. All five players are just sitting and staring at their monitors. Lake looks like he either wants to vomit or kick a chair over. This one hurt. "Come on," he says finally, with little spirit. "Go shake their hands."

It was a disappointing end to an overall strong tournament for CompLexity. Across eight matches at Lanwar, fRoD posted a +56, an average of +7 per match. Tr1p led the team at +69. But against 3D on the Nuke map, fRoD struggled as expected. The AWPer was −5 in the match, unable to find shooting lanes, and in many rounds he never even used his sniper rifle.

All that remained for 3D now was to right a wrong in the final against Pandemic, although even the TV crew here from GamePlay channel knows that match will be a walkover. They want to interview 3D now.

As Levine and his players file into the greenroom, a crestfallen Lake and CompLexity head for the exits of the Expo Center. ShaGuar gets in one more dig. "You've gotta be number one. Third ain't gonna cut it," he taunts before getting a little push from Rambo into the interview room.

Inside, the cameraman arranges the players in two rows, three sitting in front and three standing in the back. 3D has enjoyed success overseas, in Asian and European countries where gaming gets more airtime. They've done interviews with TV news reporters and had Q&As with gaming magazines and Web sites, so they're not especially impressed by GamePlay's two cameras and a boom mike. They know the drill.

Levine observes from just outside the camera frame. No one's sure what GamePlay has planned for their broadcast, but 3D's media-conscious owner Levine isn't leaving anything to chance. Gaming is his business, and in business, image goes a long way. The image of gamers has historically been a tough sell to the mass market, which still largely assumes they're either antisocial geeks or antisocial ghouls. So when his team steps in front of the cameras, Levine never quits tweaking the picture. This is where he's a coach.

"Okay, cell phones off," he says. "Sal, pull your shirt down."

Volcano's white V-neck undershirt is peeking out at the collar of his black Team 3D jersey, so he reaches under by the waist and tugs down the undershirt. "Is that better?" he asks Levine obediently.

"Let's get Dave in the first row," says Levine, meaning he wants the team's face man, Moto, front and center. The GamePlay interviewer, an aspiring broadcast journalist in his late twenties, compliantly rearranges the rows, bringing Moto forward and switching Method to the back row. Not that Method minds. He rarely speaks in interviews anyway. A rebellious Southern Cal skateboarder at heart, Method doesn't like hamming it up for the cameras. He's the one kid on the team who won't play show pony for Levine.

When the cameras roll and each player on cue recites his name, hometown, and gaming alias, Method intentionally looks up at the boom mike and says his alias is "dohtem," which is Method spelled backwards. It's a subtle act of defiance, completely lost on the Game-Play crew, but it clearly pisses off Levine. Method says nothing else for the duration of the twenty-minute interview.

The rest of the team is custom-built for photo ops and on-camera Q&As like this. They're presentable and clean-cut, confident, media-trained by Levine and beyond that, they win. The real sound-bite master on the team is Moto, who smiles and speaks directly at the camera: "I'm Dave Geffon. I'm from Los Angeles, California, and my gaming alias is Moto."

The interviewer's first question is, "What's the story of how you came together as a team?"

The benched player Dominator takes this one. Maybe he's just tired of standing around idly. "Team 3D is the big name out there," he says. "We have big sponsors, so 3D's always drawn the top players. I think we're all pretty similar in our business goals. We all want to win and make some money doing it."

The interviewer follows up: "You guys are strictly mercenaries then?"

"Yeah, it's all about the money," says ShaGuar. He adds a smirk to affect sarcasm, although it's misplaced. Team 3D are a bunch of mercenaries, in it for the money—even if that wasn't the golly-gee answer the GamePlay crew expected.

"No, seriously," says the interviewer, failing to pursue the mercenary angle, "in addition to the money and the sponsorships, what *is* your motivation besides winning?"

ShaGuar offers a wiseass response. "Pride, glory, a deeper meaning," he says, nervously scratching his face.

Levine isn't thrilled about where this is going. He tells the cameraman to stop.

"Two things, Griffin," he says, disapprovingly, to ShaGuar. "Keep your hands in your lap away from your face, and stop picking at yourself." Then he fires off a warning at Method, who's daydreaming in the back row. "Mikey, look at the camera. And everybody, when you give answers, repeat the question."

Levine is a shrewd businessman, despite being the same age as his players, and his thoughts are far beyond this Lanwar tournament. His broader aim is to push gaming to a bigger audience and bring in much greater revenue. That begins with presenting an attractive product that corporate America will take seriously. Levine demands professionalism. ShaGuar fidgeting and cracking lame jokes won't cut it.

Of all his players, Moto understands this best. He too knows the importance of image, which is why he's always handled 3D's media responsibilities in the past. With this Q&A careening off message, Moto takes the lead.

"Besides the money, the main motivation for us is winning," he says, serving up polished, clip-ready sports clichés. "Our goal is to be the best and to see the team come together as a unit."

ShaGuar, after his scolding from Levine, now falls in line, too. "There's no better feeling than winning a big Counter-Strike match," he says, "and there's no worse feeling than losing one."

Moto adds, more than a little smugly, "Yeah, especially the part about winning. You'd have to ask CompLexity about losing."

Nobody on the team had more at stake here at Lanwar, in terms of reputation, than Moto. He had many doubters coming in, skeptics who thought he'd be too old and rusty to compete at the elite level. Now, after knocking off CompLexity, no one is more self-satisfied than Moto.

The interviewer laughs in delight at Moto's putdown of CompLexity. "Cool, cool," he says, having just bagged his "gamer trash talk" quote. It's all a little too arrogant for Rambo though. There's a long season ahead, and by Rambo's thinking, 3D was fortunate today. They beat CompLexity, yes. But it was a 16–14 nail-biter on CompLexity's weak map, Nuke. 3D won by just two points in a match in which fRoD was −5. That's nothing to rest on.

"To lose on that map would have been devastating. That's not their strongest map," Rambo tells the interviewer, although the message is really for Moto, his replacement as strat caller. "But I am proud of the way we played, beating the best team in America."

Off camera, Levine looks like he swallowed his own tongue. Did Rambo just call CompLexity *the best team in America*?

"Aren't you guys the best?" asks the puzzled interviewer.

"CompLexity is number one in the rankings," answers Rambo. "We're number two."

Levine flashes an anxious look at Moto, who gets the message and steps in to put out the fire. "It's just a great rivalry," he says tersely, a hint that it's time for the interviewer to move on.

"Okay, lastly, what's at stake in the final against Pandemic?"

"First place," says ShaGuar.

The interviewer, playing sycophant for the WSVG, meant money. He's trying to prod 3D into gushing about how magnanimous the new gaming organization is with prize money. He wants a dollar figure.

Moto gives him exactly the sound bite he needs. "The prize for winning Lanwar, the first stop in the World Series of Video Games, is $12,500."

And that's a wrap.

Team 3D files out of the greenroom to set up for the Pandemic match. Since it's double-elimination and Pandemic reached the finals unbeaten, 3D must defeat them twice in a row for the title. The matches will be played on the elevated stage where the Miss WSVG pageant took place hours earlier. GamePlay will film the match, and images will be projected overhead on a giant TV. A crowd of about fifty or sixty spectators will gather to watch, half-filling the rows of folding chairs.

It wouldn't prove to be much of a contest, though, as 3D erased any memory of their earlier loss to Pandemic by cruising in the first match 16–2 and the second 16–1.

Nobody from CompLexity stuck around to watch the Lanwar finals, though. By the time 3D was accepting its oversized $12,500 check for first place, across the street at the Executive Inn a housekeeper in a maroon frock was vacuuming the carpet and replacing the little bath soaps in suite 511.

The room was empty. Jason Lake was already halfway across Tennessee driving home.

# PART III

## Intel Gathering

# Chapter 10

**W**ALL STREET IS THE FINANCIAL CENTER OF THE Western world, the place ruthless corporate raiders make their fortunes between Monday's opening bell and Friday's close. It is the epicenter of humankind's obsession with monetary gain. That's Wall Street.

Ever heard of John Street? It's around the corner from Wall Street, where brokers grab a copy of the *Journal* on the way to work, sit for a $5 shoeshine or call to get Indian food sent over for lunch. John Street is where Craig Levine calls home.

His apartment is located a few blocks up from the South Street Seaport in a former office building that only recently was converted to residential. Walking into the marble lobby still feels like business, not a house call. Instead of a doorman, the high-rise has a security desk. In the lobby is a bodega for your morning coffee and bagel.

Knocking on Levine's door nine floors up, you half expect to be admitted by a receptionist in Perry Ellis eyeglass frames and led down a long hallway to an office with a massive mahogany desk, video screens built into the wall, and a spectacular view of New York Harbor. There Levine would be staring out a ten-foot-window, arms crossed and conducting business over speakerphone.

In actuality, Levine has no receptionist or sweeping view of the harbor. His home office consists of a computer, printer, and file cabinet that occupy half of his bedroom. And instead of a mahogany desk, the most noticeable piece of furniture in the place is an old futon rolled up in the hallway that Levine's roommate promises to finally get rid of this week.

Levine isn't staring out his window, which does offer a sliver of a view of the East River. He's standing with his arms crossed and staring at the clock on a microwave oven. :03, :02, :01, *beeeeeeep.* He removes a serving of meatballs in marinara that his mom sent back with him in Tupperware last time he visited home on Long Island.

Levine's apartment is spare and unspectacular for two reasons, and neither is because he's struggling to make ends meet. One, he's on the road all the time with Team 3D, so lavishly furnishing the place is hardly worthwhile. Second, despite looking and acting older, Levine only recently turned twenty-three. How many guys his age have extravagantly decorated homes?

It's easy to forget that Levine is so young, both because of his encroaching pattern baldness and because he's been around the competitive Counter-Strike scene since its beginnings. Granted, that wasn't long ago, in 2000, when Frank Nuccio began hosting backroom tournaments at CPL. But with the retirement age of gamers around twenty-two or twenty-three, and with Nuccio throwing pizza dough, Levine has about the most tenure in the game.

"It feels like there's a changing of the guard now, " he says, sitting on a couch to eat his meatballs. "At Lanwar, I didn't know 90 percent of the people there. I see all these managers. I have no idea who they are. I guess they're with teams trying to get sponsors. I just think, hey, that was me five years ago."

That's not really accurate. When Levine started Team 3D, there really were no other managers in gaming, not in the sense of raising funds, handling expenses, and pocketing a profitable margin. Before Levine, the closest thing to a U.S. manager was a guy with a car who could drive the team to Dallas. Before Levine landed sponsorship deals for Team 3D in the winter of 2002, there was no business acumen in Counter-

Strike. There were no salaries, promotional work, TV interviews, mandatory practices, or, to a large extent, even strats.

The Counter-Strike community, per se, was just a few hundred adolescents gathering twice a year at CPL to play shoot-'em-up games for kicks. If they won some merchandise or a thousand bucks in prize money, that was great. To be historically precise, two German teams and one Swedish team landed sponsorship deals shortly before 3D, but it's Levine's model of profitability that all other managers in North America aspire to today.

Before Levine, there was only one other true manager in the world, Andreas Thorstensson of SK Gaming in Sweden. He and Levine essentially wrote the code by assembling winning teams and soliciting sponsorships to fund the enterprise. Now you might see thirty managers standing behind their teams at a CPL Summer event. All try to emulate Levine, but few have come through with any significant funding. No manager in the United States has pulled in anything close to his $150,000 a year from Intel and NVIDIA.

Most managers talk big, maybe solicit a local LAN center for a couple thousand to help offset travel costs. For that, they get a logo on the team's jerseys. Those managers usually keep a clan afloat for a year or two before giving up, and almost every elite gamer has a horror story about a manager who screwed him over. Most rip off the players by pocketing their prize money, claiming it's needed to cover debts.

In North America, only Levine has delivered on his promises. Jason Lake also, yes, but he's paying out of pocket. He hasn't delivered on his promise of full corporate sponsorship, and thus the year-to-year sustainability of CompLexity and the financial future of his players are still very much in doubt.

Levine has his share of detractors. To hear conspiracy theorists accuse him of scheming and cheating and rigging tournaments, you'd think this guy was the videogame Darth Vader, some kind of cyber–Sith Lord. The rumors are rampant. He cuts players on a whim, they say. He stealthily poaches players. He allegedly manipulates map selection. He buries demos.

But to judge Levine by his cutthroat methods, it's only fair to recognize that besides the game's designers and probably Frank Nuccio, Levine is the man most responsible for elevating competitive Counter-Strike in the United States. He alone raised the bar and gave every other clan a common goal: to knock him off the top of the mountain.

Levine may have done wrong by more than a few people in gaming, but this much he indisputably did right: He made it interesting.

Levine was raised in the town of Commack, about forty miles east of New York City in the quiet part of Long Island. He grew up in a Jewish household with his parents and two brothers. Middle son Craig's first love was hockey, and he and his dad would often make the drive into the city for Rangers games at the Garden. His dad still has season tickets, and Craig joins him for a game once or twice a week.

Craig was a big sports fan growing up, but as a gangly kid with bad eyesight, he never excelled in athletics. It's the usual Counter-Strike story. Around eleventh grade, he too washed out of high-school sports and found a substitute in competitive gaming. His first clan was called Black September, and he thought up a cool-sounding alias, Torbull.

Craig's best buddy in Commack was a kid named Ryan, who lived a half-mile down the street. The two were inseparable. Even now, Levine has a framed picture in his apartment of them double-dating to the prom. So naturally, when Craig picked up Counter-Strike, so did Ryan. When Craig joined the clan Black September, so did Ryan.

Ryan's alias was "TedDanson," which may be the greatest gamer tag ever on the grounds of weirdness alone. Torbull and TedDanson failed to turn Black September into a great team, and they routinely got trounced by a superior local clan called YGR. Torbull and TedDanson both had tryouts with YGR, but neither made the cut.

All this went on in 2000, the same year Counter-Strike debuted at CPL. Craig never went to a major LAN event with Black September. He played online in various leagues, including Nuccio's Domain of Games, which he loved in large part because of its structural similarities to the NHL.

His first computer, which he shared with his brothers, was in the family's basement next to a Fisher-Price air-hockey table. Even then, young Craig was innovating. He convinced his parents to install a second line so he could talk on speakerphone with Ryan during online matches. Basically, it was a crude antecedent of today's Internet voiceover programs, like the popular Ventrilo.

When Craig and Ryan graduated from high school in 2001, gaming was a fading interest. Craig was headed to NYU in the fall, and Ryan was bound for the University of Virginia. As fun as it was, the real joy of Counter-Strike for Craig was competing alongside his friend. The game itself was secondary, and it was certainly nothing he ever envisioned as a future business opportunity.

That all changed one fall day during his freshman year at NYU when Levine spotted a flyer taped up in the lobby of his Greenwich Village dorm. A new Internet café called web2zone, located a few blocks across town in Cooper Square, was hosting a Halloween tournament with $10,000 in cash and prizes for Counter-Strike. He immediately phoned a few friends from Long Island and pulled a team together. For a month, Levine practiced late into the night in his tiny dorm room.

"My poor roommate, trying to get some sleep," he says, laughing at the thought. "I was using a metal mousepad called a SteelPad, and every time I'd move the mouse across the surface, it would make this loud, scratchy *sccchh-hhhhaaa* sound."

The Halloween tournament at web2zone was full of glitches. Fuses blew and computers crashed repeatedly. The finals didn't even begin until 2 A.M., but Levine and his mates stuck it out and finished second. Each player's prize was a $300 ergonomic chair, which Levine carried all the way back to his dorm.

"Here it is," he remembers, "my first Halloween night in New York City and I'm walking across town with this huge chair. The thing was ridiculous. It looked like E.T. because of its long neck."

Levine kept that chair all through college. "I'd sit back in this thing, with its big head rest, and play Counter-Strike," he says. "The guys in my dorm used to call me 'Christopher Reeves.'"

Levine soon became a regular at web2zone and within weeks was hired for $7 an hour to work the cash register. Naturally, the ambitious Levine was drawn to the administrative side of the business, handling tournament schedules, troubleshooting during matches, and working the phones to solicit prizes from gaming companies.

Web2zone is owned by Samsung America as part of that company's plan to boost interest in gaming and, in turn, help Samsung sell computer hardware. In addition to LAN centers, the South Korea–based conglomerate also promotes gaming with an annual international event called the World Cyber Games (WCG).

At the debut 2001 WCG in Seoul, a patchwork of players from other games competed in Counter-Strike. But for their 2002 tourney, Samsung hoped to fly over a legitimate clan from the United States, hoping they'd generate some media coverage for the gaming event stateside.

In March 2002, a Samsung regional business developer named Jack Woo swung by web2zone in New York. After talking awhile at the front counter with Levine, he told him, "I want you to make a Counter-Strike team to qualify for the World Cyber Games, and Samsung will sponsor you."

Levine, a relative unknown in e-sports, immediately went out looking for players. Eighteen-year-old Kyle "Ksharp" Miller was the best Counter-Strike player in America at the time, and the most well known thanks to both reputation and write-ups on Gotfrag.

"I called him and said, 'Let's make a team," remembers Levine, whose only previous contact with Ksharp was getting owned by him in online play. If Ksharp remembered Levine at all, it was as a mediocre player. "He was apprehensive until I assured him I wasn't going to play," Levine jokes.

The whole idea was back-ended on the promise of a Samsung sponsorship. There was no salary up front. All Levine had was a sales pitch. "Nothing was guaranteed," he says, "and these guys had heard it a thousand times before. 'Oh, we'll sponsor you, we'll give you this, we'll give you that.' And nothing ever materializes."

Ksharp figured it was worth a shot, so he agreed to play for Levine

and brought over his best two teammates from his old team, X3—
Rambo, just seventeen at the time, and Bullseye, the player who years
later would famously sign with CompLexity. After adding a few other
players to round out the roster, Team 3D was officially born on April 6,
2002. Their manager, Craig Levine, was just eighteen years old.

The irony was, even years later, Levine never saw a dime from
Samsung, which had provided the incentive to start the team in the
first place. Even after Team 3D kept its end of the bargain and qualified for the 2002 World Cyber Games, the regional rep who promised
Levine a sponsorship never came through.

"It's a running joke now," says Levine. "I see him at events, and he
claims it was never a real agreement. I guess it was one of those things
where he says something in March to a kid behind a register at a LAN
center, then all of a sudden here we are in October and we've qualified
for South Korea. It was like I was some kid tugging on his sleeve saying, 'Hey, c'mon, you said you'd buy me a bike' or something."

For the first time in what would become a pattern, Levine would
deliver in a toddling industry where others did not. The NYU freshman had assembled the team under the supposition of a Samsung
sponsorship, and when that proved to be a hollow promise, he was left
swinging in the breeze. Plan B was landing another sponsor, so Levine
winged it for eight months while scrambling to find one.

First he used his credit card to fly the team to New York for a tour-
ney at web2zone. The $10,000 they won there reimbursed his credit
card and also covered Team 3D's expenses to CPL Summer, where
Levine assumed that as the most talented squad in the United States,
they were sure to rake in more cash. Yet with all the hype of 3D being
America's first "professional" team—which without any salaries or
Samsung's backing technically wasn't even true—Levine's team tanked.
At CPL Summer 2002, they failed to even reach the round of sixteen.

In what also would become a pattern with Levine, he responded
by shaking up the roster. Three players were cut, and in came three
replacements including Moto, the new strat caller.

Samsung sponsorship or not, Team 3D did attend the World Cyber

Games 2002 in South Korea that fall, marking the first time a U.S. Counter-Strike team had ever traveled overseas. They finished seventh, which was encouraging but for one detail: seventh place earned zero prize money. Now Team 3D was flat broke. They'd spent all their money traveling to tournaments and hadn't won anything in months.

The patience of Ksharp and his teammates, who had been promised sponsorships and big paydays, was running thin. All eyes were on CPL Winter 2002 in Dallas, where another poor performance would surely sound Team 3D's death knell.

The day he returned from South Korea, Levine again began working the phone in his dorm room, pitching the idea of sponsorship to any company that would listen. The computer retailer CompUSA was somewhat interested and told Levine to make a formal proposal at the upcoming CPL Winter.

"That's great and all," says Levine. "But we'd just spent ten thousand dollars and we're out of money. I'm thinking, shit, how are we even gonna get to Dallas?"

Levine contacted the Danish mousepad company SteelSeries, which in 2002 had no real exposure in North America. They balked at giving 3D any monetary backing but did agree to a small trial-run merchandise deal. Levine talked SteelSeries into sending $5,000 worth of mousepads for him to sell on Team 3D's Web site.

For five weeks, while also studying for final exams, Levine turned his NYU dorm room into a mail-order warehouse. "I'd get deliveries of hundreds of these things and sign for them at the door," he remembers. "You know in college how you raise your bed with bricks or whatever? Mine was raised with mousepads."

Imagine his roommate's horror upon returning from class one day and finding the room filled with metal mousepads—the same kind that had kept him awake nights with their awful *scccchhh-hhhhaaa* scratching sound, no less.

Levine made about $2,000 selling mousepads and put the rest of the team's trip to Dallas on his credit card, hoping at worst to recoup that debt by selling more mousepads at CPL. "I literally went to JFK

Airport with two bags," he says, "one suitcase packed with clothes and another stuffed with mousepads."

The first day at the Hyatt, he sold more than fifty out of his hotel room for $25 or $30 a pop, all under the nose of Angel Munoz and his sponsors, who were selling the exact same mousepads downstairs for almost twice as much.

Meanwhile, in the Counter-Strike tournament, Team 3D was gelling under Moto's leadership and powering through the brackets. They advanced to the tournament finals just hours before Levine was scheduled to meet with the CompUSA rep.

It was all coming together on cue. 3D was the right team, playing well at the right time, and CompUSA wanted in. Better still, because CompUSA stores stocked NVIDIA graphics cards, Levine also got a meeting with NVIDIA's marketing director at the event, Sheryl Huang.

"To be honest, before I spoke with Craig, I was really skeptical," says Huang, whose company was a CPL sponsor but had always shied away from backing a team. "It's too unpredictable," she says. "You're dealing with a bunch of kids just out of high school. You don't know who's gonna win or lose, or more importantly who's gonna quit or start bad-mouthing the industry. As a company, you don't want to risk that kind of embarrassment."

Huang was a tough sell but ultimately was swayed by Levine's professionalism.

"I'd gotten e-mails and phone calls from gamers before," she says. "Craig was the first guy who actually had a PowerPoint presentation in hand. Here's an eighteen-year-old kid, and he's speaking corporate language. I was still skeptical, but I decided to give it a shot. Team 3D felt like a winner."

Levine got what he wanted: full funding to cover salaries, travel expenses, and equipment. The next morning, Team 3D capped its dream weekend by winning the tournament and collecting a $30,000 first-place payday. It was a landmark event, the first time an American team had beaten the best from Europe.

Three days earlier, the enterprising college kid Levine had flown into Dallas with a suitcase full of mousepads, a growing credit-card debt, and a Counter-Strike team on the verge of disintegration. He was flying home with two major corporate sponsorships, a CPL title, and a very bright future in the bag.

"I guess it is fair to say that I'm a George Steinbrenner type of owner," says Levine, finishing lunch in his New York apartment. "I don't like losing."

Team 3D has been called the New York Yankees of U.S. gaming. They're the best funded, the most successful historically, and the most fawned over by the media. And similar to the polarizing Yankees owner Steinbrenner, Levine is likewise resented by competitors for using his deep pockets to lure players off other teams.

As it happens, the Long Island native is not a Yankees fan. He likes the Mets. In 2006, the Mets are a team on the rise, in first place in the NL East and stealing back-page headlines from the Yankees. And they're doing it the Steinbrenner way—by spending a ton of money on free agents like Pedro Martínez, Carlos Béltran, and Billy Wagner. That last acquisition, the closer Wagner, was an especially cunning move because they signed him away from a division foe, the Philadelphia Phillies. In landing Wagner, the Mets not only improved, but simultaneously weakened their archrival.

The lesson is not lost on Levine. Making your opponent weaker is every bit as effective as making your team stronger. In other words, if you can't beat 'em, sign 'em.

Levine may have little interest in coaching Team 3D, but he loves the business of running an e-sports team, assembling rosters, moving pieces in and out of the puzzle. Counter-Strike is his rotisserie baseball. If he weren't running Team 3D, the money-conscious Levine would likely be working a block away on Wall Street and holding discussions at the water cooler about his fantasy-league baseball team—who's good, who's bad, who's not performing, which players he'd like to trade.

Team 3D is Levine's roto team, except his roster moves actually affect outcome. And since he's signing real paychecks, he makes no apologies for showing underachieving players the door. "They get what they deserve," he says. "Besides, before I started paying these guys, nobody was making a salary anyway. What do they have to complain about?"

In 2003, Levine's first salaried roster brought new excitement to gaming. They played fast. They took risks. They had fun. They were the stars of the North American scene, and everyone turned to look when they strutted through a BYOC.

CompUSA and NVIDIA were happy. Team 3D acted professionally, and when asked to make appearances or sign autographs at trade shows, they happily obliged. Best of all, they were unchallenged competitively in the United States. There was peace in the 3D empire.

Then came CompLexity.

"Here's this new guy, Jason Lake," says Levine. "I've never met this guy, and the first time I see him is this infamous picture of Bullseye shaking hands with him at his desk. I'm thinking, this guy looks like a pedophile."

And so it begins.

Levine still bristles at the memory of a founding 3D member, like Bullseye, signing with a mediocre clan that nobody had ever heard of.

"That was a slap in the face," Levine says resentfully. "Obviously Jason wanted to make a splash, so he recruits Sean. He throws money at a former 3D member. Wow. Big deal."

Soon after, Lake went on air with TSN and among other boasts, vowed to dethrone Team 3D.

"He starts bashing me, bashing 3D," says Levine, "saying we're washed up, we're over the hill. I'm like, okay, the guy's an asshole. Some guy I've never met. What do I care? I still had a winning team."

Levine's dismissive attitude changed at CPL Winter 2004, where 3D finished eighth to CompLexity's fifth. For the first time ever, 3D had finished behind another U.S. clan. That was much different from placing second or third to a Swedish or German team, which was always acceptable because his North American sponsorships remained secure. Now CompLexity was a challenger on the home front and a threat to his six-figure funding from NVIDIA and Intel, which, by this point, had replaced CompUSA.

This was no game anymore. This was business. One way or the other, Levine was determined to quell the CompLexity uprising. "I had a couple of plans in mind," he says.

In June 2005, he hatched the first at a tournament in Paris called the Electronic Sports World Cup. That's when Levine's detractors in gaming might say he went to the dark side and became the Darth Vader of e-sports. *Scccchhh-hhhhaaa.*

CompLexity was also at the tournament in France, but without Lake, who couldn't justify flying overseas and leaving his family at home for a week. So with Lake's team unmonitored, Levine struck. What happened next, most in gaming would label devious. Others might call it cagey. Either way, it's not something Levine likes to discuss—but fortunately others present in Paris don't mind.

"We're in our hotel rooms trying to get some sleep one night, and Craig randomly appears at the door," says Trip, CompLexity's team leader. "He's got this whole pitch to sign us up as some clan called Team Ouch! He wanted to sign the whole team away from Jason."

Team Ouch! was a short-lived marketing idea from Tylenol to tap into the youth demographic by sponsoring a Counter-Strike team. Tylenol had already backed skateboarders and BMX riders, the marketing concept being that their many scrapes and bruises necessitated pain relievers. A stretch though it may be, hard-core gamers, Tylenol reasoned, had sore wrists and headaches from staring at computer screens all day.

The company contacted Levine and offered him a six-figure sponsorship. The deal was scuttled by the stipulation that he change Team 3D's name to Team Ouch!, which violated his existing agreements. Levine did agree to find Tylenol another clan to sponsor, for which he'd still get cut in on the deal.

And so, Levine's plan in Paris was to make CompLexity into Team Ouch!, and he offered salaries of $600 a month. He was laughed out of the room.

"We were never gonna leave Jason at that point, after all he'd done for us," Tr1p says. "I don't even know if Craig cared about the future of Team Ouch! Think about it. If Team Ouch! goes in the shitter, it's still a win for him because CompLexity is gone. There would only be 3D. And we could never go crawling back to Jason after that."

In traditional pro sports, such as the NFL or NBA, general managers are prohibited from approaching players signed to other teams with contract offers. They're not even allowed to directly contact their agents. That's called "tampering," and it's against the rules. But in e-sports, there are no rules. There's no commissioner, no players' union. There's nothing to prevent tampering, even with salaried players under contract, like those on CompLexity.

So without any organizational restraint, tampering is how Levine set out to bury Lake.

"You just never know with Craig. He's very manipulative," says Dominator, a player on his own team. "Maybe he never even really wanted to pick up CompLexity. Maybe that whole thing was just to create distrust and doubt within their team. You just never know. Craig has a secret plan for everything."

The next night in Paris, after 3D was eliminated from the event, Levine cut two players from his team. Then he returned to Tr1p's room with a second offer, but this time it was only for him and fRoD, and Levine wasn't holding back in his sales pitch.

"Craig was talking shit about Jason," Tr1p recalls. "He'd say, 'You've done well at tournaments. Why don't you have a sponsor yet? It's because he's unprofessional.' All this shit. But Jake's always been good to us, always paid us on time. We respect Jake."

Levine's plan was to simultaneously strengthen 3D while crippling CompLexity. fRoD was the prize Levine really sought, but he knew the star AWPer would never sign without Tr1p, his close friend. Levine offered both $1,000 a month in salary plus the usual perks 3D players enjoyed, like free $3,000 laptops from Intel.

Given CompLexity's cloudy financial future, Tr1p and fRoD had to at least consider the offer. They asked about the possibility of bringing along Warden, who was second on the team in frags behind fRoD.

"Any team would want Matt on board," Tr1p says. "It made sense, but Craig wouldn't do it. And it's for one reason only: Matt's appearance. Craig only goes for poster boys."

The accusation is a scathing one—that the media-conscious Levine passed on Warden because a chubby kid wouldn't look good in print ads or TV interviews.

As Tr1p puts it, "Right then, we said fuck this guy."

In the summer of 2006, Levine's goal remains the same: to keep Team 3D positioned atop the Counter-Strike world. His motivations, though, have somewhat shifted.

In the past, it was about being number one and keeping his sponsorships secure. Now Levine is focused on helping push gaming onto television and, unknown to anyone in e-sports including his own team, that's not just in puppeteering his players during on-camera interviews like the one at Lanwar.

For months, Levine has been secretly communicating with another broadcast group interested in filming a gaming competition for television, the satellite provider DirecTV. It appears, one way or another, gamers will finally be getting some major face time on television soon, and so Levine fully intends to have the number one clan when that day arrives. 3D will get the limelight, and they will be media-savvy when the cameras pull in for a close-up. He'll see to that.

Furthermore, Levine is still angling to rip the heart out of CompLexity's lineup. Lake's players are signed to six-month contracts, which come up for renewal in only a month. That's when Levine intends to get payback for Lake's splashy signing of Bullseye years ago. That's when he'll make the *next* pickup to shake e-sports.

"Mark my words, it's going to happen," he says, leaning back on his couch. "Team 3D will sign fRoD."

The pioneering Levine has been in the gaming biz for five years, a comparatively long time for a twenty-three-year-old. And he's spent far too much time building up this industry and pushing it in the media to let a guy like Jason Lake steal his spotlight now.

"I can't honestly say I admire Jason," Levine says, "because I don't think he'll ever make his money back. I know I'd never sink $300,000 into this industry. Jason is struggling to find his niche, and he doesn't want to admit defeat."

This isn't about fun and games anymore to Levine. This is dollars and cents. Counter-Strike hasn't really been for fun since he and "Ted-Danson" were playing in their basements on Long Island.

From the outside, Levine and Lake may seem alike—two guys in the same boat, managing gaming teams and pushing to advance the industry. But deep down, these two rivals are men with entirely opposite needs.

Levine is a shrewd entrepreneur who has turned gaming into a financial opportunity. Lake, meanwhile, may say he's in gaming as a business endeavor, but deep down, that's not why he's so devoted. Lake uses Counter-Strike as an opportunity to mentor young men and to keep alive the faded glories of a high-school football field.

In other words, Levine uses a game to do business, and Lake uses business to play a game. And as the hot sun rises in the summer of 2006, both are convinced of one thing: e-sports isn't big enough for the two of them.

# Chapter 11

DANNY "fRoD" MONTANER HAS A BLACK BMW 325I with silver rims, booming stereo subwoofers, and a cross hanging from the rearview mirror. He bought the car with his Counter-Strike winnings.

Danny lives with his mom, stepdad, and sister in western Miami. Their home is on Kendall Street in a honeycomb of comfortable ranch houses set among manmade lagoons. This subdivision of Miami is where many Cuban immigrants moved in the 1990s after gaining some measure of economic comfort, hoping to provide a safer environment for their kids than the inner city.

Inside the Montaner house are reminders of the family's Cuban heritage. There's an old sepia-tinted photograph of Danny's grandfather in a wide-brimmed hat standing in the countryside outside Havana. There's another of his grandmother at age fifteen in a delicate lace dress, standing in front of a 1940s Victrola.

Danny's mother, Miriam, was just eight when she flew to Miami in 1968, along with a brother, sister, and her parents. In their hometown of La Vibora, her parents were well-known critics of Castro's rule and had begun to fear for their safety.

After arriving in Miami, they continued on to Norristown, Pennsylvania, to stay with their only friends in the States. Miriam's mother found work as a seamstress, and her father worked for a steel company. The day they arrived in Pennsylvania in 1968 was the first time young Miriam had ever seen snow.

Danny's biological father, Miguel Montaner, also emigrated from Cuba as a child. He was one in 1961 when his parents arrived in Little Havana. It was years before the Mariel boatlift brought thousands of refugees to Miami virtually overnight, but fans of the movie *Scarface* may recognize Danny's dad's first neighborhood.

"You know in the beginning, when the Cubans got here and were living under those bridges?" says Danny, proudly. "That's where my father lived, except in the apartment buildings across the street, over on Eighth Street."

Miguel Montaner's dream was professional baseball. He played every day in the parks and sandlots around Little Havana, hoping to one day make the big leagues. Miguel's own dad worked as a busboy, and the family had little money. One day, when he was fifteen, Miguel realized he would never be good enough to go pro, so he quit baseball on the spot and began working for the parks department. Instead of playing, he mowed the grass on those ballfields and hung chain nets on the nearby basketball hoops.

Miguel never lamented his limited baseball ability, and he never complained about cutting the grass for more talented players. His dream had been to make money playing baseball. When it wasn't to be, Miguel went to work and never looked back.

After earning his bachelor's degree at Florida International University and a master's at Louisiana State, he took a job at a bank in Miami, where he met Miriam. She was working as a teller after returning to Miami from Pennsylvania. Miguel and Miriam married when they were both twenty and started a family four years later. Their second son Danny was born on August 13, 1986. He shares a birthday with Fidel Castro.

"I believe that if you have an education and you work hard," says Miguel Montaner, "you will have a good life."

Danny's dad lives ten miles away in West Kendall. His parents now divorced, Danny lives with his mom but sees his dad a couple of times a week. They speak often, but they don't exactly speak the same language. Miguel Montaner does not approve of his son playing videogames for a living.

Like his father, Danny also played baseball until he was fifteen. In fact, Miguel was his coach, all the way from T-ball at six years old to a teen all-star team called the Miami Braves, which traveled all over Florida. "I was never the best player," says Danny, a pitcher. "I'd always be the number-two guy. I was good but not the best, never the superstar."

Even then, Danny was conscious of personal performance in a team sport.

"He always would evaluate how he did as an individual," his mom says. "He would walk off the mound and say, 'I pitched this many pitches, and these kinds of pitches, and I had this many strikeouts.' That kind of thing."

Says his coach dad, "He used to get mad when he'd pitch well and we'd lose because the guys behind him made errors. I told him, 'Danny, concentrate on yourself.'"

At fifteen, Danny too realized he had a limited future in athletics. That became painfully evident one day in 2002, in the parking lot at a Miami Dolphins game, at an "NFL Experience"—a kind of interactive fun park where kids punted footballs into nets or caught passes thrown by a machine.

Danny dove to catch a pass and landed awkwardly, breaking the ulna bone in his left forearm. He was in a cast for two months, and it was during that time he developed an interest in computer games.

He shared the computer back then with his older brother, Michael, and mom's rule was that after an hour, they had to switch. Naturally, neither wanted to stop in the middle of a game, so that plan quickly devolved into shouting matches.

"My mom would get mad and take away the monitor," fRoD remembers. "That pissed me off. My brother and I would search around the house for it. One time she tried to hide it in the closet."

Another time, Miriam put it in the trunk of her car and took it to work, concerned also about the time Danny was devoting to gaming. "When he started playing," she says, "just like a lot of moms I got upset. I thought it was taking over him. You know, I didn't want him to be antisocial. He'd always been such an active kid."

Danny played three more baseball games after the cast came off, but his passion for athletics was gone. He'd never be the best. He'd never turn pro. What was the point?

Miguel Montaner accepted his son's end with baseball. Like him, Danny had taken his shot at the American sports dream. But when it failed, Miguel fully expected Danny to go to college and find a steady job, as he had done.

Danny had other ideas. After three part-time semesters at Florida International, he dropped out in 2005 to play Counter-Strike. Miguel did not take it well, and their relationship has been strained since.

"Of course I support him," says Miguel. "He's my son and he's not dealing drugs or anything. But I don't understand why he can't go to school."

Their conversations go around and around. "I'm making money," argues Danny, and his father says he'd be making more with a degree. "I get to travel," argues Danny, and his dad says he'd travel more with a job like his in international banking.

The irony is that after playing organized baseball for nine years in large part to please his father, Danny has risen to become the best Counter-Strike player in the world. And Miguel couldn't be less impressed. It's not that Miguel is a coldhearted guy. It's just, you know, his son is great at a *videogame*. To the older generation, number-two pitcher still carries a lot more weight than number-one AWPer.

"He'd rather I be doing something else," Danny says. "He wants me to get a business degree and work in a bank. I try to explain gaming in terms of someone making money by starting up an Internet company, like a Web server. He's not buying it."

Tyler Wood doesn't own a BMW, like his teammate fRoD. He shares a Dodge minivan with his mom and brother Sean. On the bumper is a sticker shaped like a yellow ribbon that says SUPPORT OUR TROOPS.

In Little Rock, the armed forces are a common means to venture out and see the world. That's what Tyler's dad, Jim Wood, did. After graduating high school in 1974, he spent five years in the Marine Corps. That was post-Vietnam. For a year and a half, he was stationed in Jamaica and in the Bahamas guarding two very much unthreatened U.S. embassies. "Good duty," as he says.

Jim later attended the University of Arkansas at Little Rock on the GI Bill, where he reunited with his high-school prom date, Jeannette. They soon married and after finishing college, he took a job as an accountant with the Veterans Administration.

Jim had lived a little, left Little Rock, and enjoyed the warm breezes of the Caribbean, then returned to raise a family. "I was lucky enough to get to come back home," he says.

Jim is an outspoken supporter of American troops. But as well as military service worked for him, he's not wishing it upon his son Tyler. Not now, with the war in Iraq stretching on without any foreseeable resolution. "That is definitely not something I would push at this time," he says.

And his twenty-year-old son, Tyler, isn't asking. Through videogaming, Tyler "Storm" Wood has gotten out and lived a little too. He's been to New York and Los Angeles and Paris. He's getting a peek at what's out there beyond the Arkansas River, and he's not doing it by enlisting in the service. He's doing it by playing pretend commando, firing off imaginary rifles inside a computer game.

The Wood family lives on North Jackson Street. It's by no means the depths of poverty, but it also isn't the Heights, a more affluent section of Little Rock a mile straight up the hill. Their one-story brick home is warm and welcoming. On the kitchen counters are boxes of Lucky Charms, tubs of Carpet Fresh, two big two-liter Coke bottles, and boxes of Friskies for their five cats, Collie, Max, Crystal, Misty, and Minnie.

Beside the cat food is a box of Milk Bones dog biscuits. The Milk Bones speak volumes about this family. The Woods don't have a dog. Those are for the neighborhood dogs, and the box is jumbo-size. The

Woods may not have a lot, but whatever they've got, you're welcome to share.

Tyler's mom, Jeannette, is a collector. She has presidential buttons and old Barbie dolls, but her most prized collectibles are the little bells that run along the ledges in her kitchen. They're from all over: Albuquerque, Minnesota, Memphis, Colorado.

Jeannette doesn't travel much. She doesn't even have a passport. But she's got bells from Dallas and Las Vegas and all the other cities where Tyler has played Counter-Strike. He picks one up wherever he goes.

"I love that he has this opportunity," Jeannette says. "Before all this, I had no idea anybody got paid to play videogames. Maybe for testing videogames, like for a company. But not on a team, just to play."

Recently, Tyler's mom has even begun following along with the scores on Gotfrag, picking up some of the lingo. "I know there's Inferno and Nuke," she says, except she says it "Nuuuuuuke," with her Arkansas drawl. "I try and watch online, but usually something will go wrong and I don't know how to fix it. I can barely do e-mail."

Jim enters from the carport with grilled chicken and pork ribs. Over dinner he too speaks favorably about his son's involvement in professional videogaming.

"It's comparable to any job," says Jim. "He spends his time back there in his bedroom doing the Train and so forth. Tyler has a good work ethic. I really want him to finish college and get his degree. Hopefully this doesn't get in the way there. But this could lead to other things. I think it's great."

Gaming never interfered with Tyler's grades. In high school, he graduated thirteenth in a class of 185. Now he studies accounting part-time at Arkansas–Little Rock, which he helps pay for with his Counter-Strike winnings.

Tyler is a soft-spoken and humble kid, whose voice trails off into a mumble at the end of his sentences. It's not that he's shy so much as he's unassuming. "Tyler, tell the story about your first time down to Dallas," prods his mom.

"I took a Greyhound," says Tyler, who was in high school at the time, traveling to CPL with a local clan called Agent. "That was way before CompLexity. Back then, I was buying my own ticket, paying my own way. I'd lose money even if we won the tournament."

For the ten-hour bus trip, he'd pack his computer in a suitcase, padding it with thick sweatshirts and sweaters, even in summertime. "Yeah, it was kinda makeshift," Tyler says, his voice trailing off into a mumble.

"It was hilarious," says his mom, picking up the anecdote. "Have you ever ridden Greyhound? I hadn't ridden it. But they take the suitcases and they put them underneath the bus. So that's where his computer went."

After dinner, Tyler's eighteen-year-old brother, Sean, heads off to work at Kroger's grocery store, where he was promoted last week from bagger to stocker. It's going on six o'clock, almost time for Storm to go to work, too. He's got CompLexity practice tonight.

Since finishing third at Lanwar in Kentucky, the team has upped its dedication. They're putting in four or five hours a night now to prepare for the upcoming CPL Summer tourney in Dallas.

Storm practices at a desk in the bedroom he shares with his brother. It's a little snug for two grown boys, who sleep in bunk beds with their feet sticking out over the ends of its tubular blue frame. On Storm's shelves are little trophies and plaques from both Counter-Strike tournaments and his younger days, when he was a soccer standout.

Over the knob of his closet door hangs a jacket that says LITTLE ROCK FUTBOL CLUB with a bolt of lightning and the word *Storm*. That's where Tyler got his alias.

As a soccer goalie, Storm learned the same skills that make him a peerless defensive player in Counter-Strike. "It's the same thing," he says. "Be quick, anticipate, react, and don't let anything get past you."

As vital as fRoD is to CompLexity's success, Storm's importance cannot be overstated either. fRoD leads the team in frags. He's the sharpshooter. He's the star. But without Storm, there would be no dominance by fRoD, particularly on defense.

When playing CT, a team splits up to defend the two bomb sites, A and B. That usually means two guys at one site and three at the other. T-side will typically send all five guys to attack one site for an immediate five-on-two or five-on-three advantage. That's the start of a normal round in Counter-Strike.

Let's say, for example, it's a five-on-two, and after the bullets fly, both T and CT lose two players apiece. That leaves three Ts left alive to plant the bomb. They do, and the bomb ticks down from thirty-five seconds. If it reaches zero, the bomb explodes and T wins the round. So, at this point, essentially the roles reverse. In effect, T is now defending the bomb and thus the bomb site, so they dig in and try to fend off the remaining CT players who attempt to retake the site.

There's no element of surprise in the retake, so at three-on-three, it's relatively easy to find good cover, await the attack and repel it. That's how a typical round plays out in Counter-Strike, or at least that's how you draw up a T-side attack strat.

Here's where Storm comes in. He's so good at initially defending a bomb site as a CT, he can practically do it alone. Or if he does get fragged, it's often after taking out two or three attackers first. That way, even if the bomb site falls into enemy hands, they've got too few guys left alive to protect it against a CompLexity retake.

It's a selfless job, but Storm is happy to eat the rush for the good of the team. In that way, his career fragging stats are all the more remarkable. While fRoD's career +/− is miles ahead of anyone else in the game, at +1,384, Storm is second at +995, well ahead of guys like Rambo, Warden, Method, and Tr1p, who are around +580. And he's doing it while fending off double and triple teams.

Storm's ability to adequately defend a site shorthanded is, after closer examination, the key to CompLexity's defense. And the best part is, with him locking down one bomb site, teams inevitably try attacking the other—where fRoD lurks with his lethal AWP sniper rifle.

"Counter-Strike is a mental game," Storm says. "I just position myself better, preflash a spot and then move. I'm always somewhere they don't expect. I love being a defender."

Storm is the embodiment of the values stressed by his coach. He's not an egotist. He's not selfish. He's a born team player. They exist in Counter-Strike, too.

Six months ago, in his third attempt to break up CompLexity, Craig Levine approached Storm at CPL Winter and offered him a substantial raise in salary to join 3D. It was right around the time Lake was napping upstairs in his hotel room at the Hyatt.

"I thought about it, but the two things that kept coming back to me," Storm says, "were how Craig is a businessman and Jake is loyal. We owe him a lot for this chance he's given us."

Storm was the wrong fit for 3D. The humble kid from Arkansas was not tempted by a little more money, or a little more limelight. Unlike other elite gamers, Storm doesn't dream of making the leap and becoming a household name. He's not interested in being on a Taco Bell cup. This has already gone far beyond anything he ever expected.

"I'm traveling for free, playing a computer game and making money off it," Storm says. "I'm meeting all these people and learning about different cultures. It's great to see all these cities that are so huge and so busy. But I'm a pretty calm person. After a few days, I'm always ready to come home. I still prefer it here in Little Rock."

Storm puts on his headphones for practice, sliding a chair up to his computer. For the next few hours, he'll be playing a game of make-believe war in a home that's completely at peace.

In the kitchen, his mom is wrapping the leftover ribs in foil and finding space in the fridge. His dad is in the living room, tilted back on a recliner in front of the TV, sound asleep.

When fRoD was sixteen, he joined a local Miami clan called Alien Gamers, choosing his unusual alias. "I wasn't portraying myself as a crook, like a fraud or anything" he says. "I just thought it sounded cool."

Playing online, he immediately posted huge frag totals and quickly gained a reputation as a cheater. His opponents figured he had to be using some kind of cheat hack to lock his shots on target. But it wasn't that fRoD wasn't cheating. He was just a freak talent, a cold killer with an AWP, a deadeye. He simply was too good to believe.

"When I was coming up in the scene," he says, "everybody would down-talk me. First, it was, 'You're a cheater.' Then it turned racial. 'Go cut my grass, you fucking spic.' Trouble found me."

Once in an online match he got into it with a Canadian gamer who called him a Mexican. fRoD, who is Cuban not Mexican, called his opponent a Canadian and an asshole. The league suspended them both for two weeks for unsportsmanlike behavior. "Nobody gave me any respect. I had to prove myself over and over."

fRoD can't explain why he makes shots that others can't. It's just that when he's in the zone, he feels like any other athlete who's locked in. To a baseball hitter, the ball somehow looks bigger. In basketball, the rim gets wider. To fRoD, people's heads just look big through his sniper scope.

When Kyle "Ksharp" Miller retired from Team 3D over the winter to work an IT job in Virginia, fRoD became the biggest name in Counter-Strike. He's turned down offers to play for Swedish and German teams who were willing to cover his travel and housing expenses. And predictably, with his CompLexity contract expiring in a month, Craig Levine has again come calling. Twice this week, fRoD has gotten e-mails from the 3D manager asking, "What will it take to get you on this team?"

CompLexity's contracts coming up for renewal every six months means that twice a year fRoD wonders if he could do better playing elsewhere.

It's not just an issue of loyalty. He appreciates Lake's dedication, and he has no desire to walk out on his teammates. But as the best player in the world, he's conflicted about sticking with a team whose owner can't land financial backing—and the extra promotional opportunities that come with a major corporate sponsorship.

Maybe a selfless, unassuming team player like Storm needs nothing more from Lake, but fRoD does.

"I'm not saying that if 3D comes offering me two-hundred more dollars a month that I'm going to quit CompLexity," he says. "Salary isn't the only issue here. It's the sponsors, the media exposure, the financial security."

Danny's father, Miguel Montaner, always envisioned his son succeeding in either sports or business. Danny, in his own way, is attempting to do both through a videogame. He's chasing his own version of the American dream, trying to cash in on his unmatched talents and prove that Counter-Strike isn't a waste of time. Part of Danny is ego-driven, seeking fame and fortune. Another part of him wants only to prove to his father that it means something to be the best AWPer in the world.

"I really do owe Jason a lot for this opportunity, but right now I have to make the decision I think is right for me," he says. "The reality is, gaming's been around for ten years and it's still underground. I only plan on playing this game until I'm twenty-one or twenty-two. There's only so much money out there, so I need to grab it while I can."

fRoD sums it up with a puzzling, paradoxical comment that shows how strange it is to be the biggest star in a sport that nobody appreciates.

"Right now," he says, "Counter-Strike just isn't big enough to make decisions based on friendship."

# Chapter 12

OUR PEOPLE IN TEXAS STILL SAY "HOWDY, PARTNER," and seemingly they all work at the Gaylord Texan Resort. Those four cowpokes also hook their thumbs in their chaps and tip their ten-gallon Stetsons downward, Old West–like, with a tug of a thumb and forefinger. Two wear black hats and two wear white, and you can catch their gunfight show at 5, 6, 7, and 8 P.M.

The Gaylord Texan Resort is a monstrosity of a hotel and convention center built near nothing in the open-range Dallas exurb of Grapevine. The big selling point of the Gaylord is its air-conditioned biodome with a 300-foot-high glass ceiling dubbed the Lone Star Atrium, into which most of the hotel's 1,511 guest rooms face.

The Lone Star Atrium is where tinhorns and tenderfoots can watch the phony Gaylord gunfight show or enjoy other western charms like campfires of purple and red translucent strips of paper blown upward by electric fans installed in the floor.

The Gaylord must have been built intentionally in the middle of nowhere, because all your cowboy and cowgirl necessities are made available for purchase right there on the premises. Lime-green mesh cowboy hats are $110, and imitation-leather cowboy boots start at $185.

A weekend at the Gaylord resort is just like a gallop back to the Old West, except that the spirit of the Old West was freedom and enterprise. The Gaylord Texan, on the other hand, is a monopolistic tourist trap. Then again, it is air-conditioned.

On the first weekend of July, the Gaylord is also the home of CPL Summer 2006. At least, it *was* the home of CPL Summer until four days before the tournament was set to begin. Now it's the home of the first-ever "Intel Summer Championship," presented by the World Series of Video Games.

Months ago, Matt Ringel took Angel Munoz's main sponsor, Intel. Now he's taken over his flagship tournament, CPL Summer. The marquee annual U.S. gaming tournament is now owned by the WSVG.

The official line from both camps is that it's a "partnership," but that's nothing but spin. It's really a pawn job by Munoz. After losing Intel, he scrambled unsuccessfully to find a replacement to fund the summer event. Munoz inked far less lucrative deals with microchip maker AMD and graphics-card company ATI. They were enough to salvage one tournament a year, but that will be the far smaller and much less costly CPL Winter at the Hyatt.

In stepped the opportunistic Ringel, who bought the summer event off Munoz for just under a million dollars. It was a safe bet for the WSVG. The CPL already had three thousand gamers registered at $100 apiece, so immediately they recouped $300,000 of the million.

To maximize turnout, Ringel left the CPL's well-established name attached to the event until four days before it was to start. Then he abruptly erased all mention of the CPL and renamed the event the Intel Summer Championship after his principal sponsor. Ringel never wanted the CPL name, nor any kind of partnership. All he wanted was Munoz's registration money.

CPL Summer was declared dead on July 7, 2006. And with its demise, Munoz was effectively exiled from the kingdom he created nine years earlier.

In truth, few tears were shed inside gaming for the marginalized Munoz. While no one questions his role as a founding father of e-sports, many—*many*—in gaming take issue with his methods. And immediately after he was vanquished, his enemies all descended to pick apart the man with the alias Prometheus.

Ex-employees, many of whom jumped to the WSVG, lined up to criticize their former boss. "He strung us all along for years at minimum wage, or less, with the promise that some day we were all going to be millionaires," one laments. "The only person Angel ever made rich was Angel."

His detractors weren't just disgruntled ex-employees. You could also practically fill a BYOC with gamers who say Munoz has screwed them out of tournament winnings.

"Angel?" says one top Counter-Strike player from Dallas. "He doesn't just use kids, he manipulates kids. It's like, 'Hey, come to my event and pay me to enter,' but when it comes down to paying you after you win? Sorry, you didn't fill out a form in time, and I can't give you your four grand.

"What are we gonna say? Give us our money or we're not attending? It's like, okay, don't attend. It just sucks," says the gamer. "He probably owes a quarter of a million dollars to people. It's small print. It's super shady."

Teams that won at past CPL events were required to fill out notarized tax forms, a W-9 for U.S. teams and a W-8 for foreigners. Allegedly, Munoz would "misplace" those forms for weeks and then void their prize money on the grounds that they missed some arbitrarily imposed CPL deadline to fill out the paperwork.

"Every event I worked at, there were at least one or two teams or players that did not get paid. Sometimes more," says an ex-employee who worked side-by-side with Munoz from 2002 to 2005. "Or if they got paid, it was a year after winning. There were checks going out for the wrong amount. There were checks that didn't have signatures. There were checks with signatures but no amount at all. That whole process was such complete and utter bullshit."

Even the publicized $150,000 check from the CPL presented to Fatal1ty on MTV—the stunningly large payday that, on shock factor alone, convinced MTV to run a gaming segment in the first place—was yet to be honored. Six months later, Fatal1ty was still waiting on more than $100,000. The whole thing apparently was a Munoz bluff.

As another ex-employee puts it, "Angel has held a noose around the U.S. gaming scene for years and years."

Munoz didn't set out to become notorious inside gaming. When he launched the CPL in 1997, he was an avid gamer himself and honestly believed that his cyberathletes were the sports stars of the future. He was just incapable of selling that vision.

After years of being rebuffed by the mainstream, Munoz lost faith. He quit on the kids and instead decided to pocket the CPL's revenues.

That's the reason Frank Nuccio left the CPL acrimoniously in 2004 and went back to making pizza. Nuccio wanted the CPL to run tournaments in a dozen U.S. host cities and launch a national league. That would've required significant reinvestment, and by then Munoz had already decided to cash out. In his mind, expanding e-sports was a lost cause and he stopped investing in it.

Munoz was never wise enough to effectively package e-sports to the masses, but he was smart enough to realize that he was incapable of doing so. Munoz began to realize how counterintuitive it is to sell gaming as a spectator sport. He gave it one last shot with MTV in 2005, and when they turned their backs, he was out of moves.

So now Ringel has the sponsors, and thus the control of e-sports. So far, he's using the same formula, approaching MTV with more "life of a gamer" profiles. After Lanwar in Kentucky, he contacted Moto and a few others about scheduling follow-up interviews.

Ringel's intentions are honest, and he's aggressively reaching out to all of the networks. To date, though, only a single GamePlay segment has aired on Dish Network. MTV remains skeptical, and others are taking a reluctant wait-and-see approach. The WSVG did get a nibble from CBS, which expressed some interest in a one-time Saturday morning segment. But in that time slot, violent content was out of the question, so the focus would be on kiddie games like Guitar Hero II.

Ringel, of course, is fine with that. He'll take whatever he can get. But now the avid e-sports community, the hardcore scene built around first-person shooters, may get sidestepped altogether as the WSVG spotlights young kids rocking out with toy guitars.

The whole idea of turning videogames into a spectator sport seems implausible. That's been the response from MTV and Spike TV and ESPN, and all the other networks turning their back on e-sports. But there's one thing they're all ignoring: people want to watch Counter-Strike. The evidence is right in front of Ringel's eyes, in the ten or fifteen onlookers standing behind the teams and watching the matches.

That's the key point: they're watching *the matches,* just as twenty years ago a crowd would gather around a Pac-Man machine when some ringer was clearing twenty or thirty screens in a row. Their eyes were on the screen. They weren't watching the gamer.

Just as now, the onlookers are not watching a guy like Moto move his mouse around and tap on his keyboard—which is basically the player-profile package Ringel is trying to sell to the networks. Nobody wants to watch somebody else play a videogame, no matter how many high-fives and close-ups on anguished faces are included.

After a decade running e-sports, Angel Munoz understood the appeal of hard-core competitive gaming. He just didn't want to spend any more money on it. After one tournament, Matt Ringel doesn't have a clue. E-sports may now be in a worse predicament than before. The gamers were probably better off just getting ripped off.

Sixty-six Counter-Strike clans will compete at Intel Summer, arranged in a bracket like the NCAA basketball tournament. Largely because of its win at Lanwar, Team 3D enters as number-one seed, followed by the usual U.S. suspects CompLexity, Pandemic, JaX Money Crew, United 5, and Mug N Mouse.

No new rankings have been released since Lanwar, but Gotfrag again informally handicapped the tournament with a readers' poll. The predictions were spread wider than at Lanwar, since quality European and South American teams are in attendance.

Gotfrag's poll results were: No. 1, Team 3D at 24 percent; No. 2,

Alternate aTTaX of Germany at 18 percent; No. 3, CompLexity at 15 percent; No. 4, Fnatic of Sweden at 15 percent; No. 5, g3x of Brazil at 7 percent; and No. 6, the German team Mousesports at 6 percent.

Those top teams draw easy matchups in the first few rounds, facing an array of no-name clans who've all made the trek to Dallas with the hope of shocking the gaming world. For the dozens of small-time clans who will never win any major prize money or compete overseas, this weekend is the culmination of months of practice. They've come to satisfy a curiosity, to see how they measure up against the Counter-Strike elite.

"This might not be a career thing for me, like 3D or those guys from Sweden," says Andrew McPherson, of a clan named Eximius, which is seeded sixty-second of the sixty-four teams in the bracket. "Coming here is about trying to move up the ladder."

McPherson is a twenty-one-year-old college dropout from Durham, New Hampshire. He's been working overnight shifts at a hotel to earn money for this trip. First McPherson flew to Nashville, then he and two teammates drove eleven hours in a van to get to the Gaylord.

"It's worth it just to see how good you really are," he says.

A few months ago, McPherson played against fRoD online in a pickup game, although he didn't know it at the time. When fRoD messes around on a public server, he uses a fake alias to avoid unwanted fanboy attention. For that pickup game, he was signed on as "Renatnom," his last name, Montaner, spelled backwards.

"After five or six rounds, I was positive he was cheating, like blatantly cheating," remembers McPherson. "He was shooting me through windows and things. After the match was over, my teammate was like, 'Dude, that was fRoD.' I felt like an idiot."

In the first round at Intel Summer, McPherson and his clan, Eximius, are sent packing by Pandemic, losing 16–10. "Man," says McPherson after getting his first taste of elite Counter-Strike, "at local LANs up in New Hampshire, it's not stressful like this. Nobody really cares who wins. Here it's about intimidating the other team. There are lots of egos in this place."

It's easy to forget that for every premier gamer like Warden, fRoD, or Rambo, there are hundreds of other players here at Intel Summer—to say nothing of the hundreds of thousands in America, and millions globally—who aspire to be on their level.

The Gaylord convention center is filled with gamers who play for hours a night at home but will never be as quick or precise as anyone on 3D or CompLexity, or even clans a tier below like Mug N Mouse or Pandemic. After a few days of idol worship in a place like this, it's understandable how elite gamers might develop oversized egos. It's guys like fRoD and Storm whose frag stats are unfathomable to a mediocre gamer. It's 3D's demos—like the miraculous one-on-four that Moto won while stuck behind a crate on Inferno—that are downloaded and marveled at by kids across the world.

Outside this scene, nobody knows an elite Counter-Strike player from a bag boy at the local grocery store. Here, they're stars. When you're the best, you know it. And if you forget, there are plenty of fanboys around to remind you.

"Oh my god," says one young gamer who joins his clan in the BYOC. "I just walked by this guy outside, and I'm like, 'Hey, I know you!' And he's like, 'Yeah, definitely,' and kept walking. A second later, I'm like, 'Oh, man, that was Moto.' I just froze up when I saw him."

Looking around the BYOC, it's obvious that gaming is a male-dominated activity. A handful of female clans do compete online and at small tournaments. But to date, Counter-Strike hasn't drawn in a lot of female players.

It's not that girls are universally repulsed by the violence in first-person shooters. A few are signed up here to compete in 1-v-1 games like Quake 4 and Halo 2. And when you think of it, there's no physical disadvantage to competing against boys in a videogame. The problem with Counter-Strike is that it's rare finding five girls to regularly practice together, and the few female clans that do play online have little interest in coming to Dallas just to get eliminated in the first round.

Most girls who play Counter-Strike prefer a newer version of the game called Counter-Strike: Source, which has crisper graphics and is much easier to play (meaning, easier to shoot people) than the standard version favored at LANs, known formally as Counter-Strike 1.6. Released in 2004, four years after the original, Counter-Strike: Source was an attempt by Valve Software to capitalize on the title's popularity by making it more accessible to casual gamers.

It was also, no doubt, an attempt to phase out 1.6 and force the millions of Counter-Strike fans to purchase the new Source software—a transparently greedy move by the software maker that was rejected, and ridiculed, by the hard-core community, which refused to play it.

"Source is total candy-ass," as one gamer put it. "It's a game for girls."

At Intel Summer, one female clan is signed up to compete—a Source team that's in over their heads at a 1.6 tournament. The five girls represent the PMS Clan, an all-female organization founded in 2002 by Halo 2 player Amber Dalton with a mission to provide a "harassment-free environment for girl gamers."

"Gaming is such a male-dominated culture," Dalton says, "We don't put up with comments online like, 'Bitch, get back in the kitchen.'"

The thirty-year-old Dalton, who goes by the alias "AthenaTwin," originally dubbed her clan PMS as an acronym for Psychotic Men Slayers, but later realized the name was a bit too caustic. So now PMS stands for Pandora's Mighty Soldiers.

The clan rarely place high at LANs in any game, but they do receive a disproportionately large amount of press for being girls competing in a guys' world. Recently they were featured in an article in *Entertainment Weekly* magazine.

Dalton, who refers to PMS members as "my girls," is the reigning queen over the female-gamer cottage industry. It's a calculated package that she presents to the cameras, assigning her most attractive girls the media-relations work.

"Amber puts us out there in strappy shirts and makes us talk to people," says Shannon "MaryJane" Ridge, an attractive redhead who plays Halo 2. "It's not because we did well in the tournament. It's because we're hot chicks. But I think that's okay, you know? It gets the whole clan attention, and it's good for gaming in general."

PMS are nothing like the kinds of socially awkward girls you'd expect to be into gaming. They wear low-cut tank tops and tight jeans with silver loopy belts. They wear cowboy boots and vampy leather collars with their aliases written in sparkling rhinestones. They're almost like the real-life alter egos of the Valkyrie babes that World of Warcraft geeks fantasize about (assuming they're not just fantasizing about the PMS Clan).

Before Intel Summer, Dalton inked a sponsorship deal for $15,000 with Verizon that came with the stipulation that PMS Clan field competitors in every event. That was no problem in Xbox games, where her girls always compete and have even placed as high as sixth. But with no Counter-Strike team, Dalton had to scramble to pull together a collection of Source girls, then pressure them into taking one for the good of the clan.

"Yeah, I wouldn't exactly say she gave us a nudge," says one player, Vera "Mistress Vera" Knief. "It was more like a kick in the ass."

Worse still, this PMS fivesome has only practiced together for two weeks and has yet to play a single match, at a LAN or even in an online league.

The PMS Clan was destroyed in their two matches, losing 16–0 and 16–1. In the single round they won, all five girls rushed together and blindly lobbed grenades into a spot where, luckily, all of their opponents happened to be standing.

Because they are so often overmatched yet still get a disproportionate share of media attention and sponsorship dollars, PMS Clan is often the target of gamer backlash.

"Some guys have been nice, others have been complete jerks," says Mistress Vera. "The owner of JaX Money Crew, he's like, 'You guys are gonna get rolled 16–0, and it's because you're a girl team and you can't play.' And it's just like, 'Thanks, you're a douche.' He's being a sexist douche, and I didn't want to hear it."

The derision is yet another flashpoint in the struggle between e-sports purists and those falsely packaging it for broader appeal. The clans who ridicule PMS complain that with so little sponsor funding to go around, it's outrageous that girls are getting funded primarily because they're cute.

Dalton shrugs off the criticisms. "I'm comfortable playing in a boys' world," she says, defiantly. "They don't scare me. They don't intimidate me. The attention we get is good for gaming."

It's debatable, though, whether it's good for gaming to send a patched-together girls' Counter-Strike team out to get demolished 16–0 and 16–1. It was no secret to anyone around the tournament tables that PMS Clan only entered to fulfill its sponsorship agreement with Verizon. It was transparent, too, that Ringel allowed them to play because it was good publicity for the WSVG. Despite never having competed, the girls even got a favorable fifty-third seed out of sixty-six teams, designed to give them an easier matchup in the first round and avoid getting humiliated by a Top 10 team.

"A lot of the girls were just hoping to lose quickly," says Mistress Vera. "They knew they weren't ready, and they didn't want to look like jerks in front of everybody."

Mistress Vera and her teammates didn't look like jerks. They looked like what they were: sacrificial lambs sent to the slaughterhouse so PMS Clan could collect a $15,000 paycheck from Verizon.

For PMS and all the wannabe teams at Intel Summer on day one, they came, they saw, they got owned. Now the thirty-two clans remaining in the tourney get down to the business of battle.

Mug N Mouse is here, the clan of Dallas rowdies aiming to defend their home turf. "I think we're the third-best team in America," says Punkville. "All we need is a good match to break through."

Bzrk sits at the next seat, wearing a gaudy, fake-silver medallion around his neck shaped like Texas. It's something Punkville picked up for $15 at a gas station, and he awards it to whoever's playing best on the team.

Right now, Bzrk is on his game. It's Gosu who's struggling.

"Dude," Punkville tells his teammate, "didn't I tell you to AWP that faggot?"

"I got shot through the box!" snaps Gosu, who admittedly is a bit tightly wound at the moment. An hour ago, Gosu was upstairs in a hotel room, hunched over a glass table with a rolled up dollar bill, snorting a line of Adderall that he'd chopped up with the edge of his expired driver's license.

Adderall is an ADD drug, and it's the pick-me-up of choice among gamers. Adderall gives you energy and stamina and locks in your focus, but it leaves your head clear, unlike methamphetamines. At smaller LANs and in online competition, there's no doubt plenty of meth abuse, but at a major event like this one, there's too much money on the table to screw it up by tweaking on meth. But Adderall is a different story. Lots of gamers pop it, maybe one in five. It's not even hard to get your hands on. These are twenty-year-olds, and it seems half of them are prescribed it for attention deficit disorder. This is the after-effect of living in a pharmaceutically dependent quick-fix society: a convention hall filled with kids gobbling each other's ADD drugs.

On top of the line he snorted, Gosu also swallowed an Adderall XR capsule, which is time-release, so it will keep him alert for sixteen hours. He strategically popped the XR at nine o'clock this morning so he'd at least get *some* sleep tonight. "I've got to find a couple V8's somewhere, too," he says. "I won't eat on this shit either."

Mug N Mouse is playing United 5, another clan that throws around major attitude. Before the match, the two teams nearly came to blows when United 5 sabotaged Mug N Mouse's warm-up time.

Counter-Strike etiquette dictates that the last few minutes before a match is for players to run around inside the map and test their weapons. Nobody shoots each other. They just fire at the walls or lob grenades into empty alleys. It's a courtesy thing, like tennis players hitting volleys to each other before the first set.

Before this match, United 5 warmed up early and when Mug N Mouse logged in, their opponents kept immediately ending the session. They would intentionally frag themselves by shooting each other, repeatedly resetting the game after just a few seconds. It's a total bush-league move, and after they did it a fourth time, two admins had to restrain Punkville from going over the tables and throwing punches.

Instead, they're settling it inside the game. In the first half, Mug N Mouse jumps ahead 5–3 as Punkville sneaks up on an opponent and takes him out with a pistol. "Come on, let's 12–3 these pussies," he yells after winning the round.

Mug N Mouse is amped. Gosu, still grinding hard on Adderall, is actually taunting someone inside his monitor. "Peek me again, motherfucker. See what happens," he yells at his screen.

The tide turns, though, late in the first half and United 5 runs off six straight rounds to lead 9–6 at the break. Afterward United 5 pulls away to win 16–8 and Mug N Mouse drops into the lower bracket.

There are a dozen foreign teams at Intel Summer from Europe and South America, plus another ten or so that made the trip from Canada. One top foreign team, g3x from Brazil, is playing Team 3D on Inferno.

The g3x clan, which is short for G3neration-X, is based in Rio de Janeiro, home to only a scattering of LAN centers. As g3x's top player Rafael "Pava" Pavanelli says, "Computers in Brazil usually are terrible. Not many people have them. It's not exactly a Third World country, but it's not the best, computer-wise."

As g3x battles 3D, they holler in an odd sort of "Portugueslish"—half in Portuguese and half in English terms borrowed from the game. "Nice shot" is "frag *boa*" and "Come back, smoke!" is "*Hay recua,* smoke!"

So far, it's mostly a chorus of "frag *boa,*" with the Brazilians taking a 9–6 lead into halftime. In the second half, 3D goes on the offensive, switching over to T-side and putting the dominant Banana Peel strat into action.

In Moto's tactic, three players throw smoke and flash grenades that blast simultaneously at the far end of the curved Banana alley to blind any defenders positioned there. Then 3D charges in with guns blazing.

With the strat, overcoming a 9–6 halftime deficit shouldn't be difficult for 3D. Yet it is. What Moto failed to anticipate when devising

Banana Peel at boot camp was that there may not be two or three defenders guarding the alley. Instead, only g3x's star player, Pava, is positioned there. And so far, he's wreaking havoc on the game plan.

Much as Storm of CompLexity can go it alone and repel a three-man rush, Pava is practically single-handedly holding 3D at bay. And what's ingenious about his defense is that he's actually using the strat to beat the strat.

The point of Banana Peel is blindness and disorientation from the onslaught of flash and smoke grenades. But instead of holding his ground and getting steamrolled, Pava is dropping back to safety and then *also* throwing smokes and flashes at the same point of attack. He's re-blinding the blind spot.

So every time 3D rushes in, not only is nobody there to frag, but they can't see a damn thing because Banana is still filled with smoke. By the time 3D staggers through the fog of battle, Pava's teammates have had plenty of time to rotate over and help.

After the Brazilians push their lead to 12–8, Moto starts to panic. "Go quicker!" he commands, calling for the Banana Peel strat over and over, even though it continues to fail. "Again," he bellows into his headset, cracking his neck anxiously from side to side.

After another attack is repelled, Rambo challenges: "Let's go A and set up a crossfire." He's lobbying to attack the other bomb site on the opposite side of the map and give up on attempting to overrun Banana. "We can outgun these guys one-on-one."

Moto ignores him, again calling for Banana Peel, and yet again Pava fights them off. At 14–9, g3x is just two rounds from the win. Moto again calls for Banana Peel. "We've got to get through faster!" he implores.

Rambo has seen enough. "Fuck this," he says into his headset, "we're going A." In that instant, he hobbles Moto's authority. "We're hitting A site," Rambo tells the team, leaning forward and looking left and right down the row. "Let's go left. I need a flash."

Moto says nothing as 3D rushes out and catching g3x off-guard wins the round. Before the next round, again Moto is mum as Rambo orders an attack away from Banana. This one fails, though, because Moto is hanging too far back to provide cover fire for his teammates. "Dave, you have to push up," Rambo snaps at Moto. "Stop playing scared."

It's match point for g3x, 15–10, and as the next round begins, Moto and Rambo are still bickering. "I wasn't playing scared," argues Moto. "I was trying to clear the—"

"Shut the fuck up," lashes Rambo. "Just get out there and play."

Like a confused child, ShaGuar asks, "What am I doing?"

"Do whatever you want," snaps Moto.

In seconds, the Brazilians mow them down to end the match, 16–10. ShaGuar immediately yanks off his headphones and rips into Moto. "Didn't you hear the AWP? It was right there. We walked in, and every time they were expecting it."

Team 3D is imploding.

"Get off my ass," says Moto. "Jesus."

Craig Levine may not be much of a coach, and he has little desire to play babysitter to a bunch of petulant guys his own age, but he won't stand by and watch his team collapse halfway through the tournament.

"You know what, all you guys are playing like shit!" he says, stepping between ShaGuar and Moto. "There's no sense of urgency. There's no intensity out there. You're arguing halfway into the round. Come on. Play like it fucking means something."

Rambo speaks up. "I'd be more comfortable calling strats."

Moto argues, "I don't even have time to call shit before you second-guess me."

Levine puts his foot down, again siding with Moto. "We've had this conversation for the last two months. Dave is calling strats. You're assisting. It takes five players to lose, not one guy, not one strat.

"This is a double-elimination tournament," Levine says, looking them all in the eyes one at a time. "You lose twice, you go home. Not once. I'm not ready to go home. I'm ready to win the next match, and the one after that and fight through the lower bracket. But if you think this tournament is over, you might as well go upstairs and pack your bags right now. The decision is yours."

It was Levine's finest moment. In the midst of mutiny, he rose to the occasion to become a guiding force for his team. But were they even listening?

Minutes later, with most of the gamers off eating lunch, Rambo and Dominator are alone at 3D's base camp in the BYOC, commiserating over the team's collapse.

"That pistol round, Moto totally fucked up CT-half," Dominator says. "He was pushed up to Kiwi Box. And then Sal's rotating over to help and we all got caught off-guard. No one should have been rotating to B to help him."

Dominator's beef with Moto is different from Rambo's. Whereas Rambo wants to run the team, Dominator just thinks Moto is a weak player, period. As the team's sixth man, Dominator's perspective is unique. It's a flip-flop from traditional sports. In Counter-Strike, when you're benched, you don't take a seat. You stand. And from where Dominator stands during matches, behind the chairs with a view of all five screens, it's obvious that Moto is the weak link.

Against g3X, he was −6, in most of the rounds getting picked off early and leaving the team to fight shorthanded. Or, as Dominator was just complaining to Rambo, other 3D players are getting picked off rotating over to help Moto because he's incapable of defending an area himself.

It's not that Moto is a bad player. It's just that he's not up to 3D's standards. And now the other players believe his skills have deteriorated below elite level and that he's costing them matches—and consequently, prize money.

"Even when he's standing in a guy's blind spot, he still doesn't get the kill," Rambo says. "If you can't shoot someone in the back when they don't even know you're aiming at them, there's a problem."

Rambo and the others were skeptical of Moto's ability back in boot camp. There was a reprieve after the Lanwar win, but now the team's lack of confidence in Moto is again snowballing. Rambo is convinced Moto is hiding inside his own strats, that he's afraid of exposing his weaknesses in one-on-one gunfights so he's hanging back and letting others take the bullets. "That's why he's fighting to be strat caller, so he can sit back and play quarterback. Then he won't have to step out and get frags. We all know that."

Rambo is the ninja, the lurker. He's the eyes and ears of Team 3D, as well as its conscience. He's suspected ever since boot camp that half of the reason Levine brought Moto back to the team was for image and public relations. Now the rest of the team is starting to figure it out, too. Levine is loyal to Moto, siding with him over Rambo as team leader, because Moto is an irreplaceable asset in interviews.

It's no secret that Levine's focus is the future. His goal, as it's always been, is to build Team 3D and e-sports into something larger and more profitable. But what his players are mostly unaware of is that Levine, in all the time he spends away from the team, has for months secretly been consulting with DirecTV, tutoring them on the games and clans and advising them on ways to present gaming on television.

The satellite provider is finalizing plans for a small invitational tournament in the near future to include only a few select gamers. It's all very hush-hush, as DirecTV maneuvers for its own sponsors. Besides a few rumors among the Gotfrag writers and TSN shoutcasters, few people here at Intel Summer are even aware of the plans for a TV invitational. And other than what little he's told his team, Levine is keeping it quiet.

The 3D boss has a secret plan for everything, his own player Dominator has said. Levine's secret plan now is to get Team 3D maximum exposure when DirecTV puts a spotlight on gaming.

That's fine, of course, except a gaming veteran like Rambo is far too pragmatic to hold out for some promise of an illusory future in e-sports. He's seen too many false starts and unfulfilled promises in the industry to look beyond the money available here and now. His concern is the first-place check of $40,000 to be handed out on the final day of Intel Summer.

"I don't go to school, and I don't have any other income," Rambo says. "And I've put in way too many hours to have *this* happen." By "this," he means Moto's weak play costing the team matches. "I'm not here to make friends. This is business."

It wasn't always this way. Team 3D wasn't always a fractious team of mercenaries. In the early days with Ksharp and Bullseye, when they first started traveling overseas, there was camaraderie and laughs.

"It was around two years ago," Rambo says, "when Craig started cutting friends from the team as purely business decisions, that's when this became a job. That's when I decided I'm here for one reason only: to make money."

Team 3D, the golden boys of gaming, are in shambles. Rambo and Dominator are the only players in the BYOC practicing. ShaGuar, Method, and Volcano are off with other clans, hanging out with gamers they like more than their own teammates. Moto is wandering around the Gaylord, trying to locate what's left of his leadership ability. Not even Craig Levine can save 3D now. He's already over his allotment of pep talks for one day.

These guys are dead men walking.

In the next round, 3D plays Fnatic, a top Swedish team and one of the favorites to win the tournament. In the loser-goes-home match on Nuke, Fnatic runs out to a 9–6 lead, with 3D practically silent. When Moto calls out strats, his teammates don't even bother to reply.

After Fnatic pushes the lead to 11–6, Moto pleads, "Don't give up. Come on." Desperately he even turns to Rambo for help. "Ronald, do you think we'd be better off going outside and flip-flopping the smoke?"

Rambo says nothing, freezing him out.

Fnatic goes ahead 12–6, then 13–6, then 14–6.

Levine sees what's going on, standing silently off to the side with his arms folded. The players have made their decision. 3D has packed it in. They're not even trying anymore. They're boycotting Moto, letting him hang.

"Is anyone even gonna throw a grenade?" Moto says in disbelief, again drawing no response.

In a last futile gesture, Moto rushes alone into a bomb site. It's a suicide dash, a one-on-four, and he's immediately shredded by machine-gun fire.

"What are you doing?" says ShaGuar, mockingly.

"Don't fucking worry about it," snaps Moto, his loss of control over the team now total.

Mercifully, in the next round, Fnatic ends it 16–6, eliminating 3D from the event. Moto sits at the table, head buried in his hands, as the others rise without a word and wrap up their gear.

Over the next two rounds, the curtain falls on other U.S. hopefuls. In turn, Mug N Mouse, United 5, JaX Money Crew, and Pandemic all bow out. Only one U.S. team remains: CompLexity.

So far in the tourney, Lake's team has been rolling. They trounced Function Zero, an Australian team that ousted JaX Money Crew, by a score of 16–3. Then they destroyed g3x, the Brazilians who earlier beat 3D, by a convincing 16–5.

CompLexity's final match of the day is against the only other unbeaten, Alternate aTTaX of Germany. The winner gets a guaranteed spot in tomorrow's final, and the loser drops into the lower bracket to play the Swedish team Fnatic.

Intel Summer is double-elimination, so CompLexity has one loss to burn. It turns out they'd need it. On Nuke, the map that is their Achilles' heel, aTTaX dominates throughout and rolls 16–2. It's a punishing loss for CompLexity, but one that wasn't especially consequential.

"Brush it off," says Lake, as the team exits the tournament area. "That's the one we had to waste."

In the morning, CompLexity will face Fnatic in the lower bracket, where a win would give them another shot at the Germans in the final.

# Chapter 13

THE NIGHTTIME HOTSPOT AT THE GAYLORD IS THE Texan Station sports bar, which from the outside looks like an old Spanish mission with neon signs in the windows. Inside are a dozen TVs with different baseball games on, plus a sports ticker for score updates. It's like being at a Las Vegas sports book minus the clamor of slot machines.

In front of the TVs is a lounge area with plush leather couches arranged into a honeycomb of little pods. Here's where the gamers set up for the evening.

At one couch, Amber Dalton and her two lieutenants, gamer vamps Caitlin "Venus" Buckshaw and Alexis "Tart" Hebert, are enjoying the attention that a ten-to-one gender ratio of a gaming tournament guarantees. They've traded in their pink-and-black PMS T-shirts from today for low-cut blouses with slinky skirts and strappy stiletto heels. At the moment, the girls are getting chatted up by JaX, who's hanging out with his team in an adjacent couch pod. "Let's all get another round of drinks," says JaX, who's trying to put the squeeze on PMS girl Tart.

"You guys, this place is lame," sniffs Amber Dalton, exhaling cigarette smoke up into the ceiling fans. "I heard Fatal1ty's having a party in the penthouse suite. Let's split."

Sitting at a booth on the other side of JaX's crew is Pandemic and their manager Marc Dolven. There's a noticeable tension between these two clans.

"You know why your team lost today?" Dolven needles JaX, interrupting his flirtations with the PMS girls.

"Dude," says JaX, annoyed. "We weren't even talking about gaming."

JaX Money Crew vs. Pandemic is the undercard to 3D and CompLexity. The friction comes from each team's claim to be number three in America. Neither has a convincing argument, really, no more so than United 5 or Mug N Mouse or a handful of other U.S. clans. JMC hasn't done anything since their third-place finish at CPL Winter, and Pandemic never did anything before Lanwar. That's why the feud between JaX and Dolven is so entertaining. Both of the managers are delusional.

JaX is a trust-fund kid who dresses sharp, parties hard, and networks in New York nightclubs with names like Suede and Lotus. He's night to Dolven's day. Dolven is a clean-cut jock from Montana who tucks in his polo shirts, plays scratch golf, and networks on a tee box at eight o'clock in the morning.

As a regional marketing director for Subway restaurants based in Arkansas, he's managed to loosen up about $1,000 a month in funds through his accounts to support Pandemic. They wear a Subway logo on their shirts, though as sponsorships go, that's something of an overstatement and derided inside gaming.

JaX, more than anyone, loves to trash Dolven: "He's just a guy on the outside looking in. It's like he wants to belong to a club that won't take him as a member."

Dolven, in turn, has no use for JaX: "I don't call it an accomplishment to waste your parents' money to run a Counter-Strike team. I give him no credit whatsoever."

Jason Lake is at the bar, networking as always. He's shaking hands and buying rounds of drinks, investing one pint at a time in guys like Tim Takeuchi, Intel's point man in gaming and the gatekeeper to their six-figure sponsorship. "Let's talk again later," says Lake. "You know, maybe we can meet in the middle on this thing."

Takeuchi rejoins Craig Levine at a table with a few players from United 5. Intel sponsors Team 3D fully with salaries, equipment, and travel, but they also have a far smaller, merchandise-only deal with United 5—the bad-attitude clan that sabotaged Mug N Mouse's warm-up time today. In-your-face attitude sells to the youth.

"They're West Coast," Takeuchi says of hip-hop United 5. "They have a little more edge. They've got the lingo. They're the Raiders of e-sports. Look at any MTV type of show, and there's a lot of emphasis to how much you can bling."

For Lake, it's been a fruitless couple of nights of networking at the Gaylord. With no crossover brands yet on the scene, no Nike or Mountain Dew in the mix, the sponsorship pie is still limited to computer companies. So far this weekend, he's spoken with both Takeuchi of Intel and Sheryl Huang of NVIDIA and gotten absolutely nowhere.

"We have a finite pool of dollars that we want to spend, and our dollars are spoken for," Takeuchi says privately, after sidestepping Lake. "Right now we're interested in Craig and Team 3D. They're the New York Yankees of e-sports, right? They're professional, they're reputable, and they have a long track record of being good spokespeople with the company."

Intel has sponsored Team 3D since August 2005. NVIDIA's Huang goes back to the beginning, having given Levine his big break at CPL Winter 2002. She too is lukewarm on the marketing appeal of a kids-next-door gang like CompLexity.

"They're a good group of guys," she says. "They're quiet. They're not going to destroy a hotel room and make your company look bad. But you're also looking for a certain star quality. That's what sells. Look at how boy bands are put together. That's how I see a group of guys like 3D."

So there it is. Team 3D is beloved by sponsors because they're the *NSYNC of Counter-Strike. "We saw that star quality immediately with Moto," Huang gushes. "He has that charisma. He's great with the camera. He is obviously the leader of the pack."

Moto is the leader of the 3D pack, says NVIDIA's Huang. Apparently she missed today's match when the pack sat idly by and let their leader get torn to ribbons by machine-gun fire.

No wonder Jason Lake is frustrated. The team he's competing against gets about $100,000 from NVIDIA, and all those players do is annoy each other. Meanwhile, he's got the only U.S. team still alive in this tournament and nothing to show for it but a $100 bar tab from buying drinks for marketing reps.

It's been a tough stretch financially for Lake, who's running out of time on his e-sports dream. This weekend alone he shelled out for three rooms at the Gaylord plus five round-trip airfares to get his kids to Dallas. That's about $5,000 before he picks up a single check at dinner or buys a single round. "I really need this to break soon," he says. "I can't go home without a contract or at least a *very* promising discussion."

Lake's best hope now is Dell, a newcomer at this event that's come on board with a small financial commitment to the WSVG. It's Dell's first time dipping a toe in gaming, but everyone's hoping by the end of the weekend they'll like what they see and commit to sponsoring a team.

Lake's master plan is to get in the ear of the company's CEO himself, Michael Dell, who will be making an appearance tomorrow for the awards ceremony. The WSVG has even been trumpeting the occasion with placards on artists' easels around the event bearing Dell's grinning mug.

The catch is, Lake only gets a shot at Michael Dell if CompLexity wins the tournament. After the finals conclude, the champions in every game title will join the CEO upstairs in the president's suite for refreshments and a question-and-answer session.

That's when Lake plans to make his pitch. That's when he can stand before the Great and Powerful Oz and ask for what he needs most: a six-figure sponsorship.

First, though, CompLexity must win.

Lake leaves the sports bar and takes a seat on a bench in the atrium, now dimly lit. He leans back on the bench and stares up at the glass ceiling, again searching for a little faith. Lake may be an idealist, but he's not naive. He's perfectly aware of all the opinions on why his team can't land a sponsor. "Oh, I've heard it all before," he says. "We're not what sells products. We're not attractive. We're fat, we're boring, and guys like ShaGuar or Moto are what companies want to move their products.

"I've been through finance and marketing courses, and I know that with some companies maybe there is a certain amount of truth to that. But I don't put together a bunch of pretty boys. I build my team on character and talent. I build teams to win.

"My guys carry themselves well. They've got good personalities. Hey, maybe we've got a couple of heavy kids. But look around. This is America, man."

Others quietly suggest that Lake himself has been the biggest obstacle to inking a deal. The coach is a good ole boy who likes to drink a few beers now and again, and he did make a bad first impression in e-sports with that off-putting TSN interview. And, for those unaware of Lake's paternalism with his players, his antics during matches could at first be misconstrued as belligerent.

NVIDIA's Huang, an ardent 3D supporter, backs the own-worst-enemy theory on Lake's difficulties, saying, "It can come down to the manager. If you don't have the professionalism, or you come across as a poor representative of a brand, you're not gonna get that sponsorship. It doesn't matter how many times you beat the number one."

Takeuchi of Intel, who has a better rapport with Lake, disagrees.

"If the fear is that Jason is too vibrant a character, I don't necessarily see that as negative," he says. "Vocal characters bring a liveliness to the sport and make it a better spectator experience."

Of course, Takeuchi, like the others, has yet to back up those words with an offer.

The heat of the Texas day arrives early in summer. By 8 A.M., the sun is beating sideways if not straight down, and the thermometer is already inching up on 90 degrees. CompLexity plays at eleven o'clock, which is an early call time for guys who generally sleep past noon.

The coach wants his boys at their best. He doesn't want them battling drowsiness this morning as well as Fnatic.

Warden and Trıp's hotel room is dark, with the thick drapes pulled closed. The only light in the room comes off Warden's buzzing cell phone. "Hello," he answers groggily. "A what?" he says. "Uh-huh." He hangs up.

"That was Jake," he tell his roommate, Trıp, then rolls back over and pulls the covers up over his head. Warden is a devoted sleep enthusiast.

"What did he say?" asks Trıp.

Warden's muffled complaint comes from beneath the blankets. "We're going on a *power walk*."

A half-hour later, CompLexity is gathered on the front steps of the hotel, rubbing the sleep out of their eyes and squinting into the glaring sun.

"All right, boys. Time to get the blood pumping," says Lake, full of vigor. "Let's move it on out."

As the coach leads the way down the road, the players fall in behind, sulking about the unscheduled early-morning workout. Since when is cardio part of being a gamer? "This is retarded," mutters Warden, scuffing along in bath slippers.

They look like a pack of somnambulists, dragging single-file along the side of the road. It's all the more comical because the Gaylord is in the middle of nowhere. Its long driveway leads only to another empty road, which cuts across an open expanse of prairie. CompLexity looks like a bunch of guys who made a wrong turn on a parade route.

Behind Lake are Warden, then Trıp, fRoD, and Sunman. Bringing up the rear are Storm and his gamer girlfriend, Stephanie. She lives in Toronto, and with Storm in Arkansas, major gaming events are their best opportunities to see each other. This weekend, they've been practically inseparable. Stephanie plays Counter-Strike, too, on a female clan called SK Ladies, under the alias Miss Harvey. Her teammates joke that since they started dating, Stephanie has begun playing like her boyfriend, choosing the same weapons and hiding in the same blind spots in the maps.

As a coach, Lake isn't crazy about the idea of having a girlfriend tagging along, but even he's not so competitive as to stand in the way of young love. He's allowing Stephanie to sit in on team meetings, and go along on the team's power walk.

As Storm and Stephanie walk up the road to nowhere, they talk about Counter-Strike almost like an old married couple—when she starts rambling, he tunes out.

"On Nuke, I always go up on Rafter and shoot low and high," she says. "We used to triple-flank back, but it never works."

Storm absently throws in an "Mmmm," gazing around the empty plains. Then when he starts talking, she tunes out. "You know how I sit behind my Pit Box on Inferno peeking through the hole?" Storm says, ignored. "My little spot there?" he asks.

"You know what," Stephanie says, her mind a mile away. "I think I might buy some purple pants today."

Up ahead, fRoD is stewing over yesterday's late loss to Alternate aTTaX on Nuke. Not just because he hates losing, although it was an embarrassment getting dominated 16–2. fRoD's pissed off because late in the blowout, aTTaX started hotdogging to rub it in.

At the start of the final round, instead of buying the usual machine guns like AK-47s or M4s, aTTaX scrolled deep down into the inventory list and bought Paras. Nobody ever uses a Para in professional Counter-Strike. Ever. It's a gigantic, heavy, loud, and utterly inaccurate weapon. It's cartoonish almost. Using a Para in a Counter-Strike match would be like a hockey player skating out for a face-off with a goalie stick. It's an unmistakable insult.

Then, if the Para showboat wasn't enough, aTTaX later tried to show up fRoD personally.

In Counter-Strike, every player comes equipped with a knife. Nobody ever uses it except in a worst-case scenario like, say, after they've run out of ammo. It's common sense. You don't break out a knife in a gunfight.

As the final seconds of yesterday's blowout wound down, two aTTaX players ran at fRoD with knives. It was a direct "screw you" to the world's number-one player.

"Those guys are faggots, trying to knife me," he says, still fuming at the slight. "I just stepped back and shot them. Losers."

Lake knows that the hot-dogging is a potential motivator, but the last thing the coach wants now is fRoD dwelling on the insults when they're not even preparing to play aTTaX. He doesn't want his team looking ahead. First CompLexity must get past the talented Swedish team Fnatic.

"Don't worry about it, Danny," he tells his star. "Once we're up on the big stage, on our maps, we'll teach them to show some humility. But first, let's concentrate on getting to the big stage."

aTTaX's hot-dogging is not all that's bothering fRoD. He's also torn about his future. Again, in the hallways at the Gaylord, he's been approached by Craig Levine.

It's been a distraction for him all weekend, and consequently he's not playing up to his ability. Meanwhile, the more that Lake stresses team unity and pulls them together for bonding exercises like this power walk up the driveway, the more fRoD agonizes over the decision he must soon make.

Looking back over his shoulder, fRoD sees four teammates he has no wish to abandon. He sees four guys who, if he leaves to join their rival, will be broken. It's not ego. It's the truth. And he feels guilty about it. Guilty yet also frustrated that he's not capitalizing financially on his peerless ability, that Lake can't solicit funding, that the growth of the game in which he dominates seems to have petered out.

Lake always says, "Win, and the rest takes care of itself. Win, and the rewards follow." If they can deliver Lake a major championship today, maybe he can deliver on his promises.

There's a lot of cash riding on today's matches. CompLexity is guaranteed no worse than third place, so they'll split a minimum of $20,000 five ways. Beating Fnatic would assure second place and a split of $27,000. Winning the whole event would be worth $40,000, or $8,000 a player.

A videogame is no longer child's play when a single match can mean a difference of $2,500 per player, and it's not uncommon for a Counter-Strike match to come down to a one-on-one with all the money on the line. That's why underachieving teams cut weak players. That's why a guy like Rambo has no patience for a weak link like Moto. When $40,000 is on the line, game becomes business.

And for CompLexity today, there's still more at stake than just prize money. Lake's team is playing for their very survival. They're playing for an audience with the Great and Powerful Michael Dell.

CompLexity sets up for the Fnatic match, seated left to right in their usual order. fRoD is at one end, propped up on a tucked-under right foot. Next is Warden, in shorts and barefoot after kicking off his flip-flops. Tr1p sits in the middle, where he can call strats and direct players left and right. Sunman has his ever-present good-luck charm, an old tattered teddy bear set atop his monitor. And at the far right is Storm, with his girlfriend Stephanie looking on nearby.

CompLexity has played in pressure spots before, but considering the stakes, there's an extra frazzle of nerves before the match. Lake doesn't air out his financial woes to the team, but everyone's fully aware that time is running out. And nobody knows it more than Warden, the first player ever signed by Lake.

Warden is the one who books the team's flights, so he knows Lake's credit cards are almost tapped out. It's also Warden whose weight problem is really what people mean when they say CompLexity can't land a sponsor because they're not a camera-ready boy band.

Warden has brushed off many insults since becoming a name in Counter-Strike. Not from other top players at LANs like this—they know him, like him, and respect his ability. The taunts come anonymously on the Internet.

"He doesn't talk about it a lot, so we don't really know if it bothers him," says fRoD. "But we'll be at tournaments and read Gotfrag together and he'll see a doctored photo of him in front of a McDonald's or something online. He'll just say, 'Whatever,' and if there are people around, he'll laugh at it. But obviously he's not happy about it. Who likes people talking bad about them?"

All Warden says about the insults is, "People talk shit in pro sports all the time, and I'm sure LeBron James doesn't go home and cry about it. I'm not gonna get mad over what some guy with one-twentieth of my skill says about me. I really don't care."

Win or lose, Lake would never have gotten this far without Warden. And if it's true that having a fat kid on the team is costing him a sponsorship, then Lake would have them stick that sponsorship up their ass. "Warden is one of the nicest guys you're ever gonna meet," Lake says. "The organization stands behind him."

Fnatic takes pistol round to open the match on Train before quickly running out to a 4–0 lead.

"Shake it off," says Lake, who begins seated but now is on his feet. The crowd gathered behind the CompLexity table steps back to give him room. It won't be long before he starts to pace.

Warden leans forward and looks right and left down the row of players. "Let's get going. We don't need that many. It's T-side. Come on."

Three tables away in the tournament area, Fnatic is riled up, too. They're not lacking in confidence, in their black-and-orange jerseys and spiky Swede gamer hair. *"Comiendo!"* they shout in encouragement.

In the fifth round, Warden frags a Fnatic player and then rushes over to take his victim's gun, an AWP no less. It's a heads-up move, and he immediately picks off another foe to win the round. CompLexity is on the board, down 4–1.

"Nice, Matt," says Lake. "Build on this."

Fnatic bounces back to win the next two rounds and push the lead to 6–1. fRoD is struggling. Maybe he's bothered by his future, or maybe he's thinking ahead to getting revenge against aTTaX. Either way, he's not right.

The match is starting to slip away for CompLexity. But Warden grabs it back. He gambles by purchasing an AWP. It's a little unusual, having both fRoD and Warden AWPing. Because of the game's money system, it's a big risk. But right now with fRoD struggling, it's worth a shot. Warden perches in an area of the map called Tower, high above the rail-yard bomb site, and starts piling up frags. CompLexity roars back with five straight rounds and ties the score 6–6.

"Driver's seat! Driver's seat!" shouts Lake, who's now fully awakened. "Come on, gentlemen." He hits the back of Warden's chair for encouragement.

CompLexity wins two of the next three to close the half ahead 8–7. After trailing 6–1, there's a sense of relief on the team, but not with Warden. Through the minute-long break before the second half begins, he's locked in, sitting with a focused stare at his monitor.

In the opening round after the break, a pistol round, Warden comes out blazing. He pushes ahead of the pack and kills one, two, three. He's leaning in toward his monitor, feet bare and flat on the cement floor, eyes piercing. He kills a fourth. He's roaming, roaming, hunting. Blam! It's an ace. Warden took out all five.

His teammates roar. "Nobody aces with a pistol," someone says in the crowd.

CompLexity takes the next round and pushes ahead 10–7. It goes to 12–10 and then 14–10. fRoD steps up and stops a rush. CompLexity moves ahead 15–10 and is one round away from reaching the finals.

"Backbreaker! Backbreaker!" shouts Lake, hands on his hips.

Warden screams even louder than his coach, "Right now!"

CompLexity is rolling, clearing out the map. Bodies are dropping. Fnatic is down to one last player, who's scrambling around trying to plant the bomb.

Lake shouts, "Finish them!"

The Fnatic shooter slips past fRoD's aim and takes out Trip. He takes out Sunman and rushes into the bomb site, but Warden—who else?—is waiting for him.

Warden unloads an entire clip from his M4 into the last Fnatic player, hurtling him against a concrete wall. The dead man slides down to the ground, leaving a red streak on the cinder blocks.

"Yes!" shouts Warden, pulling off his headphones and high-fiving

Tr1p and fRoD. Storm and Sunman celebrate at the end of the row. Lake pumps his fist.

CompLexity is in the finals. They're going to the big stage, and it was Warden who carried them there. His match was the stuff of legend. An ace round is a rarity in Counter-Strike with any weapon, let alone with a basic default pistol. He also had three other rounds in which he took out four of five players, plus he had six other multifrag rounds for an incredible +18 for the match. It's all the more impressive when you know Storm was only +3, followed by Sunman at −1, Tr1p at −3, and stunningly, fRoD at −9.

Fnatic leaves shaking their heads. One player named DSN says of Warden's highlight-reel performance, "He is a great player. We make mistakes and he took advantage every time. He was locked in on the kill."

CompLexity only gets about a fifteen-minute break before meeting Alternate aTTaX for the championship. And it turns out they won't be on the big stage after all. The finals were supposed to be played on the WSVG's elevated main stage in the middle of the convention center under bright, colored lights.

The problem is, the Quake 4 final is still being played up there because of earlier technical problems. Pushing back the Counter-Strike final isn't an option because aTTaX has a three o'clock flight back to Germany. They've even sent their bags ahead to the airport, so the Counter-Strike championship must be played back in the regular cafeteria-table setup off to the side of the venue. Once again CompLexity and Jason Lake are denied the limelight of the big stage.

As the teams set up for the finals, a crowd squeezes around the edges of the tournament area. The guys from JaX Money Crew and Pandemic are looking on, as well as recently ousted Fnatic. Craig Levine and Moto stand and watch just outside the penned-in tables.

Storm's mom and dad are here, too. They made the trip from Little Rock as their family summer vacation. It's the first time mom Jeannette has flown on an airplane since she was seventeen and the first time they've ever seen Tyler play at a LAN. It's also their first opportunity to meet Tyler's girlfriend Stephanie, who stands with them for the match to explain what's happening on his monitor. The Woods like their son's new girlfriend.

Circling around the tables is the two-man camera crew from GamePlay channel, as well as the aspiring NYU filmmakers, Jon Boal and Artem Agafonov. At Lanwar in Louisville, the documentary duo spotlighted Team 3D. This event the focus is on CompLexity.

Lake is thankful for the attention, and encouraged that someone else believes there's an audience out there who may be interested in e-sports. He's doing his best to accommodate both film crews, allowing them to wire him up with remote microphones. "I've got one in each pocket," says Lake, pulling them out to reveal the wires. "I feel like a goddamn Christmas tree."

Jon and Artem, the NYU guys, even asked him to repeat a few of his more colorful phrases. "They want me to yell 'backbreaker,'" Lake says, rolling his eyes. "So, what, now I'm being scripted?"

Since it's double-elimination, CompLexity must beat Alternate aTTaX twice. That's no enviable task. aTTaX is a rising force in German gaming, and in reaching the finals, they've run off four straight wins over teams ranked in the worldwide Top 10: Catch-Gamer from Norway, Fnatic, Mousesports, and CompLexity yesterday in the 16–2 rout that ended with the Para and knife hotdogging.

At the start of the match, on Inferno, Warden picks up where he left off, taking out three opponents before dropping. aTTaX clears out Banana and rushes into Bomb Site B. One player kneels down to plant the bomb while two others protect his back. The coast looks clear until…*bang!* One gets head-shot and falls dead. Where'd that come from? *Bang!* Another head-shot. That's two. Who's shooting at them? The last aTTaX player alive, the one planting the bomb, rises and spins to face the enemy.

There, aiming a pistol from across the courtyard, is fRoD. *Bang!* That's three. Lake throws a fist in the air. "Welcome to the show!" he yells at aTTaX.

This is Jason Lake sounding the battle horn. This is him leading the charge. The Germans disrespected his boys yesterday, and now they must answer for it.

CompLexity goes up 2–0, 3–0, 4–0. "Snowball this!" says Lake. It goes to 9–1, 10–1, 11–1, and at halftime CompLexity is ahead 12–3.

"Backbreaker!" shouts Lake, slapping his players on their shoulders.

When Storm wins the pistol round after halftime, it's just a matter of closing it out. The final in this one, the match that aTTaX could afford to throw away, is CompLexity 16–5.

The next match, winner take all, will be played on Dust 2, a wide-open map with a desert-outpost theme. On Dust 2, if fRoD is hot, he can lock down half of the map by himself. At one elevated perch near Bomb Site A, he can scope out two alleys at once. If the opponent comes straight into the site, he's waiting. If they try to sneak around the long way, the attackers must momentarily dart across an opening, exposing themselves for about two seconds to an AWP shot. It's a sliver of space, and to hit his opponents fRoD must fire a bullet through a narrow gap between two half-opened wooden doors.

Most AWPers barely consider it a viable shot. But fRoD is not most AWPers. Two seconds of exposure is about one second more than he needs to drop an attacker cutting past the doors.

Meanwhile, as usual, Storm is assigned to the other bomb site, holding off rushes shorthanded and forcing the enemy back fRoD's way. That's the way CompLexity draws it up on the chalkboard, fRoD and Storm each holding down half of the map. But what Lake didn't expect was that the match would end up in the hands of the quietest, most overlooked player on the team.

Justin "Sunman" Summy is a shy, almost withdrawn kid. It's not easy pulling him out of his shell. Even his home in rural Grantville, Pennsylvania, a few miles outside of Hershey, is set back and almost hidden from the street.

Inside the quirky house that Sunman shares with his dad, there's a pulley system for watering hanging plants and a couple of restored gumball machines from the 1960s. In the middle of summer, the Summys usually have about fifty quart jars and eighty pints of home-made salsa all over the kitchen and living room, ready to sell at the annual chili cookoff in Harrisburg. There's a lot going on inside that little mouse hole, if you take the time to peek inside.

Sunman was a top Counter-Strike star back in 2003 and 2004. These days, his skills have waned, and he's become a complementary player. For a quiet kid like him, that's just fine.

"Back in 2003, that was my time. That's when I was king," he says. "I'm not a top aimer anymore. So if I'm in a 1-v-1 with someone, I get into their head and think, 'What would I do if I was playing *me* right now?' And then I do the opposite. Most of my success at this point is through mind games."

In the final, CompLexity jumps ahead with another pistol-round win before running out to a 3–0 lead. Warden then takes out two, and Sunman comes up with a big head-shot. That's 4–0 for CompLexity, and then 5–0.

"Get greedy," says Lake. He walks to one end of the row, stops, watches for a half-minute and then walks down to the other end. He's oscillating between fRoD and Storm, the two ends of CompLexity's spectrum. And so far, the plan is going according to script. At 8–0, fRoD turns around to Lake and half-jokingly says, "What do you think? Should we buy Paras?"

Lake smirks. "Get all fifteen this half and we'll talk about it."

aTTaX finally gets on the board at 9–1, and the half ends 11–4. Nobody in the CompLexity row says a word during the break. It's theirs if they don't choke, and they know it. There's nothing to discuss.

CompLexity wins pistol round to open the second half on CT. At 13–4, fRoD's in a one-on-one with a perfect chance to deliver more payback to aTTaX for insulting him yesterday.

"Finish him, Danny," says Lake, as his teammates peer over at fRoD's screen, waiting for him to close out the round. Instead, he loses. The kid is human, after all.

aTTaX capitalizes to run off a few rounds and make it 14–8. "Stay calm," stresses Lake. "This is your match." After trading rounds, CompLexity is at match point, 15–9.

fRoD has another one-on-one. This time Lake stays quiet. But again, fRoD loses the duel. He's pressing. He's still not completely on his game. Someone else will need to step up.

In the next round, aTTaX rushes the short way toward Bomb Site A. fRoD, Warden, and Tr1p all fall. Only Storm and Sunman are left to defend, in a two-on-three.

Storm is locked in a firefight on the periphery, while Sunman is double-teamed inside and has to fall back. But instead of digging in for the attack, he chooses to vacate the bomb site and hide behind a wall.

Alone, Sunman crouches in his little hiding space and counts off a few seconds. Guessing that aTTaX must be in the site now and planting the bomb, he lobs a grenade over the wall. It's a blind gamble. If they're not in the site, he's just wasted his grenade and given away his position. *Boom!*

Sunman rushes around the corner into the smoky aftermath. His grenade took out both attackers, who lie dead, but they'd already gotten the bomb planted. As it ticks down from thirty-five seconds toward detonation, Sunman runs over to attempt a defuse.

It takes ten seconds to defuse a bomb, and in that time Sunman will be defenseless. He'll be crouched over, without a weapon in his hands. If he's attacked and reaches for a gun, the defuse will stop and he'll have to start over again.

It's another blind gamble. Sunman holsters his gun and begins the defuse. 10...9...

If he makes it to ten seconds, CompLexity will win the tournament. Storm tries keeping the last aTTaX player at bay but falls.... 8...7...6. The aTTaX shooter comes charging up a ramp into the bomb site...5...4...It's gonna be close.

Sunman must decide: stay defenseless on the defuse or reach for a gun. He's going for it. He's staying on the defuse.

The aTTaX player is now in the site, firing off shots that miss Sunman by inches. *Blam! Blam!*...3...2...

Warden can't stand the suspense. He pushes his chair back, stands up and tosses his headphones on the table. "Please," he begs.

...1...0. Click. The bomb is defused. CompLexity wins.

Warden turns and collides in a hug with Jason Lake. Sunman and Storm pile on. Tr1p and fRoD join in the jubilation. It's bedlam.

Fans on the sideline whistle and applaud. Jim and Jeannette Wood are laughing and smiling, and Storm steps over and gives them a hug. He gets high-fives from other gamers in the crowd, and the cameramen rush over for postmatch interviews.

As aTTaX makes their way for the exits, a Gotfrag reporter asks for a quote. "We are impressed," one player says. "We beat them yesterday. And they beat us today. They are good players. It is okay."

It's the biggest win in CompLexity's history, and their numbers for the tournament are spectacular. Warden was +33 and Storm +37. fRoD finished +74, once again off the charts.

CompLexity has its championship. They have their $40,000 cardboard check, and they got their payback on Alternate aTTaX. Now they're off to see the Wizard, heading for a meeting upstairs with Michael Dell. Much like Craig Levine four years before at CPL Winter, Lake now is hoping to head home with both a championship and a corporate sponsorship in the bag.

The jubilant gamers spill out of a packed elevator onto the top floor of the Gaylord Resort. Along with Jason Lake and CompLexity are the winners of the other games, like Day of Defeat and Halo 2, all headed to the Dell penthouse suite.

The NYU documentary duo, Jon and Artem, follow along, planning to capture the big occasion on camera. Halfway down the hallway, WSVG boss Ringel heads them off.

"Sorry, we can't allow you guys in there," he says sternly. The documentary makers are stunned. "We've been following these guys for six months," says Jon. "We can't go in there now? Why not?"

Ringel is squirming. "See, we okayed you guys to be at the event, but this is a Dell situation. We don't have clearance. It's not something we can allow."

"It's a hand-held," reasons Artem. "We'll stand in the back. We won't even use a—"

"Sorry, we can't allow it," says Ringel, slipping inside the Dell suite. "Thanks so much for understanding."

The last few players are headed in. Artem pulls one straggler from CompLexity aside. They duck inside a hallway bathroom, where Artem asks, "Hey, man. I need a favor."

Ten minutes later, Artem is sitting quietly in a fire-escape stairwell a half-floor almost directly below the penthouse suite, listening intently to an earpiece. He's wired one of the CompLexity players— whom we'll call "DonnieBrasco" to protect his identity—with a remote transmitter and a little microphone taped up under his shirt.

"If you can hear me, I'm in the third row at the end," DonnieBrasco whispers into the mike. "They've got sodas and peanuts and stuff in here, if that matters."

"I can hear him," whispers Artem, who's recording the audio. "We're in." When Michael Dell is introduced to the room of gamers, Artem recoils from his earpiece because the applause is so loud.

"Thank you very much. It's great to be here," says Dell, as he looks over the room. Of the twenty or so champion gamers in there, he can't help but notice the CompLexity fivesome all dressed alike in their maroon team jerseys.

"Hey, look at all these shirts," Dell says. "You guys really look great."

Lake isn't wasting any time. He drops a first hint. "Yeah, they'd look even better with a Dell logo on them."

The CEO doesn't take the bait, instead launching into a few minutes of pat rhetoric. "You may be wondering, what's the largest computer company in the world doing at a gaming conference like this?" he says. "Well, this last year, the videogame business produced more revenues than the entire Hollywood box office. It's an eleven-billion-dollar industry, and we're excited to be part of that."

Dell opens up the sit-down to questions. Lake immediately digs in for his first big swing. "I think a lot of people are wondering about your plans for gaming," he says. "Are you dipping your toe in the water? Are you diving in headfirst? What's your plan?"

Again, Dell evades. "Well, in September, we'll be attending an immersive game-development conference in Austin. We're very interested in hardware and software to advance the industry."

DonnieBrasco whispers into the mike taped on his chest, "Strike one."

Dell fields a few more questions, telling the gamers that he plays World of Warcraft on occasion with his son. After a few minutes of softball questions, Lake takes his second shot. "Have you considered the idea of sponsoring a gaming team?" he asks.

Once again, Dell dodges. "Well, you have to understand that this is an ongoing learning experience for us," he says noncommitally. "We like to support events like this and find ways to support the community. Right now we have ventures with XPS and Alienware, and we've got four thousand engineers putting their world-class minds into making kick-ass game machines."

"Strike two," whispers DonnieBrasco.

Lake is going down in flames. In the stairwell, Artem shakes his head. It's painful even to listen to. After five more minutes of questions, Dell asks the players what they do besides play videogames. A couple mention they have part-time jobs. He's forcing it, but Lake is determined to give it one last try. He's gonna go down swinging.

"A lot of these guys are in college as well," Lake interjects, "and in many cases they don't have the time to study, practice, *and* on top of that hold a part-time job to support themselves. So it's sad, but a lot of them are forced to choose between work and gaming. That's why sponsorship is so important."

Lake has laid it all on the table. He's tried four times now, and he can't be any more obvious than that. It's now up to the billionaire Dell to make his dreams come true, to loosen a hundred grand from the multibillion-dollar company to help a struggling clan like CompLexity.

"We have heard the demand from gamers, and again, we are very committed to supporting this community," Dell says, giving Lake a ray of hope.

And then Dell says, "So before you guys leave, make sure to check out our Series XPS 700 downstairs at the new-products expo. And we've got XPS M17-10 notebooks here, the first Dual Core notebooks with 700 DS graphics and 504 megabytes of video RAM. That's the kind of performance I know you guys love."

And that, for Lake, was most definitely strike three.

"Man, this guy doesn't want to sponsor us," says DonnieBrasco, his voice trailing off into a mumble. "He just wants us to buy his computers."

# PART IV

## Lights, Camera, Reaction

# Chapter 14

**S**IX MONTHS HAVE PASSED SINCE THE MOST FAMOUS Counter-Strike player in the world called it quits. Kyle "Ksharp" Miller was twenty-one years old when he retired from Team 3D in January 2006, hanging up his mouse after the team's disappointing finish at CPL Winter.

At the time, Ksharp was probably second in the United States in name recognition among gamers after only Fatal1ty, the 1-v-1 star featured on MTV in November 2005 and another segment months later on *60 Minutes*. Ksharp had gotten his share of ink, too. Two months before he quit, the Team 3D sniper was featured in a sprawling story in *The Washington Post,* the newspaper that had been landing for years on the doorstep of his home in Reston, Virginia.

The article was a well-written if familiar angle by the mainstream media on the underground world of professional videogaming. It expanded upon many of the same points made in past stories in *Sports Illustrated* and *The New York Times* and on CNN, ESPN, ABC's *World News Tonight,* and dozens of others. The hook was always the same: Young guys...$30,000 a year...videogames.

In the profile of the boyish, sandy-haired Ksharp, *Washington Post* staff writer Jose Antonio Vargas led with: "He drives a Bimmer. He attracts the ladies. He's got sponsors. He trains hard. He plays harder.

He's 21. No, he's not in the NBA. 'Ksharp'—aka Kyle Miller—is a full-time professional computer game player."

Later in the article, Ksharp was quoted as saying, "Whenever someone asks me, 'Oh, what do you do for work?' I just kinda shy away. Then the person asks again, and I'm, like, 'I play videogames.' Then the person goes, 'No, I mean what do you do for an actual job?' And I say again, 'I play videogames. It is a job.'"

At the end of the article, Ksharp summarized, "I understand that for a lot of people, what I do for a living is heaven."

Then, curiously, three months later Ksharp quit gaming. Why would he have walked away from such a heavenly job, especially as his star was shining brightly? Ksharp quit for the same reason all pro gamers do: it just wasn't going anywhere.

Ksharp had played Counter-Strike competitively for seven years, from age fourteen to twenty-one. He was the first player Levine phoned in 2002 to help build America's first professional clan. In 2005, he clashed with Moto and forced him off the team.

A year later, at the start of this season, he quit. At twenty-one, Ksharp decided that he was now a grown-up, and gaming was not a grown-up job. It's not that he was dying to put on a suit and begin working his way up the corporate ladder to a corner office and a parking space. Nobody in gaming wants that kind of drudgery. To Ksharp, grown-up meant making some real moolah, the $70,000 and up he could earn in programming or IT work.

"Gaming had become work anyway," Ksharp says. "Not the tournaments, but the practicing and scrimming. A lot of the fun of the game was gone. It was good work, sure, but it was still work. So if gaming was a job, why not find another that pays better?"

Now the legendary Ksharp is just Kyle Miller, as it says on a nameplate in his cubicle at the SRA data-management company in Virginia. At his new nine-to-five, he still taps away on a keyboard all day, only now he's tracking data. It's techie stuff. He's good at it.

"Some things haven't changed," he says. "As jobs go, it's still a chunk of your day that's gone. Only now I wake up at eight o'clock in the morning, instead of three o'clock in the afternoon. I don't make that much more than, say, a very good year in Counter-Strike, but it's consistent. I've got a 401(k) and full benefits. It's something I can plan around."

No Counter-Strike player had done more to push the message of "gaming as the sport of the future" than Ksharp. But after three and a half years with Team 3D, he just stopped buying the hype. "I never honestly envisioned myself as an NBA player," says Ksharp, "getting paid by a league to play. The vision didn't click in my head, which is kind of funny because I was on a team that sells that vision."

Now that he's twenty-two, most of his high-school buddies are graduating from college. When Ksharp finished high school, he was accepted at the University of Tennessee but instead enrolled part-time at Northern Virginia Community College so he could live at home and play Counter-Strike. He dropped out of NVCC after one year.

"Looking back, I don't regret it," he says of skipping college. "Yes, it would be good to have a four-year degree, but I had travel, some money, camaraderie."

Ksharp says the decision to walk away came spontaneously during CPL Winter in January, right after the team lost in the quarterfinals to SK Gaming.

"Maybe it was going to the Hyatt for the twentieth time. I don't know," he says. "But the morning after we lost that triple-overtime match to SK, I just thought, I can't keep doing this. I don't want to wake up in this hotel ever again."

So now he sits in a cubicle at a data management start-up, gets a paycheck direct-deposited into his checking account every Thursday, and feeds $40 a week into a 401(k).

"I loved being a gamer," Ksharp says. "It was a once-in-a-lifetime opportunity, and I'm glad I took it. But after seven years I had to ask myself, is this going anywhere?"

That remains the question on the minds of everyone who's invested their time or money in professional gaming: is it going anywhere?

Nobody really expects gaming to be the NBA, but the hope is still that it breaks even half as big as Texas hold 'em poker. Five years from now, nobody in gaming wants to still be reading the tired "gamer kid makes $30 grand a year" angle in the newspaper.

Matt Ringel of the WSVG would probably tell Ksharp he retired a year too soon. At the start of the 2006 season, Ringel boasted of expanding the appeal of e-sports beyond "the same fifteen hundred people that always go to the CPL events."

Yet at Lanwar in Louisville, the WSVG pulled in about 6,000 across three days, or roughly 2,000 a day. That's not a whole lot better than Munoz's 1,500. At the Intel Summer Championship, 15,280 people showed up, about the same as past Summer CPLs. Attendance-wise, it seemed the WSVG and CPL were pretty much a wash.

The numbers that truly matter—prize money—remain below a high-water mark of three years earlier, when SK Gaming won $60,000 for first place at CPL Summer 2003. Top prize at Lanwar this season was $12,500 and first at the Intel Summer Championship paid $50,000. And similar to the CPL, it would take a half-year for the WSVG to pay out its prize money.

It's a mystery to those in pro gaming how even as the popularity of videogames on a recreational level continues to climb to unprecedented heights, interest in gaming at the elite level appears to have stalled. The biggest paydays were in 2003. One of the biggest U.S. gamers, Ksharp, now works a nine-to-five. The best U.S. team in the world's most popular game, CompLexity, has spent three years of futility searching for a sponsor.

Why isn't the market growing? Why hasn't pro gaming gone to the next level? Why is Ksharp sitting in an office cubicle, instead of appearing on the cover of a newsstand magazine? The answer is simple. Gaming hasn't made the leap to TV.

"I think the mistake that guys like Angel Munoz and Matt Ringel are making is assuming that a wide audience cares about all this," says Salli Frattini, the MTV producer who lost interest in e-sports after shooting one CPL event in 2005. "The truth is, they don't. The people who care about professional gaming are already into it.

"They say, well, look where extreme sports are now. But the difference is it's something you can watch. You see someone do a 720 on a skateboard, and you're like, wow. It's a little different than five guys sitting and staring at a computer screen."

MTV is an entertainment network. Salli Frattini's job is not to broadcast competitions. That's what sports networks do. Her job is to find extroverted, entertaining young people and put them on the air. MTV is not the answer. The mistake made by both Munoz and Ringel was forcing that mentality on gaming when it required a more imaginative approach.

The truth is unavoidable: *nobody wants to watch somebody else play a videogame.* It seems self-evident. But that begs the question of televised hold 'em poker. Who would've ever thought viewers would tune in to watch other people play poker? If they can pull it off, maybe e-sports can too. How did poker crack the code?

Two types of viewers watch hold 'em telecasts. The first group, the smaller of the two, are avid poker players who want to learn. The second, a much larger group, watch because of the simple concept that competition—if well presented—is entertaining. That's why poker, despite not being a sport, per se, is a hit on ESPN.

The key to poker is that it's compelling, and compelling TV requires two things: first, the viewer must have a basic understanding of the game being played; and second, the viewer must have a rooting interest. A spectator should either love one side or hate the other. Doesn't matter which. It works either way.

Then it comes down to drama. That's the real hook in televised poker. With pocket cams giving a secret peek at hole cards and likelihood-of-victory percentages on screen for every player, drama is built in every hand. Drama exists at the moment of triumph and loss. But for that drama to take root in the mind of the viewer and make the showdown entertaining, the viewer must understand that drama. They must understand why one player wins and the other loses at the very moment the final card is revealed. You've got to know that three-of-a-kind beats two pair. To make it compelling, the viewer must understand the game.

That's why the World Series of Poker works on TV. It teaches viewers the game so they can enjoy the drama. That's why MTV's spotlight on Fatal1ty failed to connect to viewers, just as WSVG's segments on Game-Play are a bore. In circling around the tables at Lanwar and Intel Summer, all the cameramen were doing was capturing one clan's joy and the others' disappointment. They were spotlighting the winners and losers without bothering to explain how and why one differs from the other.

If nobody understood tennis, nobody would care what Roger Federer has to say. People care about Federer because they know he's got a wicked down-the-line topspin backhand and if he puts it past Rafael Nadal at 40–15 on serve, he wins the point. They understand the game, so they understand the drama. They understand the drama, so they're drawn to the guy who wins.

Expecting to push gaming to a wider audience through TV by focusing first on the personalities like Fatal1ty won't work. That's Matt Ringel's big mistake.

Personalities are part of the formula. That's where rooting interest comes in. But it's the second part of the formula, after the game action. If the aim is to expand the audience, then putting the focus on personality without spotlighting the competition itself isn't merely putting the cart before the horse. It's the cart without a horse. The cart goes nowhere, just like gaming so far on TV.

What's frustrating, even to a relative newcomer, is that the answer is right there at every LAN, in the groups of ten or twenty spectators around the Counter-Strike tables. That's the existing audience, so in them lies the secret of how to make gaming compelling. The trick is figuring out what's drawing them in, where the hook lies, and then presenting it on TV.

And the lesson is this: Those gaming diehards behind the tables are not staring at Rambo and fRoD and Warden. They're hearing their shouts and seeing their celebrations after victories. But during matches, their eyes are glued on the monitors. So, if gaming is to have a chance on TV, that's where the cameras must focus. That's the hook. The rest is just window dressing.

Nobody wants to watch someone else play a videogame. Period. But what about getting people to watch the videogame itself?

It's the best thing to happen to football since the advent of the forward pass, and it doesn't even really exist. It's the yellow line. On TV broadcasts, the yellow line is a superimposed first-down stripe running across the field from sideline to sideline.

The yellow line is now standard, but it was first added into a broadcast by Fox Sports in 1998. That's the same network that pioneered other superimposed elements over sports action such as the FoxBox in the corner of the screen showing the score as well as scrolls along the top or bottom with updates from around the league. Those are standard today for every sports broadcast, too, but the yellow first-down line was innovative in a whole new way. It was more than just an informative element. It added drama.

Each time a player is running with the ball, his quest for the first down becomes a mini-goal unto itself. The tension of every play is heightened watching a football player run toward that imaginary yellow line.

And like most of the visual and auditory extras Fox Sports has added to its broadcasts over the past decade, it was directly inspired by videogames.

The president of Fox Sports, Australian TV veteran David Hill, is a self-confessed gamer. "I've always been huge on videogames, ever since Pong," says the boisterous Aussie, who says he's currently hooked on the first-person shooter Medal of Honor.

Hill's first job in media was as a newspaper copy boy in Australia, where during breaks he'd hang out at an amusement parlor playing pinball. Then it progressed to videogames. "Later on," he says, "when my son Julian was ten or eleven, he became addicted to Sega, so I got totally addicted, too. He had the space aliens, and all the rest of them. We had a whole bunch of games. My favorite was Penguin Land."

By the late eighties, Hill and his family were living in London, where he was working for BSkyB television. It was then that Hill became fascinated with videogames for a different reason: as inspiration for sports TV.

"At the time, I was directing soccer matches or boxing, and I would feel that it was two-dimensional," Hill says. "But when I'd play videogames, I would be in this very vibrant world. When sprites moved, there'd always be a noise, a whoosh or something."

Julian Hill was a lucky kid. He and his dad would regularly run around the corner from their London flat to a huge arcade called the Trocadero, which was stocked with all the latest games. Arkanoid, Street Fighter, Tetris, you name it.

"I'd have a pocket full of pound coins, and we'd try every single game there. What I'd do is analyze what made each game good, bad, or indifferent. I'd see what was exciting about the videogame world I was in, and then I started trying to duplicate that into sports production."

The first innovation was audio. Hill approached one of his engineers about laying in a special effect. "When you wipe a screen, it transmits a computer pulse. I asked one of my sound guys if he could use that pulse to trigger a little digi-tape recorder with a one-and-a-half-second *shhhheeeewww* or *eeeee-ahhhhhhh* or whatever it was. He went in his garage at night and a few days later came up with a device. He and I were the only two who knew what was going on."

During an English Premier League soccer match, Hill fired off the whoosh heard 'round the world. "There was a goal scored, and I looked over to the audio guys and said, 'All right, let's go.' As we ran the replay, when the picture came across the screen we added a little *whhoeeeeewwww.* Everyone in the truck said, 'What the bloody hell was that?' They were all looking at each other.

"I always wanted a live production to look post-produced," Hill says. "To get sound effects like that, ordinarily the only way to do it was to add it later. Sports are live, though, so that's what we did. And that was the very first time. I don't even remember what the game was, probably Manchester United versus Aston-Villa or something."

Old-timers and purists would soon long for the days of simple, uncluttered sports coverage that simply let viewers feel like they were at the ballpark. But there was no going back. Sports television would never be the same.

"All the guys in my crew were dead against it," Hill says. "They wouldn't even drink with me and the audio guy at the pub that night."

The tide of opinion shifted, by random luck, the next day at the office, when a soccer player from the English national team happened to swing into Sky TV to shoot a spot. "He stuck his head in my office," Hill remembers, "and he says, 'Hey, that was cool. My son and I were watching and he said, 'Dad, that sounds like a Sega game.'"

Hill led the soccer star into the bullpen, where his producers were in a meeting, to repeat what he'd just said. "After that, they said, okay, the whoosh can stay."

In December 1993, Hill arrived in the United States to lead Fox Sports, which along with *The Simpsons* would build Rupert Murdoch's two-day-a-week TV curiosity into America's fourth network. With a goal of assembling a staff to share his vision, Hill again turned to videogames.

"I had one guy from ABC, one from CBS, one from ESPN or whatever, and I wanted them all on the same page about how I wanted sports produced. I wanted to recreate that kind of enveloping world that videogames are, with a lot of information, where you always know where you are, a place where the geography is always apparent."

Hill sent out interns to buy Sega and PlayStation console systems and a stack of games. Not just sports games. Hill likes the world of first-person shooters as well, with their radar displays and ammo counts and pull-down weapons menus. He mandated that every member of the new Fox Sports crew play videogames for at least a half-hour a day.

"By the time we got to the telecast of our first NFL games, everyone— and especially the young guys—got what I wanted to do. That was to build a complete world that the viewer would enter during a telecast."

As games continued to evolve, Hill began playing at home on his computer. He got hooked on the World War II game Medal of Honor. "I was addicted," he says. "I'd tell my wife that I was in my study writing, and really I was storming the beaches of Iwo Jima."

The president of Fox Sports is, by his own admission, hooked on a first-person shooter. This is very good news for professional gaming.

In April 2005, in addition to his post at Fox Sports, Hill was also handed the responsibility of overseeing the development of original programming at News Corp's satellite provider DirecTV. It was a side job for Hill, a pet project. He was moonlighting, basically, and given free rein. With DirecTV, Hill was playing with house money.

One day, he was sitting around with an assistant named Eric Shanks discussing ideas for original programming. Shanks had read about a LAN in South Korea that had drawn thousands of spectators. "We looked at each other and said, 'Hell, that's it,'" says Hill. "Here was an existing sport, it already had its devotees, and we'd all seen what had happened with poker."

There it is, once and for all, the answer to the question of whether competitive gaming is a sport. The answer? Who the hell cares. The president of Fox Sports thinks it is. "Of course it's a sport," Hill says. "Anyone who doesn't consider it a sport has obviously never played."

Beyond that, Hill shares the belief that for the bulk of teenagers in the United States, videogames are fast becoming a substitute for traditional athletics.

"In this country," he says, "unless you're an elite athlete, you stop playing competitive sports around the age of fifteen. The rest of the world gets out there, gets sweaty, gets hit, goes to the showers until they're eighteen. Not in America. Here, unless they're unbelievably good, they become spectators, bystanders.

"What videogames do for adolescents is give them this unbelievable world where they can be athletes. They can be great footballers, basketball players, soccer, whatever. Or they can go kill dragons. It forms this ersatz world that they're denied because of the mores of this country, where only the elite can participate."

In March 2005, it was decided. A made-for-TV videogame competition was going to happen on DirecTV because David Hill wanted one. And it would happen about a year later, sometime during the summer of 2006. The only question was how.

Nobody in e-sports had any idea what was happening at the time. In the summer of 2005, as early planning was ongoing at DirecTV's offices in L.A., Craig Levine was over in Paris, trying to poach Jason Lake's players, and the WSVG did not yet exist as a challenger to the CPL. Nobody had any idea how big a role DirecTV would play in determining their futures.

The job of planning the first TV showcase went to Hill's underlings Shanks and Steven Roberts. Their assignment was to produce a pilot episode that cracked the code and made videogames compelling content for television. If it worked, if the pilot connected with viewers and both appealed to existing hard-core gamers and brought in new fans, the long-term windfall to DirecTV and its parent company, News Corp, could be enormous.

The best-case scenario: DirecTV would one day launch its own gaming league with a regular season and playoffs, maybe even a world championship pitting top teams from around the planet. With sister satellite TV properties BSkyB in Europe and Star from China to the Middle East, tapping a global viewership would be easy.

The potential benefits were threefold. First, viewership and subscriptions would climb for DirecTV's service, in early 2006 at about fifteen million for North America and another four million in Latin America. Second, sponsors and advertisers would come calling, and DirecTV was thinking beyond the usual gaming companies. Their push would be mainstream, companies like Mountain Dew and Best Buy.

Down the road, there was licensing potential. Just as NFL or NBA or Major League Baseball videogames are more popular than generic versions featuring no-name teams, DirecTV hoped to eventually offer licensed DirecTV versions of the games used in their high-definition TV broadcasts.

One thing the DirecTV planners hadn't considered, but which also seems entirely feasible, is the idea of a fantasy league for gaming itself. E-sports insiders are prone to argue about players—"Who's better, Trip or ShaGuar?"—in the same way sports fans argue about which ballplayer should be MVP. In a league structure with an even playing field and statistics, fans at home could even draft "fantasy" Counter-Strike teams in the same way baseball fans have a rotisserie team of various players. In the virtual world of e-sports, that would make it a fantasy league on top of a fantasy league.

But all those possibilities were hypothetical. In 2005, the first order of business was putting together a pilot episode.

The duo running the project, Roberts and Shanks, at first considered partnering with existing gaming organizations, such as the CPL or WSVG, and simply filming one of their tournaments. They met with Angel Munoz and later Matt Ringel. But after getting a look at their bare-bones cafeteria-table tournament areas, they knew those LANs were nowhere near camera-ready.

DirecTV had something glitzy in mind, something more like a game show. They wanted a set to echo *Who Wants to Be a Millionaire,* with gamers facing each other in seats on elevated stages. They envisioned a crowd-stirring emcee and player entrances through smoke and lights, like a smaller-scale WWE *Friday Night SmackDown!* but with the dust-up inside computers instead of in a wrestling ring. The CPL and WSVG offered nothing anywhere near that compelling visually, so DirecTV opted to go it alone. They could do glitz. They could do smackdown. They only had one problem, really. None of the execs at DirecTV knew a damn thing about the competitive gaming world.

In the fall of 2005, Shanks called up an old roommate named Alex Gomez at Van Wagner sports marketing in New York City. Gomez was assigned the task of tracking down a gaming know-it-all. DirecTV needed a consultant, somebody who could tell them which games to pick and what glitches and pitfalls to avoid. They needed an expert who already knew all the top professional gamers, knew their backstories, and knew which ones could be charismatic on TV. They needed someone who knew gaming cold, but who wasn't already working for their competitors at the CPL or WSVG.

Gomez told his old roommate he'd probe around for a couple of weeks and come up with a name. He did. Craig Levine.

Levine was first brought on as a consultant to the DirecTV

endeavor in November 2005, the same month his team won its second straight World Cyber Games title and a month before the CPL Winter where this season began.

"What I told them from the beginning was that you don't need to buy anything. You don't need to partner with anyone. Just build it," says Levine.

DirecTV began drawing up blueprints for their first-ever event, dubbed the Championship Gaming Invitational, to be held in San Francisco in late July 2006. This was a trial-and-error pilot, so they wanted a wide sampling of games from both console and PC formats to test viewer response. Levine recommended five: Halo 2, Project Gotham Racing, and Dead or Alive 4 to be played on Xbox, and Battlefield 2 and Counter-Strike for PC competition.

Initially, DirecTV was hesitant about including Counter-Strike. As the most widely played action computer game in the world, they knew it came with the largest built-in audience. The fan base was nearly three million strong, and to ignore the game would cost DirecTV credibility coming out of the gate. Their hesitation was over the technical challenges of a team game in which ten players are running around the field of play. It wouldn't be a live telecast, but still, how do you put "cameras" on ten different guys?

Levine lobbied hard to include the game, no doubt thinking of his own potential windfall with Team 3D. "From a competitive standpoint," he told the DirecTV executives, "if you don't include Counter-Strike, you leave open the opportunity for the CPL and WSVG to prosper. If you lock up the top Counter-Strike teams with exclusivity deals, who's going to attend a CPL event? Nobody. If you do this right," he told them, "you will own this core community."

Craig Levine has a plan for everything. Four years after starting Team 3D while a freshman at NYU, Levine has done well in professional gaming. At twenty-three, he is the one guy significantly profiting from his own peer group's devotion to e-sports. The money he's made through pro gaming has made him comfortable—but far from content.

"It's got to grow," says Levine, always with an eye toward the future. "What it is now isn't sustainable. Yes, 3D is a top pro team. But now it's like, okay, how can I push this sport forward otherwise? How do you get more companies into this? How do you build something bigger and more profitable? If the pie stays the same as it is now, it's not worth it for any of us to be here."

In the DirecTV initiative, Levine saw his springboard. While his team was gathered at Mug N Mouse café in Dallas for its preseason boot camp, Levine was holding meetings with DirecTV's executives.

This was much bigger than just Team 3D. If they benefited, fine. If they won DirecTV's event, great. For Levine, this was about numbers. This was about the million people in North America who play Counter-Strike and the millions more kids that a TV showcase might draw to the game.

Levine has revenue streams in competitive gaming besides Team 3D. Since August 2003, he also has co-owned an online venture called E-Sports Entertainment Association, or ESEA.

To play Counter-Strike, anyone can go online and jump into a public server with fifteen or twenty other players and shoot around for fun. Dedicated players who join clans participate in organized leagues or otherwise schedule their own scrims by combing through Internet sites until they find a suitable opponent.

But until Levine launched ESEA, there was nothing for the gamers in between. All the semiserious players who didn't have a clan were slipping through the cracks.

On the ESEA site, for $6 a month, members are sorted out individually by skill level. When a member signs on to play, the site's admins pool other players of similar skill and schedule 5-v-5 matches. In other words, ESEA organizes pickup games.

"It's like basketball," Levine explains. "If you're a pretty good player and fairly serious about it, you can only shoot around for about thirty minutes before you get bored. But you can play pickup hoops for three hours. Same concept."

Additionally, ESEA keeps stats for its members and occasionally holds tournaments with small prizes. It's also where 3D's players give their Counter-Strike lessons for $30 or $40 an hour. "The Web site isn't even necessarily for the kinds of guys going to CPL events," he says. "It's for the next level down."

ESEA has a little over eight thousand members, each paying $6 a month, so Levine and his business partner Eric Thunberg are bringing in $50,000 monthly. Operating costs, including servers, four full-time admins, and a few part-timers to help with the site, cut into the profits, perhaps as much as $30,000 a month. Still, Levine is pulling in $10,000 or $15,000 a month, to go with his Team 3D profits.

When DirecTV came knocking, Levine's light bulb went on. If this TV venture managed to stir up a Counter-Strike craze even half of what ESPN did for poker, hundreds of thousands of new players would be drawn to the game. Maybe millions, eventually. And driven by the dream of playing someday on TV, those newcomers will soon enough become serious about it. They'll stop horsing around in public servers and start looking for five-on-five pickup games. And that is when they'll all come to ESEA, each with $6 a month in hand, or whatever price Levine sets.

Levine knew right then that *this* was how he'd make his fortune. He'd do it the old-fashioned way, off the masses. And he'd use DirecTV to make it happen.

"You know, it is entirely possible that at the end of the day, it may not work," he says. "Not everything is meant for TV, and maybe gaming will always stay niche. But I don't think so. I think they're going to put it on TV and it's going to be a huge magnet."

The key for Levine is that DirecTV's broadcast be hugely aspirational. It must have the same effect on a young kid that watching an NBA game does, sending him running down to the playground to try reverse layups like LeBron James. Except in Counter-Strike, with ESEA, Levine owns those playground courts.

"You're ten years old, and you see these stars on TV holding up a check for fifty grand for the game that you play? You're going to be drawn to that," he says.

Beyond that, Levine was a realist. While his peers in gaming remain dumbfounded as to why their pastime hasn't caught on yet with the public, Levine recognized that beyond its schoolyard five-on-five simplicity, what keeps Counter-Strike compelling to veteran players are its details—things like strats and weapon selection and map variations, which do not exist in other games. Unfortunately, those details are also potentially confusing and therefore an obstacle in making Counter-Strike viewer-friendly for TV.

Watching a match couldn't feel like walking into a CPL for the first time. He would advise DirecTV on how to streamline the package, make it less overwhelming to a first-time viewer, with the aim of piquing their curiosity.

Levine knew that nobody would ever really watch gaming on TV unless they also played the games. The only kids who would watch videogames on TV over *Monday Night Football* are the same kids who choose to play Counter-Strike on a Sunday afternoon instead of going outside to throw a ball around.

Levine's foresight was knowing that the real aim of TV was getting people to give the game a try. Then, the game itself could set the hook and the industry could grow upon itself. More gamers, more viewers. More viewers, more gamers.

But to close the deal, Levine still had to convince DirecTV to include Counter-Strike in the show. He had to convince them that the technical hurdles of packaging a sprawling ten-player shooter game was worth the trouble because it would make great TV. Once he did that, he was golden.

So Levine, the Team 3D founder and gaming pioneer, played his ace in the hole. He sold them on CompLexity.

Levine, who had spent the last two years trying to undermine Jason Lake and destroy his team, now saw the bigger picture and reversed tack. He began pitching the sports-minded execs at DirecTV on the fierce rivalry between the two top U.S. squads.

Despite the fact that CompLexity had jumped ahead of 3D in the Gotfrag world rankings in May, Levine packaged Team 3D as the juggernaut world champs, the titans of the Counter-Strike world. And he pitched CompLexity as the scrappy kids-next-door, the ragtag Bad News Bears of e-sports.

He sold them on a scenario for their pilot: scrappy CompLexity trying to shock the world and knock off powerhouse Team 3D.

Basically, Levine was bullshitting. He knew full well that CompLexity was every bit 3D's equal now, but what mattered was that nobody outside gaming knew it. Levine would bend the truth and give DirecTV something it could use, something it could sell to American audiences. He gave them an underdog, CompLexity.

Meanwhile, Jason Lake was oblivious to it all. He had no idea that DirecTV was even planning a gaming show. With Lanwar approaching, he was busy watching practice in his living room and packaging CompLexity to a list of sixty-two companies as the premier team in gaming, "the Cadillac of Counter-Strike," in his own words.

Turns out, he'd have been much better off packaging his guys as the likable kids-next-door, a rootable gang of misfit underdogs. That was their appeal all along—commonness, not elitism—even if Lake was too competitive and bullheaded to see it. Levine wouldn't make the same mistake. He knew how to market a team, even if it wasn't his. Levine was taking over sales.

Besides, the fact remained, CompLexity still had never beaten 3D at a major LAN tournament. They still hadn't defeated 3D on the big stage under the lights. And the lights had never been as bright as they'd be on national satellite TV.

Levine was no longer sure that his team could hold off CompLexity. So, he figured, if you can't beat 'em, use 'em.

# Chapter 15

**S**EVENTY-FIVE OF THE BEST GAMERS IN THE WORLD ARE gathered in a banquet room at the Hilton in San Francisco, on the border of Chinatown and North Beach. Everyone is mixed together, sitting in rows of chairs, waiting for the DirecTV organizers to begin their orientation meeting.

Competitors in the other games—Halo 2, Dead or Alive 4, Project Gotham Racing, and Battlefield 2—are all here, including a few girls from PMS Clan. Also in attendance, of course, are the Counter-Strike clans. Four squads made the invite list: Team 3D and CompLexity, plus JaX Money Crew and a top Swedish team, Ninjas in Pyjamas.

DirecTV's gaming event was officially announced July 12, just a few days after Intel Summer, and the invitations took everyone but Team 3D by surprise. In the few weeks since, the gaming world has been abuzz with curiosity and hope that deep-pocketed DirecTV will be the group to finally lift e-sports out of the underground. Yet no one in gaming, besides Craig Levine, has any clue how they're going to do it, not even the players gathered here at the Hilton.

Even 3D's players know little, other than what their manager's let on. But really, all they need to know is that it's a four-team invitational with a first-place prize of $50,000. Two wins takes the payday. They also know it was Levine who got them here, so their insubordinate attitudes are in check.

After the fiasco at Intel Summer, the manager did defer to the will of the players and Rambo will now call strats. Moto has been deposed as in-game team leader, but on one condition: nobody speaks a word of it. For DirecTV's sake, Moto remains the team's unchallenged leader, its captain. That's Levine's edict, so that's how they'll play it for the cameras.

Jason Lake is noticeably absent at the orientation meeting. He's home in Atlanta, on conference calls with potential sponsors and helping Danielle with the baby. It's hard for him to justify any days away from home that aren't necessary, so he won't arrive until tomorrow's walk-through on the DirecTV soundstage.

His team is here at the Hilton, seated a few rows behind Team 3D. But ironically, while Levine's typically dysfunctional squad is in a state of relative accord, it is CompLexity that now grows fractious.

As high as they were after winning the title at Intel Summer, they were equally crushed after the fruitless postmatch meeting with Michael Dell. Minutes after the team's greatest triumph, the players saw firsthand Lake's desperate bid for financial backing crash and burn.

Now just a few weeks away from the end of his team contract, fRoD has concluded that his future lies elsewhere. For years he'd listened to Lake preach about the victors getting the spoils, the faithful getting their just rewards. It was all another false promise, fRoD decided, regardless of how earnest Lake's intentions were.

This is 2006, and maybe a guy like Lake belongs to another time and place. Sports is business. Tony Hawk is not the best skateboarder at the X Games, but he's the richest. David Beckham is not the best soccer player in the world, only the most famous. CompLexity is better than Team 3D, and yet 3D has all the money.

fRoD is the best player in the game yet still unrecognized by the outside world. And here's Moto, the Anna Kournikova of Counter-Strike, a guy who doesn't even belong in gaming anymore, and he gets all the media limelight.

The truth, to fRoD, can no longer be ignored. In 2006, image wins over integrity.

Tr1p is fRoD's closest friend on the clan. The two were teammates together even before CompLexity, while playing for United 5, and in years past, when Levine came calling or when fRoD received offers to move to Europe, it was Tr1p he'd always turn to for advice. But fRoD has shut even him out since Intel Summer, out of guilt as much as secrecy.

"I'm convinced Danny is gonna leave the team after this event," says Tr1p, with resignation. "Everyone knows he's been talking with Craig, and because of that he's not really communicating with anybody else on the team right now.

"Look, I know how huge he is to this team," says Tr1p. "It's reality. There's no other player in America to replace Danny, and if he goes to 3D, they'll be unstoppable."

Warden in particular has clashed with fRoD lately in practice. As the son and grandson of longshoremen from the docks of Galveston, to Warden union and loyalty are bedrock. You just don't break ranks, period. Last week during some downtime in practice, after fRoD spoke noncommittally about re-signing with Lake for next season, Warden called him out as a traitor. fRoD lashed back and called Warden a liar for flying off to meet a girl in Hawaii months back. The two have hardly spoken since.

"Meanwhile, here I am," says Tr1p, the team leader, "trying to keep the peace and get us ready for this TV thing. And at the same time, trying to keep all of this from getting to Jake. To be honest, I really just want to get this tournament over with."

The seventy-five players here in the San Francisco Hilton were hand-picked for DirecTV's pilot episode—called the Championship Gaming Invitational, or CGI. Each gamer was flown in, provided lodging, and handed a gift bag containing, among other souvenir goodies, an envelope with five $100 bills for spending cash.

The free cash has gone far to quell any jaded skepticism the gamers may still harbor from a past of unfulfilled promises. This was no Cyber X Games, nor was it just another CPL or WSVG tourney. This

DirecTV project was an entirely new business model. This was made-for-TV, made to showcase the spirit of gaming competitions—not just another ploy to milk kids for entry fees.

Years ago, Angel Munoz quit on the gamers, sponging them $75 at a time and pocketing the money instead of reinvesting in every-one's future. Matt Ringel has likewise been stuffing his pockets with entry fees, even if he is more sincere in his effort to reach out to the media.

This was different. This was the seeds of a partnership. For the first time, nobody was cashing in on the gamers. On the contrary, these seventy-five invitees had all been flown in and handed $500 cash for showing up.

DirecTV intended to profit, of course, but from sponsors and ads. Not from the players. If this new model worked, they'd be making money *with* the gamers.

"I'm fascinated by what you guys do," says Mike Burks, the pro-ducer assigned to run gaming's TV debut. And with that opening line, he immediately ropes in the crowd. "I've been fortunate to cover a lot of teams and a lot of sports around the world. And as I researched the gaming culture, what I kept hearing was this: we need to be treated like a sport. Am I right?"

"Yeah!" comes the enthusiastic response from the audience.

"So that's what we're gonna do," Burks says. "Our mantra is sim-ple. Treat the games like a sport, and treat the gamers like athletes."

Burks is a veteran producer in sports television. First at CBS and now Fox Sports, he has worked twenty-five NFL seasons and eight Super Bowls. In twenty-four NBA seasons, he's produced ten Finals and eleven All-Star Games. He's done eighteen NCAA basketball tour-naments, five NHL playoffs, and five Olympic Games. The guy's been around sports as long as AstroTurf.

When David Hill green-lighted the DirecTV project in 2005, he recognized the unique challenges it posed. There was no template for gaming, no footprint for this assignment, no tape to watch. For every cut, splice, close-up, and fade-out, they'd have to wing it.

Hill wasn't messing around. He went straight to Burks, a guy who's produced over two thousand sports broadcasts in his career.

"I get an e-mail one day from David, who's my boss at Fox, and it says, 'What would you think of producing gaming?' Just a one-liner," Burks remembers. "I had no idea what he was talking about. I thought it was a typo and he meant 'gambling.' I wrote back, 'Hell, we can't put gambling on television.'"

Burks is a middle-aged Californian whose standard work outfit is a T-shirt and jeans and whose long whitish hair and mustache give him a passing resemblance to David Crosby. He's the kind of guy who probably has a photo in his office of himself holding a ten-foot surf-board on a beach somewhere in Mexico. But despite the easygoing beach-bum exterior, Burks is as sharp as they come. The guy has won eleven Emmys.

He's covered Bird and Magic, Montana and Rice, Tonya and Nancy. He's covered major sports, and he's covered minor ones like rodeo and acrobatic flying. But before CGI, he'd never attempted anything like producing a videogame tournament.

"Meeting these gamers was like getting an invitation into a private club," he says. "You've got to educate yourself, prepare yourself, talk to the people in the game. It's been a great challenge, but I've never had the feeing it couldn't work."

Since last winter, Burks has met repeatedly with Levine to learn the intricacies of the various videogames, learning how best to simplify their content for broadcast without stripping away what's compelling. He's on board with the concept of game play first, player spotlighting second. He's eyeing about a 70-30 split, with the majority of airtime devoted to the on-screen action. Of the five titles at CGI, Counter-Strike presents the most advantages and the most obstacles to the production team.

In the same way gamers can watch a match in demo mode, so too can Burks have invisible, free-roaming "cameras" inside the maps. The headache is trying to follow all ten players around without knowing which one will make a key frag.

"Counter-Strike is hard for television because scoring can occur anyplace within the game," he says. "When you think about sports on TV, they're somewhat linear. A football team kicks off left to right. A batter hits the ball into the outfield. Cars go around in a circle.

"If anything, this is most like golf, where in eighteen holes you've got a lot of guys out there making shots and you've got to figure out where to cut it. Of course, Counter-Strike moves a lot faster."

To help viewers differentiate between teams and players, Burks will superimpose colored, numbered vests on each character on-screen, something akin to the pinnies kids wear in gym class.

To speed up matches, the winning team is first to 10 points, instead of 16. And to add a bit more drama, the map chosen for each match won't be announced until one minute beforehand.

"All of a sudden, you've got excitement generated at kickoff time," says Burks, who will mike all players and managers to capture their reactions. "In the NFL, it's like everybody wearing half-inch cleats and suddenly there's a big rainstorm and the field's wet. 'What are we gonna do about it?' Now, team unity, team strategy, ability to communicate, these are all heightened."

For those introductory segments where DirecTV profiles the competitors, Burks will draw upon past experience covering the Olympics.

"Think about those obscure sports," he says. "Biathlon, curling, ski jumping. At first, it's just a lot of people with hard names to pronounce. But then, all of a sudden, you find out something intriguing about an athlete, and now you're rooting for them.

"I met CompLexity a month ago," he says. "I was just walking through an event, and there were these five guys—some big, some tall, some squatty, some small, some shy, some gregarious. But they were great. My flash on them was the TV show *Entourage*. Or the Bad News Bears, the guys nobody wanted.

"And meanwhile, here's Team 3D carrying the banner for full financial support, playing internationally. They're both cool stories. It's good theater."

As he continues his greeting at the orientation, Burks tells the gamer crowd how they're following in San Francisco's great trailblazing tradition, worthy successors of the Mexican settlers of the 1800s, the miners of the gold rush, the hippies and the dot-commers.

"It's a pioneering city," Burks tells his rapt audience. "We think what you guys have to offer belongs here, too."

After orientation, the gamers split up for B-roll interviews shot against green screens, which producers would later enhance for broadcast with logos and effects.

As the Counter-Strike teams wait their turns outside in the lobby, the topic of discussion is a reflex test they'll be taking tomorrow at the set. It's called "h2i" for "hand to eye," a series of coordination drills to measure quickness and dexterity on a computer. DirecTV brainstormed the test as something like a forty-yard-dash of videogames, to further make the show aspirational to kids at home. After the show airs, the test will be available online so viewers can try it and compare their results to the pros.

"I think I'm gonna tank it," jokes Warden, sitting on a bench in the hotel lobby.

"Yeah," says Tr1p, with a grin, "just blow it on purpose so people think you suck. Let's all do it. We'll all score shitty, so they're like, 'Here's CompLexity. These guys are horrible.'"

"Right," says Warden. "Imagine on TV, they're like, 'Here's Warden. He scored thirty. That's lower than a Down syndrome kid.'"

A production assistant steps out of the interview room and asks for Team 3D to come inside. On their way in, ShaGuar takes a dig at CompLexity: "That's right, boys, remember who gets called in first."

Method, Rambo, Volcano, ShaGuar, and Moto line up in front of the green screen, wearing colored CGI team jerseys. To match their characters in-game, 3D's are red, CompLexity's are yellow. CGI's uniforms resemble hockey jerseys but with a medieval shield logo to add a gaming undertone.

As they line up in front of the camera, Levine tweaks them in the usual manner. "Mikey, take off the black undershirt," he tells Method, who predictably doesn't appreciate the puppeteering.

DirecTV's interviewer is Art Lyons, whose last job was shooting Ultimate Fighting events for Spike TV. He runs the team through some poses, like all five drawing imaginary guns or looking tough with their arms crossed and heads tilted back. 3D even does the old *Dating Game* sign-off, kissing their hands and waving good-bye.

CompLexity is next up for group shots. As they enter, Warden jokes, "Hey, when we do this, let's all start talking like WWE wrestlers. Get all into it. Call out McMahon. They'll be like, 'Who the hell's McMahon?'"

Warden is wearing his usual attire of shorts and flip-flops, to go with the yellow CGI team jersey. Trip asks, "They don't care if you're in shorts?"

Warden laughs. "No, I asked the camera guy if I should go get pants. And he's like, 'No, man, keep the toker look.' The toker look. That killed me."

The interviewer Lyons instructs them to say, "We are Team CompLexity and we're here to throw down."

As the cameras roll, they all say, "We're Team CompLexity and we're here to throw down," except Trip, who says "We are" instead of "We're" so he's a beat behind. Trip was actually the only one who said it as requested.

"You screwed it up," Warden ribs him.

"No, I didn't. He said to say, 'We are,'" argues Trip.

"No, he said, 'We're.'"

"No he didn't. He said, 'We are.'"

This is going nowhere. Lyons breaks it up. "You know what," he says. "It's not that important. Let's just give it another try."

The next take is a success, and after a few poses CompLexity is finished in the greenroom, except for Warden, who's asked to stay behind for a one-on-one interview. "Here he is, the Warden Dickens," says Lyons' cameraman, Ray, combining Warden's alias and his real name, Matt Dickens. "The Warden Dickens," repeats the cameraman in a fake southern drawl, apparently because Warden Dickens sounds like the name of a guy who'd be running a Louisiana prison. "We've got the Warden here. The Warden Dickens."

Warden just stares at Ray, waiting for the guy to get it out of his system. He asks the interviewer, "So, do I have to be all arrogant and cocky?"

Lyons tells him, "No, say what you want, but say it with confidence."

Lyons's job is to coach as much personality as possible out of these gamers, many of whom are going in front of the cameras for the first time. It's no small challenge. Gamers are much more comfortable staring into screens, not being on them. So far it's been trial and a lot of error for Lyons.

"Say, 'We're here to battle. We're on a roll. We can take this' or whatever," Lyons tells him. "But tap into the confidence you have as a world-class competitor."

"Yeah, but I'll sound like a prick," says Warden. "I'll sound full of myself."

"Okay, tell me what winning DirecTV's Championship Gaming Invitational means to Team CompLexity."

"And we're rolling," says Ray the cameraman. Action!

"Uh," says Warden, already effectively blowing the take in a single utterance, "winning DirecTV's Championship Invitational means a lot to CompLexity because then everybody in the world would know who the real best team is. Is that worded wrong?"

"Let's try it again," Lyons encourages, "but say DirecTV's Championship *Gaming* Invitational."

"Oh, did I say it wrong?" asks Warden, who needs five or six more takes before finally getting it right. Or close enough.

Next, Lyons calls in two players from Team 3D—Moto and Method. Moto's a no-brainer, a pro at the public-relations drill. But Method is an odd choice. He's the least obliging player on the team in interviews. Even he's baffled by the request, shuffling over in front of the cameras slowly, as if maybe they'll change their minds.

As he sits, Method has a little smirk on his face, as if, in a strange way, he's almost looking forward to how terrible this interview will be.

"Okay," Lyons says enthusiastically, as Method takes a seat in front of the green screen. "Look into the camera and say, 'I'm The Method.

My competitors say I'm the man to beat in this competition. Let's see if they've got the skills to bring me down.'"

Method couldn't be less comfortable. "I don't normally do that but…"

"It's okay. It's cool."

"So say I'm the man to beat?"

"Say, 'I'm the man to beat, and let's see if they've got the skills to bring me down.' And tell them who you are. Say, 'I'm The Method.'"

He smirks again. He's not The Method. He's just Method. But he doesn't bother to tell the interviewer.

"And we're rolling," says Ray the cameraman. Action!

"Um, my opponents say…" Method has already forgotten his line. He stops and looks at the floor. Cut!

Another trial, another error. Maybe the skeptics at MTV were right. These guys are awkward. Lyons tries coaching him. "Okay, you're looking at me. Just relax and tell me very conversationally, but like you mean it, man, 'I'm The Method, and my competitors say I'm the man to beat in this competition. Let's see if they have the skills to bring me down.'"

Take two. And…action!

"Basically, uh, wait. What do I say again?"

Cut, cut, cut.

"I'm The Method. My competitors say I'm the man to beat," Lyons repeats, growing impatient.

"We're still rolling," says the cameraman.

Method tries again. "I'm The Method. Basically, my *computitors* say I'm the man to beat. And I'm here to basically head-shot. Is that good?"

Uh, not exactly. And did he actually just say *computitors?* What's that, like a cross between "computers" and "competitors"?

"You know what, that's great," says Lyons, waving the white flag in surrender. He looks over at his cameraman. "Who's next on the list?"

Moto takes a seat in front of the camera. "Don't worry," he says, primping his hair up a little. "I'm better at this."

Lyons knows what he's angling for. He wants to play up 3D as the big favorites. He's looking for some "team to beat" stuff.

"Got it," says Moto, and the cameras roll.

"Team 3D's biggest advantage in this tournament is our experience," Moto says effortlessly. "We're the most established team in the United States. We have the most experience of anybody here, and we're gonna win this tournament."

"Wow," says Lyons, surprised. "That was great. Okay, um, now tell me about the rivalry between you and CompLexity. You know, in the shortest way possible."

"The rivalry between 3D and CompLexity," says Moto, succinctly, "is like the Yankees and the Red Sox. It's back and forth, and either you love us or you hate us."

"Again, great," says Lyons. "So, what professional sports team would you say Team 3D is most like?"

"Of all professional teams, Team 3D is most like the Yankees," says Moto, even crafting his sound bites to include the questions. "We have the best-known, most skilled players. We have the best funding, the best support, and the most accomplishments of any team in the United States."

Moto's hitting homers on every swing.

"Lastly, tell me how important winning this event is for Team 3D. You know, winning DirecTV's Championship, uh…"

Now Lyons is flubbing the event's formal title, and it's Moto who helps him out. "Championship Gaming Invitational," he tells him, more in control of the interview than even the interviewer.

"Winning DirecTV's Championship Gaming Invitational is important to Team 3D," says Moto, "because we want to be the best in the world. And nothing but being the best is good enough for Team 3D."

Lyons swaps a satisfied look with his cameraman.

"That's awesome, man," he tells Moto. "You've got this down."

# Chapter 16

A BUS WINDS THROUGH THE STREETS OF CHINATOWN, making its way toward the Bay Bridge and a trip out to Treasure Island, where the CGI soundstage awaits. Inside, the gamers are kicking back with big, padded headphones and nodding along to rap music. They'd remind you of a bus full of NBA players. In other words, they're starting to buy into this whole star-athlete thing. A few gaze half-interestedly out the tinted side windows of the bus at unintelligible storefront façades with Chinese lettering.

This morning the players were shuttled out to various postcard-quality locales to shoot exteriors. Team 3D went to Union Square and did pan-up shots on the stairs in front of the Admiral George Dewey statue. Later they were filmed walking at the camera, like gunslingers on their way to the OK Corral.

CompLexity went out to a hillside beneath the Golden Gate Bridge and later gathered in a hotel room to shoot one of Jason Lake's pep talks.

Lake flew in early in the morning from Atlanta, and now he's sitting in the back row of the bus. Out of earshot of his players, he quietly admits that the news he'd been dreading for a month finally arrived from Dell. Sorry, but regardless of their win at the Intel Summer Championship, Dell just wasn't interested in backing a gaming team at this time.

"Yeah," laments Lake, shaking his head, "we didn't get shit from Dell. They offered us two laptops. *Two.* I've got five kids playing. It was insulting. Plus they wanted us to endorse their products on our Web site, have our kids work the names into interviews. They actually wanted me to get my kids to say they *wished* they had Dell products. Unbelievable."

It was the latest in a seemingly endless string of financial disappointments. Earlier in the summer, Lake thought he had a deal in place with Adidas. "By the time it was all said and done," he says, "their best offer to us was a discount on clothing for the team. A *discount.* Not even, say, fifty team jerseys a year we could sell on the Web site. Discounts. Like, half off. They wanted us to advertise Adidas on the back of our shirts, and still pay for the goddamn shirts."

There's something new in Lake's voice now, a tone that hasn't been present at any time this year. It's near-resignation, a fatigue. He's clearly at the end of his rope, floored by the disappointment that not even winning a big tournament like Intel Summer could translate into any kind of real financial support. His team is on a roll, coming off its biggest victory ever, and Lake is ready to pull the plug. The running tab on CompLexity is now pushing $300,000. Enough is enough.

"I'm not going to keep spending my family's money on this," he says. "My wife's had it. My whole business model hasn't amounted to shit. Nothing's worked. I've spent a fortune on this thing. I'm upside down. With interest rates up, even my law business has been choking the chicken for a year and a half."

It's surprising to see Lake so dispirited as he's en route to a DirecTV event that could reinvigorate his entire effort to forward e-sports. The creeping resignation is partly because he knows little about DirecTV's plans. He wasn't at the orientation meeting last night, so he remains pessimistic that this production will be anything more than another attempt at TV that fails to convey the allure of Counter-Strike.

On top of all that, minutes before boarding the bus, a not-so-tactful Gotfrag reporter outside the Hilton pulled him aside to ask about the rumors that fRoD was planning to sign with 3D.

As the bus veers left off the Bay Bridge to Treasure Island, it's looking like Jason Lake's final exit. He's spent, nearly broken. And if the exposure from this DirecTV pilot doesn't help him land a sponsor, he will close up shop.

The sad thing is, part of him knows he's merely ahead of his time. He hasn't lost faith in gaming. He's just tired of trying to get people to care. Gaming may take another five or ten years to finally break through, but if it does, Lake won't be around for it. If the engine doesn't turn over this time, he's done. "It's now or never, man," he says.

Treasure Island is a strip of land in San Francisco Bay that until the mid-1990s was owned by the U.S. Navy. There are few residents on the island and no real town to speak of. It's mostly a spooky grid of untended athletic fields and vacated military barracks. The only real inhabitants out here are the seagulls, which fly over across the bay from San Francisco.

Upon driving in, the first building you see is an air terminal with a con tower on the roof. Next door is Hangar 180, a building where until a decade ago the Navy maintained its seaplanes. They'd roll them in, tighten down the bolts, and roll them back into the water. Now vacant, Hangar 180 is where the Championship Gaming Invitational will take place.

As the gamer bus arrives, production trucks are lined up along the cross streets California Avenue and Avenue C. The crew is in full swing, hustling in and out of the set or stopping by the craft-services tent for a soda. Giant yellow air-conditioning tubes, like octopus legs all twisted together, run from generators in the parking lot up through second-story windows to pump cool air into the set.

Since the 1990s, Hangar 180 has been used periodically to shoot movies and TV shows. On a chipped cement wall inside the doors is an expanding list of projects scribbled in marker: *James and the Giant Peach 1995, Flubber 96/97, EdTV 1998, What Dreams May Come 97,* and *Battlebots May 2001.*

As the gamers file into Hangar 180, their eyes grow big in disbelief. The sprawling, multilevel staging looks like something from an Aerosmith concert. Platforms at different heights, all connected by ramps and stairways, are constructed in a futuristic metal mesh and Plexiglas. Green and red bulbs glow from beneath the stage, and smoke rises up through its grates. The motif is raw galactic, like a spaceship in one of the *Alien* films.

The hangar is sixteen thousand square feet with a thirty-two-foot ceiling, and more than three hundred lighting instruments hang from its roof. Below grandstand seating, enough for about a thousand spectators, are the two stages to be used for CGI. One is for PC games, with two rows of seats facing each other along a catwalk that extends out across the floor. The other is a semicircular riser with three seats facing inward, which is where the Xbox games will be played. Both feature contoured, futuristic seats and tabletop surfaces highlighted with glowing boxes of purple and green lights. The place is gamer nirvana.

"A lot of tournaments have stages, but I've never seen anything like this," says Rambo. "It's like *Wheel of Fortune* or something. I didn't really think it'd be this cool."

Gazing around in awe, there's a glint in Rambo's eye that's been missing all season. The veteran player, for whom so much of the joy of gaming has been drained by its evolution into business, isn't thinking of prize money at the moment. He's reminded of the thrill he felt walking into his very first CPL years ago.

"This could really be it," says Rambo. "This could be our X Games, the real start of gaming in America."

Off to the side of the stages are indications that gaming might truly be headed to the big time: banners bearing the names Mountain Dew and Best Buy, the two nongaming sponsors DirecTV landed to go with traditional e-sports backers Intel and Xbox.

DirecTV's Steven Roberts is giving Jason Lake and a few others a tour of the set. "Since the players are relatively static, there's a whole dynamic where spectators can go right up to the stage," he says. "They can go watch from above, up on a platform that's fifteen feet high overlooking these two stages.

"We've got seventeen cameras, which is more than the NBA conference finals," says Roberts, pointing out various vantage points. "We'll have sideline reporters, analysts, commentators, a pregame show, a postgame show. You name it."

Lake is reborn. Ten minutes ago, he was ready to throw in the towel on his e-sports dream. Now he's as happy as a little kid in some kind of space-age candy store.

"I wish my wife could see this," says the CompLexity coach, grinning and peering around the set in wonderment.

"Maybe now, all the people in my real life will understand what I've been talking about all these years. My law partner, all my friends. I mean, they never said anything negative because they don't want to second-guess my dreams. But I know they don't get it. They all think I'm nuts. But once they see this on TV…"

Years in gaming have worn Lake down. For all his contacts and colleagues in this world, he is alone here. Lake stands out in the gaming subculture because he is not really from it. Sure, he'll buy a round of beers and talk Counter-Strike with the guys from Gotfrag or the TSN shoutcasters. But he's not really of this world. He's isolated here in gaming, and a little bit lonely.

Hundreds of times in the last three years he's reached outside the sphere and pitched to marketing execs from mainstream companies, and each successive rejection deepened his isolation a little more. These DirecTV people speak Lake's language. They too come from the traditional sports world of grit and sweat and smash-mouth. These are his people.

As Lake stands on the set and gazes around at the busy production crew, his renewed optimism is partly from the prospect that all this glitz may soon help him find profitability. Part of it, as well, is the relief that finally he is no longer alone.

"You know," Lake says with a smile, "it feels like the cavalry has arrived."

The crew has built a players' lounge backstage. It's geometric and sleek, filled with cushy couches and chairs and flat-screen TVs for viewing tomorrow's matches. In the back of the lounge, there's a snack area with Chex mix, nuts, fruit, and bottles of sodas submerged in a plastic Mountain Dew ice bucket.

Two computers are set up for the h2i hand-eye coordination test the gamers were joking about yesterday. The test consists of five segments of about a minute apiece. In one part called "Speed," players react to a flashing image with a mouse click. In another part, "Tracking," players use directional keys to chase objects around the screen.

Each of the seventy-five invitees gets one shot at h2i. Of the twenty Counter-Strike competitors here, the top finisher was Rambo. He scored a 49.40, whatever that means. Second was Volcano of 3D, followed in the top five by Hostile of JaX Money Crew and then Robban and Ins, both from the Swedish team Ninjas in Pyjamas.

No one from CompLexity cracked the top five, a further testament that their success comes more from teamwork and coordination than individual skills. Either that or they tanked it on purpose, as they'd joked about.

All of the CGI competitors, regardless of their chosen game, are mingling in the players' lounge, laughing and swapping stories about their on-location shoots this morning. The foxiest PMS Clan gamer, who goes by the alias Tart, went with a film crew to a beach by the Golden Gate Bridge, where she lazed around in a bikini. "They did this thing where I acted like I was on vacation, kicking back at the beach," Tart tells her girl-gamer friends. "But I'm like, I am *not* going swimming in that freezing cold water."

PMS Clan is in over their heads competitively at this invitational, but they really weren't brought here to win anyway. It's a calculated play by DirecTV to work a few cute girls into the broadcast and help push the message that gamers, despite the stereotype, are not nerdy. It's a theme they'd hammer home throughout the show in each of their player profiles. Repeat, ad nauseam: gamers not dorks.

Amber Dalton came on board with DirecTV months ago, early in the planning stages, and she sees the big picture. Dalton and her PMS girls will play along with DirecTV to help dispel the stereotypes that gamer girls are geeky, fat, and uncool. It's good for gaming, and, more important, it's good revenue for PMS.

So despite the segment producer putting Tart in a bikini for cheese-cake shots, PMS won't be staging any sexism protests at CGI like the one months ago in Louisville over the misguided WSVG beauty pageant.

Naturally, the B-roll producers tried pushing the sexy-gamer segment a little too far before Tart straightened them out. "They wanted to shoot stuff here at the set in shorts and a bikini top," she tells the other PMSers. "Like, me walking around with temporary tattoos or something. But I am so not doing that."

The other PMS girls shake their heads in empathetic disapproval.

"The beach is one thing," says Tart, holding out the palm of her hand for emphasis. "But I'm a gamer. When I'm here at the set, I'm here to compete."

A production assistant enters the lounge and informs the gamers they'll soon be shooting the intro, so they put on their official CGI jerseys and gather backstage.

The host of the Championship Gaming Invitational is L.A. radio personality Stryker, who works the afternoon commute at KROQ. He's here to provide the "rad, dude" energy to the show. With his faux-hawk hairdo, black Converse All-Stars, jeans, and Ramones T-shirt covered by a linen jacket, Stryker himself is choreographed, too—he's right on the edge where cool guy meets professional guy.

For the intro sequence, he begins in the players' lounge and follows a camera out into the backstage hallway, walking through a gauntlet of more gamers while delivering his lines. It's only a thirty-second bit, but Stryker can't get past the first sentence.

"Remember back in the day, when you first started playing videogames," he says to the camera, "and the only way to figure out who was best in the neighborhood was to go to your friend Larry's basement, get loaded up on a bunch of caffeine and play the game…"

Then, time after time he flubs the next line. After six or seven takes, the gamers grow restless. It's the first lesson of making enter-tainment: it's not always entertaining.

Stryker is probably blowing his lines because last night he closed down Larry Flynt's Hustler Club strip bar, around the corner from the Hilton. A few gamers, out getting a slice of pizza in North Beach, actu-ally saw him running down the street toward the strip club at two in the morning.

"Remember back in the day, when you first started playing video-games, and the only way to figure out who was best in the neighbor-hood was to go to your friend Larry's basement…"

And again Stryker blows his line.

"Again with Larry's basement," says the manager JaX, growing impatient. "I wonder what else was going on down in Larry's basement." After two more flubbed attempts, JaX needles Stryker, "Dude, how about mixing it up? What about Gary or Barry or Herbert's basement?"

The next time through the gauntlet, a few of JaX's players slap Stryker on the ass as he passes, blowing his concentration. The cam-eraman tells the struggling host, "Don't slow down once we're in the hallway. You've got to keep walking toward me and catch up to the camera."

Stryker takes a deep breath. "Yeah," he says, shaking out his arms to loosen up. "Just like Rocky coming up the stairs at the museum."

JaX drops his head into his hands in dismay. "He just compared himself to Rocky."

After a break for lunch, a stage manager leads Team 3D and Com-pLexity through a quick rehearsal up on the PC catwalk, walking everyone through tomorrow's choreography. The teams will enter from backstage, ascending steep metal stairs behind the set. They'll be intro-duced over a booming PA system and descend from a fifteen-foot-high elevated platform, taking their seats on opposite sides of the PC stage.

"Okay," says the stage manager, running quickly through the step-by-step, "the first five will come around the corner in a kind of V. Another camera here will pick you up. The first player comes down and drops in, two drops in, three drops in, four drops in and five drops in.

Once those players are in position, we will bring out the next group in that same V formation. Managers come down last, behind your teams."

3D and CompLexity walk through their entrances, taking their seats and facing each other. "If you're going to be roving," the stage manager tells Lake, who stands in his usual spot behind the team, "we need to see that now so we know what the problems are lighting-wise."

Lake gives them an approximation, pacing back and forth behind the seats. It's narrow where he's stepping. This stage wasn't built with anxious managers in mind. There's only about four feet of space between the backs of the gamers' seats and the side of the stage. One wrong step, one out-of-control "Backbreaker!" and Lake will tumble into a spectator pit.

"Okay," continues the stage manager, "when it's over, we need a reaction. If you won, show us you're happy." He raises his arms exaggeratedly in celebration. "If you lost, show us you're disappointed." He hangs his head to illustrate.

With so much action taking place inside computer monitors, DirecTV is trying to pull out as much emotion as possible. The more high-fives the better. The stage manager arbitrarily picks a winning side. "Okay, you guys win." Naturally, he picked Team 3D. Poor Lake. He can't catch a break, not even in the hypothetical.

"So let's see a reaction," says the stage manager, and 3D's players pump their fists. CompLexity feigns disappointment. Warden slaps the table. "Son of a bitch."

The players stand and exit, one on each side meeting at the end of the stage, shaking hands and walking out together. After they all depart, Levine and Lake are last to go. They meet at the end of the stage, still playing out the scenario.

Levine pretends to console Lake, putting a hand on his shoulder. Lake throws in a downcast "Not again." Both can't help but smile as they walk off the set together.

That night, on the eve of the event, DirecTV surprises their guests with a party-boat ride around San Francisco Bay. It's money well spent for the hosts. Humility doesn't play on TV, especially not to the youth demographic they hope to attract, so they're using a yacht to build up their gamers' egos.

Downstairs is a full dinner spread of salmon and prime rib. For dessert, there's a mound of Ghirardelli chocolate with a heavy chef's knife for carving off pieces. Upstairs is an open bar, stocked with Anchor Steams and Napa Valley reds, and there are hand-rolled cigars for anyone interested in a smoke on the deck.

As the sun begins to set, the yacht circles beneath the Golden Gate Bridge and makes a close pass by Alcatraz Island. Seagulls fly alongside and sprays of seawater drift up to the deck.

Storm is hanging over the railing, looking down into the water for dolphins. "I've got to get a photo of this," he says, holding a flute of champagne in one hand and taking a cell phone picture with the other. It's the first time the humble kid from Little Rock, Arkansas, has ever been on a boat.

Warden strolls up to the bow with an unlit cigar in his mouth that must be fourteen inches long. "My first cigar ever," he says with a grin, trying in futility to strike a match in the wind of a boat doing about twenty knots. "How do you light it?"

Inside, the Swedish team Ninjas in Pyjamas, or NiP, are lounging on couches. They're more accustomed to the star treatment than their American counterparts. In Sweden, because of a high standard of living, universally fast Internet, and less competition for the entertainment dollar, computer games are much more widely played than in America.

Ninjas in Pyjamas was the subject of a prime-time reality TV series, and their biggest stars, Emil "HeatoN" Christensen and Dennis "Walle" Wallenberg, have appeared on morning talk shows and been featured in men's magazines.

"Everybody in Sweden between fourteen and twenty—all the guys at least—know who I am and know who plays Counter-Strike," says HeatoN, Europe's most famous player. "So everybody recognizes you on the street. They keep looking and taking pictures with a cell phone. Every day, you feel like people are looking at you."

DirecTV's project may give him the chance to match that celebrity in the United States. "TV shows and movies, everything is from America," HeatoN says. "*Prison Break, One Tree Hill*. Of course I'd love to be a big star in America, too."

The SS Cyberparty is going full-bore, motoring under nightfall past the docks of the Presidio and Fisherman's Wharf. Everyone's mingling and laughing. The PMS girls are leading onboard karaoke. JaX is getting in schmooze time with the DirecTV execs. His team has no prayer to win this tournament, and everyone knows it, but JaX is just happy to be aboard. At least for this weekend, he's made it into Levine and Lake's exclusive little Counter-Strike club.

"I'm thankful for the opportunity to get in on the ground floor," he tells the DirecTV execs, transparently angling in on whatever plans they have for the future. "And the teams here will help launch any league you may have in the works, is that safe to assume?" he hints.

Out at the stern of the boat, Craig Levine is crafting his own future. With Jason Lake up at the bow of the yacht, socializing and perhaps helping Warden get his cigar relit, the 3D boss is leaning back on a railing and deep in discussion with fRoD. "This year, it's been back and forth," he tells the CompLexity star. "We win one, then you guys win one. What I'm really planning for is next year, when all this TV exposure breaks. I'm putting together a team to dominate in 2007, and I want you with us. What's that going to take?"

Moments later, they shake hands and fRoD walks back inside. Levine takes a seat on a deck chair next to Moto, who leans over discreetly and asks, "Well, what did he say?"

Levine takes a sip of his Jack and ginger ale and looks out at the wake of the yacht. "Consider it done," he says.

# Chapter 17

"**R**EMEMBER BACK IN THE DAY, WHEN YOU FIRST started playing videogames, and the only way to figure out who was best in the neighborhood was to go to your friend Larry's basement, get loaded up on a bunch of caffeine and play the game?" says Stryker, exiting the players' lounge and walking down a hallway through a multicolored chute of gamers.

"Well, those days are over. DirecTV has flipped the script. Gaming is the hottest sport on the planet. And these players are fast becoming twenty-first-century sports heroes. Oh, yeah. And Larry's basement? It's about to get a whole lot bigger."

Stryker steps through a black curtain into the bright lights of the CGI set. "This," he says, "is the Championship Gaming Invitational."

An audience of a thousand spectators roars in approval, cheering and making a thunderous racket by smacking together inflatable Thunderstix.

Stryker keep rolling. "It has gone from old-school Pong to Donkey Kong to this Vegas-style madness, man. It is official. Gaming is no longer an underground sport."

He's joined by his co-host, videogame insider Tommy Tallarico. "All right, Tommy. What does all this mean for gaming right here in the U.S.?"

Stryker and Tommy are getting right to the exposition. When your audience has generational ADD, you spell out the message.

"Videogames," says Tallarico, "have become the new entertainment of choice for the twenty-first century. And this event here is going to be the elevation of gaming in pro sports. It's gonna move it up the ladder."

Stryker wraps it up. "And all you parents at home, you said your kids would never go anywhere with gaming. Well, shame on you."

The moment has arrived at last. Gaming is making the leap to television. A rowdy audience is packed into the grandstands and in spectator pits around the stages. The lights are bright, the house music is pumping, and the cameras are rolling. Let the gaming begin.

Well, that's how it played weeks later on TV. But CGI wasn't airing live this night in late July. The broadcast would be tightened down in postproduction at DirecTV headquarters over the next few weeks. The actual event on Treasure Island didn't go nearly as smoothly. There were more than a few takes, more than a few technical delays, and frequent rearranging of booms and cameras.

The thousand-plus spectators, lured in with flyers posted around San Francisco and Oakland, were here mostly for the chance to win raffled-off Xbox 360s. But to ensure the appearance of rooting interest, each audience member received either a red or blue wrist band upon entering the event. For each match, red would cheer for the first player or team introduced, and blue would cheer for the second.

And to keep that crowd pumped up during the numerous production delays, DirecTV called in "The Troof." Part stand-up comic and part emcee, The Troof is Faruq Tauheed, a bit actor who's had small parts on *The Shield* and *The Bernie Mac Show*. To stir the crowd at CGI, the Troof was a geyser of hip-hop jabberwocky. Never has a man spoken more and said less.

"All right, y'all," says the Troof, in the same voice Will Smith does when he's being all street. "Let's bring some noise, y'all, you know what I'm saying. And we gots to keep bringin' it all night. Shake somethin'. Move somethin'. We shakin' it live. I'm bringin' it. Aw, yeah."

The funny thing about Troof's over-the-top homeboy shtick is that last night on the yacht, he was keeping it real in tan khakis and a powder-blue argyle sweater vest.

"I got one question," Troof tells the CGI crowd, raising his hand rapper-style. "Who here from Philly? Who here from Philly?"

Backstage the gamers are waiting around for the show to begin. To calm their nerves, most are either playing poker or listening to iPods.

CGI's two sideline reporters, the foxy Jessica Chobot and the smooth-talking Aaron Boulding, are conducting prematch interviews. Naturally, Moto is their go-to guy.

"I'm here in the gamers' lounge, and I've got David Geffon from Team 3D," says Chobot. "David, what does it all mean to you? What's it all about?"

Moto puts on a made-for-TV smile and says, "The Championship Gaming Invitational brought in the top gamers from around the world. And it's all about showing who's the best and having a great time."

"Okay," says Chobot, kicking it back. "Let's get this party started."

First up is the futuristic one-on-one shooter Halo 2 on the Xbox console stage. A top gamer named Fiddyownz will play the PMS girl Tart. DirecTV is wasting no time breaking out the babe. For her intro, Tart stands before a giant screen bearing an icon made especially for this event. Each gamer or team gets their own bad-ass icon. Tart's is like the red, white, and blue NBA logo except instead of a basketball player, it's a silhouette of a sexpot toting a machine gun.

As she stands on the intro platform, her profile video rolls on a massive video screen. Over the bikini shots, Tart describes how she used to be a 200-pound geek in high school and hung out with all the nerdy kids playing videogames. Then she went on a crash diet and started turning heads. She took her alias, Tart, after she got an e-mail from a guy in England whom she played against online. He'd showed his girlfriend a photo of her from the PMS Web site, and the Brit gamer's jealous girlfriend said she looked "like a tart." So she proudly made it her tag.

Troof, in his best "Let's get ready to rumble" voice, brings her to the stage with, "Here's a girl who wants to turn her glass slipper into combat boots and kick some serious butt. Say hello to Tart."

It's an unlikely marriage between the long-ignored gaming sub-culture and the deep-pocketed resources of Rupert Murdoch's News Corp. Yet it's impressive to see how Burks and his production team are instinctively spotlighting the handful of gamers here who can handle the attention. For DirecTV, this event is about separating the winners and losers, and that's also in terms of who's good on camera—who's willing to play the show-biz game.

By the time Tart takes her seat on the console stage, her work at CGI is essentially already finished. PMS Clan wasn't brought here to win anyway. Of the six girls competing at CGI, only one would advance past the first round—and she defeated another girl.

In the opening match, Tart gets demolished 9–1 and scuffs back disappointed to the players' lounge, where on top of losing she has to endure pervy consolation hugs from guys like ShaGuar who feign sympathy just to cop a squeeze.

Between other matches, DirecTV weaves in a few more human-interest profiles: PMS girl MaryJane dates one of her Halo 2 foes here at the tourney; Dead or Alive 4 star Master will square off against his gaming protégé; one of the Project Gotham Racing competitors also races cars in real life.

Finally it's time for the real action, the Counter-Strike semifinals.

First up is CompLexity against JaX Money Crew, with Team 3D versus Ninjas in Pyjamas to follow. The pairings aren't much of a sur-prise. Everyone knew DirecTV would split 3D and CompLexity to set up a possible showdown in the finals.

Still, it's single elimination and nobody's looking past the semis, especially with the unknowns of DirecTV's revised format. Since it's first to ten and not sixteen, coming out fast will be key. Also each round has been shaved from one minute, forty-five seconds to 1:20, and the time between rounds is condensed, too. Instead of the usual fifteen seconds to buy gear and come up with a strat, it'll be just five seconds. It's all designed to turn up the pressure on the teams, as is revealing the map just one minute before the match.

Still, nobody's complaining, not with such a fat payday. Winning just two matches, the semi and a final, pays $50,000. Second place is $15,000.

Before their match against JaX Money Crew, the "up close and personal" with CompLexity plays on the big screen. In the thirty-second clip, they're gathered in a hotel room for Lake's pep talk. The coach tells them, "This event is monumental. Millions of kids out there are about to find out that professional gaming exists, and they're going to decide who their favorite players and their favorite teams are, starting now."

The segment cuts to Warden. "One thing our team really prides ourselves on," he says, "is that everyone has been cut from a former team before. But we can still build a champion together."

The clip ends with one of the green-screen shots, the five guys pointing imaginary guns at the camera, as Lake says, "The story of CompLexity is the story of that kid next door that always had the heart but no one ever gave him a chance."

CompLexity and JaX Money Crew take the stage to applause and the beating of Thunderstix. Boom mikes attached to crane arms arch overhead like brontosaurus necks, recording any audio not picked up by the mikes on the players and managers.

Lake stands, as always, behind his team. Not only is the space narrow, now the computers are all plugged in with thick cords running back over the edge of the stage—five extra speed bumps when Lake inevitably starts pacing.

Across the stage, JaX also stands behind his five guys. For the big show, the dapper young manager is going with a blue oxford and yellow tie. Lake, as always, has the varsity-coach look: red tie on white shirt.

The crew is ready to roll. The cameras swing into place as the referee steps forward to announce the map.

Of the usual four—Inferno, Train, Dust 2, and Nuke—three will be randomly selected for the matches, with no repeats. After a map is played, it's taken off the board. CompLexity, it's no secret, hopes to avoid Nuke.

"The map," says the ref, pulling a card from an envelope and pausing for effect, "is Dust 2."

Lake begins to pace. "You've got these kids. You've got them. Let's go!"

JaX slaps his guys on the shoulders. "We've got this! Right now, right now."

Since they won a coin toss earlier backstage, JaX Money Crew gets to choose which side to start on, T or CT. They opt for T, although going on the offensive against CompLexity is no enviable task. Dust 2 is the map where fRoD camps out and picks off opponents with a precise shot through the gap between two wooden doors.

In the opening round, JMC charges up a catwalk directly at fRoD, but they're stopped dead. CompLexity goes up 1–0.

"Light 'em up, Danny," yells Lake, pumping a fist.

In the second round, fRoD picks off two through the wooden doors. Tr1p takes out a couple more. It's 2–0 for CompLexity. The next round, JMC attempts an unusual split attack, testing Storm in the other bomb site. Warden roams freely, fragging three, and the score goes to 3–0.

CompLexity is untouchable. Everyone is locked in. Sunman closes out a round. Warden pushes up to disrupt JMC's rushes. Tr1p is scoring frags. It's 8–0, and CompLexity is two rounds from the win.

The shoutcaster calling the action, Jeff "Smeagol" Dickinson, verbalizes what everyone already knows. "Right now, JaX Money Crew is coming up with no answers. The steamrolling continues. And if we see a shutout today, I wouldn't be surprised."

JaX himself is silent and still. At the very least, he was hoping for a good showing to impress the DirecTV brass. Now his team is getting owned on national TV. In the last round before halftime, JMC finally gets on the scoreboard, making the score 8–1.

"Bring it home," Lake says calmly, as his guys crack their knuckles and loosen up their wrists.

During the break, a segment airs on the big screen about quirky gamer superstitions, like Sunman setting his teddy bear atop his monitor for good luck. Another is how lots of gamers loosen up their hands before matches by running them under warm water in the bathroom. A few guys on JaX Money Crew stifle smiles. The joke is on DirecTV.

Everyone knows that prematch "superstition" is bullshit. It's just an excuse for guys to duck into the bathroom and smoke a quick bowl before a match.

DirecTV got hoaxed. It's still their subculture, and the gamers aren't just going to hand it over. DirecTV will have to work for it.

In the second half, CompLexity shifts to T-side and wastes little time closing out the match 10–1 to advance to the finals. In the postmatch interview, Lake is gracious. He wanted to beat JaX's team, not embarrass them.

Months ago, JaX may have been quick to gloat at CPL Winter, but those times are a distant memory now. This was the time to stick up for a guy from the old guard.

"They're a great team. Great ownership," says Lake, throwing his fellow manager a compliment. "We didn't want to give those guys a chance to get back in the game."

In the match, Tr1p led the team at +11 and fRoD was an effective +6.

"I'm really proud of my guys," Lake tells the interviewer.

Next up is Team 3D versus Ninjas in Pyjamas. As they await their introductions backstage, a profile of Craig Levine's golden boys plays on the big screen.

Moto is standing before a backdrop of the San Francisco skyline. "Team 3D is probably the most consistently winning team at this tournament," he says. "We've represented our country multiple times as the best team in the U.S."

A quick cut shows Moto putting on shades and checking himself out in the mirror. Another shot shows the team stepping out of a limo. Just as Burks and his production crew established the underdog angle for CompLexity, they're now pushing Team 3D as the vain and cocky all-stars.

That was more or less the template Levine laid out months ago as a consultant, packaging Team 3D as the world-champ juggernaut. But it's Burks's instinct to add just a touch of villainy for the sake of good theater.

"Team 3D has been together since really the beginnings of Counter-Strike," Moto continues in the clip. "We are the team to be feared. We're here, we're prepared, and nothing but first place will do for Team 3D."

Moto adds a smug little smile for the camera and says, "And we're pretty cool guys. I can't lie about that."

As the Swedish clan NiP heads onstage, Craig Levine is backstage frantically looking around for Method. "Oh, God. Where's Mikey?" he says. 3D is due onstage, and Method's gone missing. "I think he's warming up his hands in the bathroom," someone says.

Method comes strolling around the corner. "Mikey, come on," says Levine, and 3D takes the stage to loud applause. Rambo sits in the middle of the row, with Moto all the way at the end. If DirecTV knew gaming, it would be obvious from the arrangement that Moto's been forced out as team leader. Rambo is running the team now, and in most rounds he sends Moto off alone to do little but guard the flank. Moto has been ostracized both outside and inside the game.

As the referee steps up to reveal the map, there's a technical problem on the NiP side. Something's wrong with their headphones. The volume is set too low, or the crowd's too loud. Either way, their strat caller Walle can't hear a thing. He can faintly hear the voices of his teammates, but he's deaf on game sounds. He can't hear gunshots or grenades going off, and most important he can't hear the approaching footsteps of the enemy. Walle's half-deaf, and he's the team's strat caller.

NiP's players are pleading their case, but the referee isn't listening.

"Let us run back and get another pair of headphones," says manager Peter Hedlund.

"You'll have to play on," says the ref, who sheepishly doesn't bother to ask producers for a time-out. "It's a tight schedule."

NiP is in disbelief. They've been sitting around for six hours of shooting and reshooting, and now the ref won't give them ten minutes to get another set of headphones. "This isn't even live," argues their manager, Hedlund.

"I can't do anything about it," says the ref, again refusing to consult

Burks and his crew. "We've gotta roll. Get ready to play." He reaches into his little envelope to announce the map.

Across the way, Team 3D is waiting. Their equipment is just fine.

"The map," announces the referee, "is Inferno. You have sixty seconds."

The NiP players are livid, lambasting the referee in their native language.

Inside the players' lounge, a few Swedes who play Battlefield 2 are watching the action on widescreen TV and hearing all the audio come through unedited. They start laughing, and one translates for the Americans in the room.

"Walle just called the ref a 'fucking cocksucker' in Swedish," he says.

3D begins on T-side, and Rambo shouts out, "We're going War-song. Let's take this shit proper!"

It's live. 3D rushes Bomb Site A. Unable to hear their approach, Walle is immediately overrun in the blitz, and Method frags four of NiP's five. 3D jumps ahead 1–0.

Repeatedly 3D pounds away on the same spot, running out to a 4–0 lead. When NiP adjusts, 3D switches it up and charges Banana alley. Rambo is in the center of 3D's rushes and racking up frags. 3D pushes the lead to 6–0.

NiP is in disarray. Walle is getting picked off early in every round, and as strat caller he's not alive to call out rotations or retake strate-gies. 3D is essentially playing five on four, and they're unrelenting in their assault.

Even NiP's star HeatoN is ineffective. Known for his ability to head-shot even with inaccurate spray-fire rifles like an AK-47, in this match the Swedish legend can't buy a frag. NiP is the best team in Sweden, arguably the best in the world, yet 3D cruises through the first half 9–0.

The trash-talker ShaGuar jumps up out of his seat and pulls off his headphones. "What up now, Swedes?" he taunts across the stage.

The shoutcaster Smeagol, unaware of NiP's technical disadvantage, inacurately comments, "I expected more of a challenge from Ninjas, but they're obviously having trouble adjusting to this accelerated format."

After the half, NiP goes on offense and pretty much scraps running strats altogether. Since Walle can't effectively communicate, they just start winging it and dueling 3D in one-on-one gun battles. Less disadvantaged, the Swedes take the first four rounds after the break and trim the deficit to 9–4.

"Play smart, guys," says Levine, growing a little uncomfortable and shifting on his feet. "Let's go now."

In the next round, 3D quashes the comeback and advances to the finals with a 10–4 win. As they exit the stage, Hedlund gives the unsympathetic referee an earful. "I'm not saying we would have won the game," reasons the Swedish manager. "But we should've been given a fair chance."

In the match, NiP's half-deaf leader Walle predictably posted the worst numbers, at −9. HeatoN was −5. On the 3D side, Rambo was unstoppable, finishing +11, followed by Method at +5. Moto was a respectable if unspectacular +2.

Up in the host's perch, Stryker tells the audience, "Team 3D's rep is intact."

One way or the other, DirecTV had its dream finals, the scenario Levine sold them on: scrappy underdog CompLexity against powerhouse Team 3D, with $50,000 on the line.

# Chapter 18

IN THE PLAYERS' LOUNGE, THE CLOCK TICKS SLOWLY toward the final showdown. Out on the set, one by one, other competitions are wrapping up. Champions are crowned in Halo 2, Project Gotham Racing, Battlefield 2, and Dead or Alive 4. Each winner is presented a check and handed a glowing Mountain Dew trophy.

It's a ridiculous-looking award, to be honest, a trophy lit up in the phosphorescent green color of Mountain Dew soda. Its jagged, glassy top looks like a relic from Superman's Fortress of Solitude, all luminescent shards of mysterious crystal. But the players vying for the Mountain Dew trophy don't think it's ridiculous. At this tournament, that trophy is as cherished as a Stanley Cup.

As the champions from other games return to the players' lounge with trophies in hand, nerves mount for Team 3D and CompLexity.

Sideline reporter Boulding does one last interview before the main event with CompLexity's star. "I'm here with my man, fRoD," says the interviewer. "You're facing your big rivals, 3D, who you know very well. But you've never faced them on a stage this big with $50,000 on the line."

He points the microphone at fRoD, who replies, "It's the biggest rivalry in gaming, and this just adds more fuel to that fire."

Boulding says, "You guys are known as the Bad News Bears, the patchwork kids. How will you keep your composure in the match?"

On a couch nearby, Jason Lake is sitting back and listening. On that question, he just rolls his eyes in disbelief.

"Jesus, they're really pushing this Bad News Bears thing. What am I, like, Walter Matthau?" sighs Lake, who in truth isn't all that dissimilar to Matthau's movie coach Buttermaker. "I'm trying to build a brand here," vents Lake, "trying to turn CompLexity into the Cadillac of gaming organizations, and they're interviewing me, like, 'Talk about your patchwork kids.' Like we're a bunch of fucking losers."

He looks across the room at Craig Levine, who true to form is still hard at work. He's got one hand typing e-mails on a laptop and the other holding a cell phone to his ear. With Levine's nonstop networking, that phone has gotten so much use today that even as he talks, it's connected to a wall charging.

When Levine wasn't on the phone or up onstage today, he was huddling with the DirecTV execs. The CGI shoot isn't even wrapped and Levine is already one step into the future, discussing follow-up events and throwing out ideas for a DirecTV gaming league in 2007 in which, naturally, Team 3D would be showcased.

Levine is in good with this DirecTV outfit. A few minutes ago, one of the organizers was so sure 3D would beat CompLexity for the championship, he threw out this idea: "Hey, Craig, how about if the team dumps the Mountain Dew ice bucket on you. Like, instead of a Gatorade bucket?"

Lake overheard that one, too.

"I knew going into this that 3D would be the sweethearts and they'd get preferential treatment," he says. "Because if Craig is involved, that's how it always goes. I tip my hat to him, to a certain extent. He always makes sure his guys come out looking shiny clean regardless of what the reality is.

"I knew they wanted to play up this underdog thing versus the powerhouse, and we gave them what they wanted because I want this to be successful. I knew Craig would get more publicity from this. That's why it's so important that we win: so we can't be brushed aside."

Lake is too close to the subject for objectivity. He's right that Burks is playing the underdog card, but that doesn't mean it's not valid. Lake is too much of a competitor to ever admit that his team is still the underdog here. Inside the game, because of their teamwork and trust and friendship—and fRoD—CompLexity has surpassed Team 3D. They are a better team now, no doubt about it. Yet they're still underdogs for the simple reason that everyone thinks they are. That goes not only for the audience here and all the viewers who'll eventually see this at home. Most important, CompLexity is the underdog because deep down they believe they are, too.

They've beaten 3D at small tournaments, and they've placed higher at major ones. But in three years of pursuit, Team 3D always wins in the end. CompLexity has still never beaten 3D on the big stage. And no matter how many LANs they win or where Gotfrag puts them in its rankings, until CompLexity beats their tormentors under the bright lights, they will always remain number two. That's in the eyes of the public, in the heads of the players, and in the heart of Jason Lake.

A production assistant steps into the lounge and gives the teams a heads-up. They're going on in twenty minutes. It's countdown time, and around the room the virtual warriors prepare for battle in their own ways.

Trip and Warden are playing poker against NiP and JaX Money Crew. They look loose and relaxed.

Two years ago, as the first pro player signed to CompLexity, Warden pledged to help Lake build the best Counter-Strike team in the world. With CompLexity's win at Intel Summer, he delivered on that promise. Warden had pledged to build the best team. He never said anything about convincing the American public to recognize CompLexity as number one. And as much as this CGI event is about competition, it's also about appearances and perceptions, and a chubby guy like Warden has spent his whole life brushing off judgments based on appearance. He's not about to start worrying about it now.

Across the room, Storm is sitting back on a couch with his eyes closed. It's been an eventful weekend away from Little Rock. Tomorrow he'll be flying home with photos of the boat trip around Alcatraz and stories to share with his family. He's also bringing something extra home for his mom. Stuffed into his backpack is a little souvenir for the prized collection in her kitchen, a bell that says SAN FRANCISCO.

Down on the couch, Rambo is deep in thought, running through strats for the upcoming match. After a tug-of-war season, Team 3D is in his hands now, and it's his job to haul in that first-place payday of $50,000, not the runner-up $15,000.

As he said a month ago in Dallas, gaming is all business now for Rambo. This season, business has been below expectations. To Rambo, that's for one reason only.

"The whole team has known all season that Moto couldn't cut it, that he was our weakest player," he says. "We hoped he'd improve but he never did. And we've known for a while now that no matter what we're ranked in the polls, we're not even a top five team with him on the roster."

Bringing Moto back was a questionable decision from the start. A look at his career fragging stats even before the hiatus shows he was never more than a mediocre player. At the time of his return, Moto's career +/− of +84 ranked him number fifty-five in the United States among active players. Half of the guys on JaX Money Crew, United 5, and Mug N Mouse had more fragging ability than Moto, and all would have leapt at an offer to play for 3D.

Moto never had the skills to return, and Levine knew it as well as anyone. The goal was never truly to beat CompLexity, not as long as they had fRoD on the roster.

After his attempts to poach Lake's players failed, Levine restrategized for the larger picture. In January, when he brought Moto out of retirement, Levine was already consulting with DirecTV.

The win at Lanwar was lucky, a 16–14 squeaker on CompLexity's only bad map. Levine's real plan this season was to use Moto to beat CompLexity in the media game. Since arriving in San Francisco,

Moto has taped five interviews for DirecTV while his teammates have barely spoken a word. The weak link on the team, the player costing them tournaments, is being celebrated as 3D's biggest star.

It's worked. Levine's grand plan has gotten them all this far, to San Francisco for a TV showcase and a free yacht trip around the bay. The only problem is, Rambo and his teammates don't get a back end on the DirecTV project. They don't get a piece of the profits Levine stands to make through ESEA. Their income is prize money, and there's been too little of that this season.

In naming Moto the new team leader, and then backing him even as the players careened toward mutiny, Levine wasn't standing behind Rambo and the others. In a sense, he was selling them out.

Off to the side of the players' lounge, Moto sits alone. Six months ago, he returned to Team 3D as a strat caller with the goal to outsmart, outwit, and outstrategize all who opposed him. The team's revolt denied him that chance.

A shrewd kid from a family of trial lawyers, Moto tried to make the case that precision and tactics were the way to beat CompLexity. He may have been right, but it matters little now. In the end, he couldn't sway the jury of his teammates.

It's been a bittersweet weekend for Moto. He's a Team 3D company man at heart and eager to help Levine push gaming forward. Yet every time he went before the cameras and spouted off about 3D being some kind of unbeatable juggernaut, he knew he was putting on a show. He knew they were beatable, and he knew the reason why as well.

In bringing him back last winter, Levine may have used Moto as a public-relations pawn. But in a way, he used Levine every bit as much as Levine used him. Moto leveraged his invaluable worth as team media ambassador to get one more chance to suit up and compete. "Honestly, this year has been a struggle," he says, "and I wish people had just given things a chance. But no, I don't regret coming back. I've had more fun playing than I've had in a long, long time."

The oldest player here, at twenty-three, Moto looks to be at the end of his run. Levine got what he wanted, a face man for his DirecTV springboard. That's done. Now, with one more match to go, Moto is through playing good soldier. In this final match, Rambo can go ahead and exile him out on the flank. Fuck it, he'll go it alone. He'll show everyone that he's no has-been.

Outside the hangar, by the generators in the parking lot, fRoD has one last cigarette before the finals and thinks about his past, present, and what may soon happen after gaming hits TV.

To fRoD, the son of Cuban immigrants, playing Counter-Strike is about chasing the American Dream. It's about being the best and some-day cashing in on his talents. For months, despite the loyalty he's felt to his teammates, he's believed that joining a financially secure clan with lots of media exposure like Team 3D was his ticket to bigger stardom.

Now he's not so sure. After all, he is here at CGI with CompLexity. He was just interviewed as the star of CompLexity. In a few minutes, he'll be onstage playing in a nationally televised championship match as a member of CompLexity.

Smoking a cigarette in the darkness outside Hangar 180, fRoD remains torn. "Jason did me a huge favor by giving me this chance, and of course I'm grateful," he says. "I also feel like I've done him a favor by staying with CompLexity the last six months. I could've left in January, the last time our contracts came up. But instead I stayed and helped him accomplish all this."

He exhales smoke into the air. "I don't know the answers."

All day here on Treasure Island rumors have swirled about the DirecTV execs liking what they're seeing and pushing through with a gaming league for next year. No one's sure what that means for the current lineups, but either way, they'd all be on TV.

fRoD had told Craig Levine last night on the yacht that he intended to sign with Team 3D after this event. But now, minutes before the CGI final, there's nothing he wants more than to beat them. He can't walk out on his teammates now. Just as he can't walk out on Lake, a man who's put his marriage and financial security on the line to turn this team into winners, even if they never felt like losers in the first place.

Lake has always stressed to the players the importance of sacrific-
ing individual goals for the sake of a greater good for all. And nobody
has sacrificed more for this team, this game, and this industry than
Lake himself.

"Maybe it wouldn't hurt to sign another six-month deal," fRoD
says, flicking away the glowing stub of his cigarette. "We've come this
far together. Maybe I owe Jake that much."

There's another reason for fRoD's sudden change of heart. His goal
of cashing in on his ability in Counter-Strike is also about winning
the approval and respect of his dad, Miguel. This is about proving he's
great at something, even if it's a videogame and not baseball. This is
about proving that being the best Counter-Strike player in the world
counts for something.

Gaming going on television has done much to win over Miguel
Montaner. It's gone far in helping him see Counter-Strike as a worthwhile pursuit for Danny. The last few weeks at work, Miguel has even
begun sneaking peeks online at the Gotfrag scoreboard and stats
pages, seeing his son's name at the top of the list.

Yesterday fRoD and his dad talked on the phone while Miguel was
at a Florida Marlins baseball game in Miami. His dad was watching
from the BellSouth skybox with other international-banking execs.
One was visiting from China, and after chatting awhile, Miguel happened to mention that his son Danny was a professional videogamer.
The Chinese businessman knew his own son enjoyed videogames and
called home to see if he'd ever heard of a gamer named fRoD.

His teenage son not only had heard of fRoD. The kid played
Counter-Strike on a clan and was an AWPer even. He hadn't heard of
a guy named fRoD. He idolized him.

The Chinese businessman leaned over to Miguel in the skybox
and said, "My son says fRoD is the best player in the world. He wants
me to ask, do you think you could get him an autograph?"

For years, fRoD had grown used to the sound of disapproval in his
father's voice when the subject turned to gaming. As he listened to his
dad tell that story, for the first time he heard something else: pride.

Earlier tonight, after CompLexity's win in the semis, fRoD got a text message from his dad offering congratulations. Miguel had been following along with the CGI scores on the Internet. Just a few minutes ago, as fRoD waited around for the finals, he received another text message from his dad. It was just one line: "Kick 3D's ass."

# Chapter 19

**B**OOM, BOOM, BOOM, BOOM! THE HOUSE MUSIC IS PUMP-ing and the crowd is stomping the bleachers. The house lights lower and purple and green bulbs glow through smoke rising through the mesh floor of the CGI stage. White spotlights swirl as the music pounds. *Boom, boom, boom.*

In the narrow, darkened space behind the set, sound engineers spin dials on control panels and production assistants hustle past and chatter into wireless headsets.

From this backstage blackness, a set of metal steps rises up past scaffolding to a platform above splashed in spotlights. For these gamers, it's an ultimate ascent from the underground to the limelight. At last, gaming had the validation that it wasn't just some basement-dwelling activity for pasty-white nerds.

The teams are standing ready, Team 3D in their red jerseys and CompLexity in yellow. They're shaking out their wrists, cracking their necks from side to side, finishing off cans of Red Bull. Nobody says a word.

"Okay, 3D you're up first," shouts the stage manager, waving them over to the bottom of the steps. "You guys ready?"

Craig Levine pulls the team in for a huddle. "All right," he says as everyone comes in close, draping their arms across each other's shoulders. "This is why we practice. This is why we boot-camp. This is what we've been playing for all season. You guys are ready. You're better than every other team here. Keep it simple. Keep it basic. Call out who's doing what, get the strategies down and take your shots. Very simple."

Rambo jumps in. "We can do this. We're better than them. Don't play scared."

"Just run them over," says ShaGuar.

"All right," Levine says, "one, two, three."

"Desire! Discipline! Dedication!" they yell and break huddle, climbing the steps, followed closely by two film crews.

"And there go the cameras," jokes Storm, standing with his CompLexity teammates. Warden wisecracks, "Desire! Dedication! Douchebags!"

Over the house PA, the announcer's voice booms: "They're an international powerhouse, considered to be the world's premier Counter-Strike squad. They live hard and play hard. Everybody make some noise for Team 3D."

The audience hollers in approval and pounds on Thunderstix as Levine and his team step out into the lights.

Backstage, the stage manager gives CompLexity its cue. "Okay, come on over."

Jason Lake calls his team in for a quick huddle, although these guys really don't need another pep talk right now. They've gotten enough pep talks from him in the last two years. They know what needs to be done. Lake's concern is the pressure of the moment. He needs his guys loose up there, so he reaches deep into his bag of coach tricks to try and break the tension.

"*Jeremiah was a bullfrog…*" Lake begins to sing, poorly no less, "*…he was a good friend of mine. I never understood a single word he said, but I helped him drink his wine.*" His players are looking at each other like, okay, Jake's finally lost it.

"*Joy to the world…*" the coach continues, just when they thought he'd stop, "*…all the boys and girls. Joy to the fishes in the deep blue sea. Joy to you and me.*"

His players are all laughing, falling out of the huddle. "Jake, man, that's terrible," says Warden.

"Okay, good," says the coach. "I don't want you guys too serious. Let's stay loose out there, have some fun, all right? Now, come on, let's go win this thing."

CompLexity breaks huddle and heads for the stairs. The five players ascend to the platform, as the announcer bellows: "From Atlanta, they're a ragtag band of gaming outcasts. Please put your hands together for team CompLexity!"

Lake pauses at the bottom of the steps. "This is my life," he says. "I've got it all on the line." Then he begins to climb.

CompLexity makes its entrance and files into the seats across the stage from 3D. Lake steps in behind the chairs, as usual. He's here at last. He's finally made it to the big stage.

The players warm up, double-checking their settings and ensuring their headsets are loud and clear. All their prematch quirks are on display. Warden kicks off his flip-flops under the table to go barefoot. Across the way, Rambo is fastidiously picking specks of lint off his mousepad. Behind him, Craig Levine stands with arms crossed, as serious as a chess master eyeing the board.

fRoD is sitting perched up on his foot. He looks at ease, confident, unburdened by the weight of his future. As he fine-tunes the settings on his keyboard and mouse, he's like a real-life sniper calmly calibrating the scope on his rifle before battle.

*Click-click-click.* fRoD sets his screen resolution to a preferred 1024 × 768 and refresh rate to 100 hertz. He adjusts his mouse sensitivity to a factor of 2.4 and locking his focus on the little green crosshairs on his screen, the AWPer fires two warm-up bullets to test the precision of his weapon.

Satisfied, fRoD slowly sits back in his chair and takes his hand off the mouse.

The referee steps forward to reveal the map. Lake can't bear to watch. He stares down at the floor. Dust 2 and Inferno came off the board in the semis, and with no repeats that means this championship match will be played on either Train or the dreaded Nuke. The map was determined earlier by referees in a secret coin toss backstage. It was heads for Train and tails for Nuke.

Staring down at the floor, Lake is thinking *Please, for the love of God, don't let it be Nuke. Don't let it be Nuke.* He stops even thinking the word *Nuke,* trying to keep the energy positive. *Please be Train, please be Train,* he thinks over and over.

Lake said, way back at Lanwar, that all his team needed was one little break. This would qualify. *Please God,* he thinks, *just this once let it be Train.*

"The map," says the referee, pulling the card from an envelope, "is Train."

Lake raises a fist in the air, with a "Yes!" All the spectators behind him in the pit, with no clue how important that was, must think he's nuts. The guy is actually celebrating over the map reveal.

At that moment, after many months, it all suddenly makes sense. Not just the game of Counter-Strike, but the fact that it could bring out such passion in someone who understands its intricacies.

None of the walk-in spectators here, lured in with the hope of winning an Xbox, has any clue what Train is. Not even Burks and his production team have any idea why Lake just celebrated the map reveal. But in those details lie the hook, the context, the why to go with the what, where, and how. This isn't two teams playing a videogame. It's CompLexity playing 3D on Train, and not on Nuke. In this world, that's as significant as Federer and Nadal on clay, and not hardcourt. It affects everything. It makes all the difference.

And in knowing what Train means, and why it's such an important distinction that Jason Lake just raised a fist in the air over it, the outsider becomes an insider. Indifference about e-sports gives way to absorption. A skeptic becomes a fan.

The ref walks over to Tr1p. "CompLexity, you guys won the toss backstage," he says. "Do you want to start on T-side or CT?"

Before Tr1p even answers, again, to one who's now an insider the answer is obvious. Train is set in a rail yard with long, open shooting lanes. It's a perfect map for a defensive team to dig in and await the rush, especially with a deadeye AWPer like fRoD, who can spot from atop a train at one end of the yard and snipe the far end.

It's a no-brainer. CompLexity wants CT.

"We want CT," Tr1p says.

"Okay, you've got sixty seconds," says the ref, starting down the clock.

Tr1p calls into his headset for CompLexity's standard defensive alignment. Of the two bomb sites, the one called Inner sees most of the action, so that's where fRoD will snipe. As usual, Tr1p has his back. Storm will defend the other site, Outer, with help from Sunman. Warden will roam between the two through an area called Z-Hall.

Across the way, Rambo is wracking his brain. Train was the map where Moto's complex smoke-and-mirrors strats were most useful. All those heavily orchestrated fakes might have proved crucial in cloaking 3D's rushes and reducing fRoD's AWP advantage.

But it's Rambo's show now, and all those boot-camp strats are scrapped. He's not sending fraggers like Method and ShaGuar out to run misdirection ploys. He's not getting them picked off while they're trying to synchronize flash-grenade tosses. Rambo is putting them into the fight. Screw the choreography. 3D is an all-star team. They'll run and gun and win this on raw ability.

"Okay, let's go Outer Fast," he says, ordering a rush on the site Storm will defend. The gaming veteran Rambo has played CompLexity plenty enough to know where fRoD will lurk, so he'll try the other side first. "Come on," Rambo says. "Let's do this."

It's go time. ShaGuar stands and yells across the stage, "Let's see what you got, CompLexity. Bring it. Whoooo!"

Across the way, Storm says calmly into his mike, "God, I hate that fucking kid."

The match commences, and four 3D players descend a ladder and rush Outer while Moto goes alone the other way as a decoy. It's a four-on-one for 3D at the point of breach, but Storm is waiting. He ducks behind a box, lobs a grenade and frags two.

"Get 'em, T. Storm," yells Lake, stepping over behind his chair.

Storm jumps out from his cover and mows down a third. The fourth attacker, ShaGuar, abandons the rush, fleeing in panic. Three down, and one running. That is how Storm keeps teams honest.

Moto is already dead across the map, so ShaGuar is 3D's last hope. He circles around slowly to the other bomb site, stepping right into Sunman's sights. *Bang!* ShaGuar drops to the ground dead. CompLexity has the first round.

"Nice," yells Lake. "That's one." He begins pacing back and forth behind the chairs, a tiger in a cage. "Let's go now!"

The cameras swing down to capture the looks on 3D's faces. All the gaming insiders who've been waiting years for their showcase can only hope that DirecTV is capturing the essence of the game as well. Do they know Rambo called Outer Fast in the first round to avoid fRoD in the Inner site? Do they know Storm's going it alone? Can they convey that to a TV audience?

In the second round, Rambo tries the 3D bread and butter, Inner Push, with all five converging on fRoD's site. They charge down a ramp, led by Moto, whose gut explodes with a bullet from fRoD's rifle. Method falls next, and in turn the others. That's 2–0 CompLexity, with fRoD flawless in his first test. Three shots, three kills.

Okay, Rambo, what else you got?

3D tries a three-one-one divided attack, with three rushers on fRoD's site. No dice. This time Moto is the last player left in a one-on-three. That means 3–0 CompLexity.

"Play smart, guys," Levine tells his squad, shifting nervously. "Come on. Back to basics."

3D tries sneaking behind Storm's position through a back alley, but he takes out three again for his second hat trick in four rounds. The score goes to 4–0.

With fRoD in the Inner site, no matter how Storm makes them pay, 3D's only real shot is to keep testing him, and Rambo knows it. The thing is, Tr1p knows it, too. So he reads Rambo's mind, and for the next round sends fRoD over to join Storm. They're basically abandoning the other site, but 3D runs right into the trap. It's five-on-five at the breach, a spray-fire bullet festival.

"Get, 'em, Danny," says Lake, as fRoD drills two through the cloud of battle. Again, Moto's the last one left.

"Let's see what Moto can do with this one-v-three," says the shout-caster Smeagol. Levine steps over behind Moto, who manages to get the bomb down and quickly ducks behind a train car to await Com-pLexity's retake. The veteran knows all the hiding spots, but in a one-on-three it's only a matter of time until they find him. He can't wait here. He's got to try something.

Moto leans out of his hiding spot, slowly peeking around the side of the train, and the bullet from an AWP sniper rifle whistles into his forehead, filling the air with a pink mist.

"Nice, Danny!" yells Lake, kicking the leg of his chair. That's 5–0.

CompLexity is halfway home, and fRoD has yet to be killed. Meanwhile he's turned the lights out on six.

"Come on," pleads Rambo. "Keep the intensity up."

It's 6–0 when Method is drilled by Warden after planting the bomb. Storm gets two more in the round. He's now got eleven frags and also has yet to be killed.

"Snowball it," yells Lake, and CompLexity picks up another round when the one-minute, twenty-second time limit expires on 3D.

"When you're the number-one team in the world," says the shout-caster, Smeagol, "you don't find yourself down 7–0 in a game very often. Not with fifty thousand dollars on the line."

When it goes to 8–0, Levine starts pacing. "Pick it up," he pleads. "Come on."

In the next round, 3D gets three early frags and has a rare num-bers advantage. It's a three-on-two with Rambo, Method, and Volcano against Warden and fRoD. When Rambo gets the bomb planted, 3D digs in and awaits the retake.

Now with the roles reversed, and CompLexity forced to go on the offensive, fRoD leaves his sniper's perch. He spots Volcano in a back alley and nails him. One shot, one kill. "Get 'em, Danny," says Lake. fRoD slides over and jumps atop a flatbed train car to get a shooting angle on Rambo below. Death from above. Two down. "Light 'em up, Danny," yells Lake. "Light 'em up, Danny." Only Method remains. fRoD leaps off the flatbed past Rambo's dead body and charges into a back alley. Method turns and gets drilled with a shot in the stomach. It's a hat trick.

"Backbreaker," shouts Lake, pumping a fist in the air, as CompLexity ends the half 9–0, just one round away from the title.

Rambo sits back in his chair and crosses his arms across his chest. As strat caller, he delivered zero rounds on offense. Zero. He had nothing that CompLexity couldn't counter, and now his team is on the brink of elimination.

Two seats away, at the end of the row, Moto is vindicated, but he's hardly pleased about it. Ousted as team leader or not, he didn't come here to get embarrassed. He didn't come here to get shut out.

As the referee signals for the second half, Moto tries firing up his teammates. "This is not impossible. One round at a time. Be the aggressors."

CompLexity comes out on T-side with a five-man rush on the Inner site. It's a free-for-all, with bodies dropping right and left. It's a one-on-one with Moto against Storm, who gets the bomb planted and awaits Moto's reappearance. The bomb ticks down from thirty-five seconds, but it's pointless for Moto to try a defuse. Storm would drop him easily as he stood over the bomb. If it detonates, CompLexity wins the match. He must duel Storm.

Moto slowly circles around the edges of the railyard, stepping cautiously and peering through the gaps between train cars. The bomb ticks down, 20, 19, 18, as he climbs up to an elevated walkway. There, across the yard and crouching low is Storm. *Bang! Bang!* They exchange fire, and it's Storm who drops to the ground dead.

"Yeah!" screams Moto, seemingly venting an entire summer of aggravation, and 3D survives to play another round.

CompLexity hits the Inner site but runs straight into machine-gun crossfire. The score is now 9–2. "Play smart now," Levine tells his team. "One at a time."

The next round comes down to a one-on-one with fRoD against Rambo. Lake says nothing and steps over behind his star player, his eyes glued to the action on fRoD's screen.

Like Moto a moment ago, Rambo's not going down without a fight either. The lurker steps from the shadows and catches fRoD by surprise, making it 9–3. Suddenly there's life on 3D's side of the stage.

"One at a time," Levine says more excitedly. "Play smart."

CompLexity gets caught trying a delayed attack around the back of the Outer site, and it's 9–4. "3D has all the momentum now," says the shoutcaster. "They've got all four rounds this half, and five more will force an overtime."

The shoutcaster isn't just manufacturing drama. He knows that Train is a CT-sided map. Defense has the advantage here, and 3D has run entire CT halves at LAN tournaments in the past. It's possible. They've just got to keep the pressure on.

fRoD scales up to the roof of a train car. All the way across the yard, spotting him from atop another train is ShaGuar. Both AWPers fire. ShaGuar's bullet sails high, but fRoD's whistles into ShaGuar's chest, hurtling him off the car to the crushed rocks below.

CompLexity now has a five-on-four advantage. Rambo answers with a frag, evening it at four on each side. Two more fall for CompLexity. Warden and Sunman are left to battle shorthanded, two-on-four.

They circle around together, stepping along the side of a cargo train. Sunman squats down to peek beneath, but Rambo's there to drill him in the stomach. Warden gets picked off coming around the end, and it's 9–5. Team 3D is reborn and now actually halfway to winning the match itself.

"CompLexity has been waiting five rounds to clinch," says the shoutcaster, "and the longer it goes, the scarier it gets."

Lake has hardly said a word all half. His team needs just one more round. Just one more. CompLexity tries rushing the Inner site, but Warden and Tr1p are dropped immediately by Moto, who falls, too, in the exchange. 3D has a quick four-on-three advantage.

fRoD inches out to a platform above the site and drills Volcano, evening the firefight at three players apiece. "Got one," he says calmly into his microphone.

Storm spots ShaGuar and terminates him with a head-shot. "Nice, T. Storm!" says Lake, coming to life. His boys now have a three-on-two for the championship.

fRoD crosses the rail yard and scales up to the top of a train car, spotting Method coming around the back side of the site. He drills him. It's now three-on-one, with only Rambo still breathing for 3D.

Lake's eyes are full of fire. He hovers behind his AWPer. "Bring it home, Danny! Bring it home, Danny!"

Rambo crouches in hiding, low to the ground between two train cars. He rolls a smoke canister out onto the rocks, filling the yard with a white haze. Slowly, into the thinning concealment of smoke, he steps from his hiding spot and sneaks along the side of a railcar. Across the bomb site, fRoD trains his scope on Rambo. He rises from a crouch and fires. The bullet whistles into Rambo's chest.

Owned. Rambo falls dead to the rocks. It is done.

"Yes!" exults Lake, thrusting both arms overhead and looking skyward one last time, finally in absolution. 3D is dethroned. CompLexity is champion.

fRoD and Warden leap out of their seats and practically fall off the stage in an embrace. Lake piles on next, and then Sunman and Tr1p and Storm, and all six bounce up and down together in a circle of triumph.

"It's all over!" Warden screams. It's pure jubilation, euphoria, freedom, as the applause rains down from the grandstands. "Number one," says fRoD, pointing a finger at the sky. "Number one!"

Lake puts his hands behind his head and lets out a long, satisfying exhale.

Across the stage, Moto is pitched forward with his head in his hands. He can't bear to watch. Although even in crushing defeat, he still found his redemption. The supposed weak link on the team, Moto had 3D's best performance. It wasn't pretty, but his +1 was tops.

For the victors, fRoD was a monster at +13, and Storm was +7.

CGI's sideline reporter Boulding climbs onto the stage for a postmatch interview with the champions. These five CompLexity guys—chubby, shy, passed-over kids next door who doubters said would never play well on camera—were ready for prime time now. "Hey," says Boulding, leaning in with a microphone, "you guys were up 9–0 at halftime. That last point must have really been working on your nerves."

"Not really," says fRoD, brushing it off with a big smile and putting his arm across Warden's shoulder. "We knew we'd eventually get our break."

Warden leans in and says, "You know, winning an event like this really opens up a lot of doors for a team like us."

And then he gives Lake a grin.

Offstage, DirecTV's other sideline reporter is with Moto and 3D.

"You guys were the ones favored to win these matches," she says, leaning in with a microphone. "What went wrong?"

Moto answers tersely, "CompLexity took the momentum from the first round and ran with it."

"Is there anything that you'd go back and change?" the reporter follows up.

An entire season of turmoil seems to flash through Moto's head, and yes, of course, there's plenty he'd go back and change. But right now, after a long three days in front of DirecTV's cameras, Moto's had enough of the show-pony act. He came here to win, not to play chagrined locker-room loser.

For the first time all weekend, all season maybe, he plays it honest. "We just got off the stage. We're all down about losing," he says sincerely. "A week down the line, maybe I'd have an answer for you."

3D exits, and back up on the big stage, it's time to crown the victors.

"All rise, everybody," Stryker says, getting the crowd on their feet. "This is team CompLexity, your Counter-Strike champions."

Four spotlights converge on Lake and his boys as the audience stomps on the bleachers, won over by the team's display of emotion. Stryker hands Lake an envelope with a first-place check for $50,000. And this time, for the first time, this was no fake oversized check with a promisory IOU. This one was signed and ready for deposit. Lake hands fRoD the check to hold and enjoy for the moment. Why not? It belongs to him as much as anyone. Probably more.

"And I have one more piece of hardware for your mantel," Stryker says. "We give to you the coveted Mountain Dew award. Raise it in the air."

Lake grasps the glowing green trophy and hoists it overhead like the Statue of Liberty's torch. The job is finished. CompLexity has toppled its nemesis at last. And they did it on the big stage, under the bright lights, for all the world to see.

This is Jason Lake's moment. For all his sacrifice and faith, this is his players' gift to him. He is redeemed, validated, affirmed in the belief that good things happen to the right people.

One at a time, the team descends the metal stairs behind the sound stage. The last one down is Lake, his tie loosened and his shirt half-untucked around the waist. At the bottom of the steps, he lets out a long exhale and says with a smile, "These kids keep saving my life."

The Championship Gaming Invitational is a wrap. A half-hour later, the crowd has gone and the production crew is breaking down the set, packing up all the lights and spooling up all the wires. After many congratulatory embraces and handshakes backstage in the players lounge, the gamers begin making their way to the bus.

As Lake walks across the parking lot, Craig Levine is headed the other way, walking back toward the hangar.

"You coming?" Lake asks. "I think we're about to head out."

"No," says Levine, motioning with a tilt of his head to the set. "Got a few things to finish up inside."

The 3D owner isn't going back to the hotel with his team. He won't be with the team much at all, from this point on. As of this night, Levine is essentially done running Team 3D from day to day. CGI has been closure for him as well, and a new beginning. DirecTV is his future, helping them push gaming to the masses. He's headed inside to throw around ideas about a DirecTV league.

"Listen," Levine says, extending his hand. "I just wanted to say congratulations."

The two rivals shake hands and share a moment of mutual appreciation.

From this point on, it would all be different. Gaming was making the jump to TV, and wherever that may lead. Maybe it would be the next big thing, like poker before it, and maybe it wouldn't. But regardless, bigger things would be happening next for gaming. It was in DirecTV's hands now. The cavalry had arrived. But it never would have made it this far without these two guys carrying it. They got it here. With Levine's brains and Lake's heart, they got it here.

It turned out there was room for both of them in gaming, after all. The old Iowa linebacker Lake had his victory, his affirmation, and after this event goes to broadcast, maybe even a return on his investment. The ambitious capitalist Levine, meanwhile, had his long-awaited opportunity with DirecTV to drive the industry to new heights.

Both got what they wanted, and each needed the other's help to get it.

Lake nods to his old foe and walks to the bus. As he boards, Levine says out of earshot, "Funny thing about Jason and me, there's no one I'd rather lose to...and there's no one I hate losing to more."

In the front of the bus, the PMS girls are singing and joking and hanging over the seats. Everyone is sky high from the event, swapping stories and laughing.

In the back, the Counter-Strike players sit quietly, drained from it all. In two adjoining seats, Moto is beside Rambo, who's down on himself for failing as strat caller. "Forget about it, Ronald," says Moto, graciously. "That's just Counter-Strike."

The others are all mixed in together: Warden and Method, Trip and ShaGuar, Volcano and Sunman. Storm is a row back, texting his girlfriend about the victory. And in the very last row, beside the bathroom, Lake takes a seat and leans exhausted against the window, still clutching the glowing Mountain Dew trophy. "I can't wait to get this home and show it to my wife," he says. "I think I'll give her the five hundred dollars from the gift bag and tell her to go shopping, too."

Lastly, fRoD climbs on board the bus and walks to the back, taking the open seat next to his coach. The bus pulls out of the parking lot at Hangar 180 and begins to wind its way through Treasure Island back up to the Bay Bridge.

Lake gazes around at all these man-boys who play videogames for a living. He thinks to himself, tonight maybe they all grew up just a little. After tonight, maybe e-sports will learn to stand on its own two feet and he can spend a little more time at home just being dad. Yeah, that would be okay.

It's been nine years since America's marginalized teenagers began showing up in Dallas to compete in videogame tournaments. It's been five years since Counter-Strike clans went professional and three years since Jason Lake first began chasing the dream of reaching the top of the e-sports world. Now, gaming was finally going on TV.

Lake again looks across the rows of gamers before him and then gazes out at the glinting city lights of San Francisco. As the bus pulls onto the Bay Bridge and accelerates into traffic, he thinks to himself, maybe we're all finally headed somewhere.

fRoD pulls CompLexity's $50,000 first-place check out of his pocket. The coach had forgotten about it after handing the check to his star player at the award ceremony. Now fRoD was handing it back so Lake could deposit it in the bank and mail each of them their $10,000 shares.

"Hey, by the way," says fRoD, "we chopped it 40–25."

Lake stares at his star player in disbelief.

Unknown to the coach, CompLexity and 3D got together before the match and secretly agreed to divvy up the prize money more evenly. No matter who won, the players all figured, $50,000 for first place and $15,000 for second was too much of a gap. It wasn't right. They'd all been scraping by in this game too long for any one player to leave with just $3,000 for the effort.

So they agreed to *chop* the payout 40–25, meaning they'd split it up after the fact with $40,000 to the winning team and $25,000 to the runners-up. It's not like a fix was in, not by a long shot. They were still

playing for the difference of $15,000 in the championship match, or an extra $3,000 apiece. That was plenty of motivation. But 40–25 seemed right, not 50–15. These guys would all get a better taste, whether DirecTV planned it that way or not.

Lake can't believe it. His guys just gave away $2,000 apiece to 3D because of the chop. Oh, well. Why should he care? It's their money.

The coach can't help but smile, thinking of these hustlers playing the angles and cutting deals behind DirecTV's back. Then the greatest irony of all occurs to Lake. He's the one depositing the winning check into the bank and then mailing the individual payouts. So now, because of the chop, he'll have to reroute $10,000 of it directly to Team 3D so their five players can get their own cuts.

After everything he's endured over the last three years, Lake now has to write Craig Levine, of all people, a check for $10,000.

"Son of a bitch," Lake says with a smirk, shaking his head and turning to see his own expression of disbelief reflected in the side window of the bus.

# Afterword

**E**VEN THE HOTTEST SUMMER TURNS TO FALL. DAYS shorten. Nights get chilly. Dried, scratchy leaves are blown across the road.

The contentious Counter-Strike summer of 2006 had drawn to an end with CGI in San Francisco and the airing of DirecTV's pilot episode in September two months later.

For the rest of the year, the world beyond gaming continued to turn. The St. Louis Cardinals won the World Series. Democrats reclaimed control of Congress in midterm elections. *Borat* had a *"niiiiice"* run at the box office.

In gaming, though, from September to the close of 2006, the planet effectively stopped revolving as DirecTV's inner circle huddled at their offices in El Segundo, a few miles from LAX, and debated whether it was worth their while to launch a pro-gaming league in 2007.

And if they did, what would that mean for the top Counter-Strike teams? Would they be absorbed? Would the managers be retained? Would Jason Lake finally get some back end on his investment in e-sports? Or, as rumored, would DirecTV muscle him out by luring his players away with doubled salaries of $25,000 a year?

"If that's the case, talk about a major kick in the stomach," Lake said over the winter, as he awaited his fate with equal parts hopefulness and helplessness. "They wanted our cooperation. They said it was gonna be great for our team, great for gaming. When in reality, they may have just been using us."

A handful of smaller tournaments remained on the Counter-Strike schedule for 2006, but to the gamers who'd been at CGI, those lesser LANs had no more appeal.

Nobody felt much like sliding metal chairs up to cloth-covered cafeteria tables anymore. DirecTV had pulled gaming out of the basement—from the anonymous darkness in cellars across America and from the basement days of the Hyatt Regency in Dallas—and the thought of going back underground was all too depressing.

No one could bear the thought that DirecTV might walk away and relegate them to a future that all-too-familiarly resembled the past. Was it possible? Would they really just pull the plug and leave gaming as they found it—a fringe subculture ignored by a mainstream that just doesn't get it?

Either way, the gamers had no choice but to get back to work. There was still money to be made at those lesser LANs, after all.

The WSVG held a few more tournaments in 2006, further shifting the focus of its events toward youth-targeted games like Guitar Hero II and Dance Dance Revolution. After getting a look at the CGI airing, Matt Ringel knew he couldn't compete with DirecTV in competitive e-sports, so he sought safe harbor in kiddie games.

To give Ringel some credit, he did improve upon what the CPL had previously achieved for TV airtime. In 2006, the WSVG had its own half-hour on MTV, plus a Sunday afternoon spotlight on CBS. Predictably, it was more of the "ain't gamers cool" approach, and among the players spotlighted was, of course, Moto. It's worth noting that at the time of the CBS segment, Moto had been benched and replaced in 3D's lineup by Dominator.

Over the final months of 2006, CompLexity and 3D squared off twice more at LAN events, with CompLexity winning both times. The first was at the DigitalLife tech expo in New York City. The second was fittingly back where this tumultuous season began, at the Hyatt Regency in Dallas for the downsized CPL Winter 2006.

In what would be the final such meeting between these two fierce rivals, the match went into three overtimes before CompLexity sealed it 25–23. It was an appropriate end to a knock-down, drag-out 2006 season, a year in which CompLexity took four of five against its former nemesis and supplanted 3D atop the gaming world.

Lake finally had what he'd long sought: recognition as the top Counter-Strike team in the world. His boys went to number one in the Gotfrag worldwide rankings. Team 3D slipped all the way down to number five.

For the year, CompLexity's players raked in about $38,000 apiece in salary and prize money, while Team 3D's guys made about $24,000. Not bad for a bunch of twenty-year-olds with no bills, but ultimately not a whole lot different from the payouts in years past.

As the calendar flipped to 2007, Craig Levine summed it up best. "E-sports must continue to grow and reach a broader audience," he said. "If the pie stays the same as it is now, it's not worth it for any of us to be here."

The gaming world waited on DirecTV's answer.

"What's more important to you guys, sex or videogames?" asks Julie McCullough, *Playboy* magazine's Miss February 1986, dressed in a green bunny outfit and standing lasciviously by the pool at the Playboy Mansion. As hard as it is to believe, the gamers are at the house of Hugh Hefner. Those supposed outcasts, geeks, and misfits are partying at the Mansion with the bunnies. Well, if you call awkward eye contact and staring at the ground "partying."

"Actually, most of them really don't talk to us," says Miss February McCullough with a coy smile. "They pretty much just take pictures and run off."

Raven-haired Deanna Brooks, the Playmate of the Month for May 1998, adds, "They've got no time for us. There are videogames to be played."

Truer words were never spoken, by a woman in rabbit ears or otherwise. Yes, there are games to be played. Lots of them.

It's June 2007, just shy of a year since CGI in San Francisco, and the Playboy Mansion is the intentionally conspicuous site of the player draft for DirecTV's pro-gaming league, the Championship Gaming Series (CGS).

Hef isn't on the premises today. He and his *Girls Next Door* girlfriends are in Monaco for the weekend, which is how DirecTV was able to rent out the estate and set up cameras under a tent in the backyard for the draft.

About 150 gamers are here in the lushly vegetated hills above Hollywood, roaming around the grounds of this den of debauchery, checking out the macaws and parrots in Hefner's aviary and sneaking peeks at the forty-five Bunnies hired to throw seductive glances around the party.

The Playboy Mansion is not an accidental location for the CGS draft. All of the activities are being filmed. DirecTV figures if the videogames don't immediately lure in the crucial male-teen demographic, a little cleavage should do the trick.

The Playboy party made it official. DirecTV was taking the plunge, launching the first-ever made-for-TV pro videogaming league in history. E-sports apparently had found its savior in Fox Sports boss and DirecTV overseer David Hill.

Counter-Strike pioneer Frank Nuccio, the old hockey fan, would be proud. Just like the NHL back in 1942, the first year of the CGS league would likewise feature an "Original Six" teams. The squads would be named after major cities and regions—New York, L.A., Dallas, Carolina, Chicago, and San Francisco—although those designations really had no point other than to further replicate traditional pro-sports leagues.

None of the players were actually moving to those cities. Instead, the sixty elite players drafted tonight would live for two months in corporate housing in Marina del Rey while shooting season one on a nearby L.A. soundstage.

CGS would feature four games: Counter-Strike: Source, FIFA

soccer, Project Gotham Racing, and the fighter game Dead or Alive 4. To maximize viewer appeal, Dead or Alive 4 would feature both a male and female division, ensuring that each of CGS's ten-player franchises would have at least one girl player on the roster.

Through the summer of 2007, CGS would air twice a week, completely live. In the fall, the league's top two teams would advance to a CGS World Championships, to also air on News Corp satellite entities BSkyB in Europe and Star TV in Asia.

In the first season, teams from other global regions would qualify through tournament play, not through a structured league as in the United States. But the idea was, if year one was a hit, CGS would replicate that full league structure worldwide.

CGI producer Mike Burks was back on board to run CGS, and a sports-minded exec named Andy Reif, who previously had built AVP pro beach volleyball into a surprise TV ratings grabber, was named league commissioner.

At long last, the gamers were cashing in. Starting salary for each of the sixty players drafted tonight would be $30,000, and that's just for a two-month shoot in L.A.

Beyond that, a reported $5 million in prize money was up for grabs in the first year alone, which includes payouts for promotional events, global qualifiers, and the World Championships in December. The bottom line: $30,000 was the least anyone drafted tonight would make, and players on a U.S. team that ran the table to win the World Championships would easily clear six figures. That's *six figures*.

DirecTV had surveyed the e-sports landscape, concluded that it was littered with incompetence, misguided vision, and flat-out thievery, and set out to conquer it.

Craig Levine would get his back end. Since CGI last summer, he continued to be an invaluable consultant to DirecTV, both in planning the league and overcoming its technical hurdles.

"We had to figure it all out," Levine says, "from the number of franchises to what games we'd include, to making sure every kid's mouse works when the cameras go on."

Levine relocated over the winter from New York to L.A. so he could work more closely with Burks. Together they further tweaked the rules and scoring of the various games and upgraded the visuals. The best touch for Counter-Strike was putting the aliases on each character's vest in-game, like names on a sports uniform, to match the jerseys worn by the actual gamers on stage.

Beyond consulting, the second stage of Levine's master plan was to cash in on the aspirational carryover of a DirecTV showcase, figuring kids at home would turn off the TV and go looking for a pickup game on his ESEA Web site. He was right. In the year since the CGI pilot, ESEA subscriptions have already jumped 50 percent, from six thousand to more than nine thousand members.

Last, Levine planned to sell Team 3D in entirety to DirecTV, which could then make it a founding franchise in the CGS league.

The appeal for DirecTV, of course, would be to preserve the rivalry between 3D and CompLexity. They were the only two clans being considered for absorption, since they had the biggest fan bases and the clout to give CGS instant credibility in the gaming community. Taking one without the other was pointless.

Levine wasn't overly concerned. A back end on Team 3D would be a nice bonus, but he now had bigger revenue streams with consulting and ESEA. His future in gaming was secure.

Jason Lake, conversely, was at the mercy of DirecTV. If they brushed him off and signed away his players, he'd be done in gaming, a bust, some kind of delusional failure who'd blown $400,000 of his family's money chasing after a fool's dream.

Lake had a top team and a loyal fan base. He had the respect of the gaming community. But the truth is, he had nothing DirecTV couldn't live without. Lake had no real leverage whatsoever, and everyone knew it.

"The work that Jason has done to build up the CompLexity brand, in terms of the industry and community, is admirable," DirecTV's Steven Roberts said at the time. "But let's face it, if we choose to go a different direction, we can make all of his hard work for naught."

Even Lake was forced to agree. "What am I supposed to do," he asked, "go out and find some scrub team to bring to CPL events? Then what? As soon as they got some exposure on my dime, they'd just go sign for the big bucks with DirecTV anyway."

In November 2006, Lake boarded an early-morning flight to L.A. for a do-or-die pitch meeting at DirecTV headquarters. For six hours, he sat stuffed into a coach-class seat, flipping through a *Maxim* magazine and steadily wrinkling his button-down shirt.

When he arrived at DirecTV's offices in El Segundo, Lake ducked into a bathroom to splash water on his face. Half of it wound up spotting his gold tie.

"There I am sitting in the waiting room before the most important business meeting of my life," Lake recalls, "with a wrinkled shirt, a lack of sleep and a head cold I'd picked up from my daughter. I felt like a linebacker going into the Rose Bowl with a broken leg."

A voice came from across the waiting room, a sign to Lake that everything might work out okay. "Holy shit," said the voice, "is that *you?*" It was an intern pointing at the wall behind Lake, where there hung a four-by-six-foot action photo of the CompLexity coach at CGI, standing behind fRoD and screaming at the top of his lungs.

Lake knew then exactly what his leverage was with DirecTV. It wasn't his clan's recognition in the gaming community, or their fan base or the traffic on his Web site, or even his top-ranked Counter-Strike team itself. It was him, the coach.

DirecTV's challenge was pulling the drama out of the computer monitors and into the real world where viewers could connect to it, right? Well, every sports league has its Bill Parcells or its Phil Jackson. What DirecTV didn't have was a coach. Not like him. There were no others like him. There just had to be a place for a sideline-pacing, chair-kicking lunatic like Lake in this gaming league.

Six franchise general managers are on stage in the draft tent at the Playboy Mansion, sitting behind illuminated consoles and beneath splashy new team logos. One of them is Jason Lake.

CompLexity is now the property of DirecTV, and for all intents and purposes, so too is their coach. His clan has been reborn as the L.A. CompLexity, complete with a new logo using the old lettering but with the capital *L* descending and crossed with an *A*.

Lake got his back end, more or less. After a series of meetings, he sold CompLexity to DirecTV for an even $100,000 and the opportunity to remain on as GM, with its $50,000 salary.

A few incentives were built into the deal, based on CGS viewership and ad revenues, that could conceivably double or triple that $100,000 payday over the next half-decade or so. Yet the odds are slim, really, that Lake will ever recoup anything close to the $400,000 he's dropped on e-sports to date.

Of course, considering the alternative of being kicked to the curb, he gladly took DirecTV's $100,000 parachute and handed them the reins of marketing and promotion.

"Now I can stop spending half of my day trying to chase down people like Adidas," he says. "It's not my problem anymore. I'm a coach. That's what I'm good at—taking gamers and making them into world champions. That's the reason I'm here."

Onstage, too, are the five other GMs. Seated next to Lake is JaX, who will manage the Dallas Venom. The nineteen-year-old's hint-dropping on the yacht in San Francisco with DirecTV's execs paid off, and perhaps so too his penchant for wearing flashy suits. "Never underestimate the power of lilac in your wardrobe," JaX says with a wink.

Ensuring that their undercard rivalry continues onto the airwaves, JaX's archrival Marc Dolven made the big show, too. The clean-cut Pandemic boss will now run the Carolina Core in the CGS.

Two of the other GMs are longtime gaming insiders from beyond the Counter-Strike circle. Industry journalist Kat Hunter will lead the San Francisco Optx, and former Quake champion Brian "DKT" Flander will run the Chicago Chimera.

Last, sitting beneath the logo of the renamed 3D.NY is Craig Levine's handpicked successor, Dave "Moto" Geffon. The embattled former team leader has hung up his mouse for good and moved up to the front office.

It was never easy for Moto to admit he couldn't cut it at the elite level, so he doesn't. "Honestly, I see more potential for myself managing and leading than being a player," he says, no doubt relieved deep down to have scrambled back from retirement and found a niche in gaming after an unpleasant peek at the nine-to-five world.

"Hey, I'm good at motivating and leading people. I'm good on camera," Moto says. "It's a win-win for everybody."

The house lights dim inside the tent, and the cameras swing into place. Back to host the draft is Stryker, the emcee of the CGI event in San Francisco. Wearing a Hefner-like bathrobe, he takes the stage and tells the audience, "Playboy turns fantasy into reality, and we're doing the same with videogames."

Shoutcasters Marcus "DJ Wheat" Graham and Paul "ReDeYe" Chaloner discuss the top talent in the room, joined by Johnathan "Fatal1ty" Wendel, whom CGS hired as an expert analyst.

The first pick in the draft is female Dead or Alive 4 player Vanessa Orteaga, who's selected by San Francisco. At the announcement by CGS commissioner Reif, Orteaga jumps out of her seat in the crowd and bounces up a few steps onto the stage, where she smiles and preens and tries on a green ball cap bearing the Optx logo.

Next on the clock, with the second pick overall, is Lake.

"L.A. CompLexity," says the host, "you have two minutes."

An oversized clock above the stage counts down from 2:00, and Lake dutifully plays along for the cameras, feigning indecision. It's a given that both Lake and Moto will select their respective Counter-Strike teams.

In two minutes, Lake will hand a card to a Playboy bunny with the words "Team CompLexity" inside, which in turn she'll sashay over to the commissioner to announce the pick. So for the next two minutes, Lake really has nothing to do but enjoy the moment.

"In America," Lake would say later, "you're brought up to believe that if you follow your dream, it will all work out. Sitting on that stage, I honestly felt like I'd reached my dream. I'd finally made it. I mean, who does this happen to?"

From his seat onstage, Lake looks over the gamers in rows of chairs on the floor, all eagerly leaning forward, hoping to hear their names called. The familiar faces are out there, all of Lake's Counter-Strike friends and foes alike. And in some cases, those foes are now friendlies.

In the front row sits Ronald "Rambo" Kim, who parted ways with Team 3D in January, after a frustrating year spent watching Levine and Moto prioritize public relations ahead of victories. More shockingly, days later Rambo signed with CompLexity.

It was a seismic roster shift that caused a ripple effect across Counter-Strike. Days after Rambo's exit, Levine cut Josh "Dominator" Sievers and Griffin "ShaGuar" Benger from 3D and found replacements. One of the players who returned was retired legend Kyle "Ksharp" Miller. With CGS now a go, Ksharp figured gaming *was* finally going somewhere, so he quit his IT job in Virginia and picked up the AWP once more.

The only clan noticeably absent here at the draft is Mug N Mouse, the group of Dallas waywards who failed to qualify during CGS's online run-up. After a disappointing 2006, Punkville hit the road to join his buddy Bzrk in Kuwait City, where he hoped to likewise land a military-contract job while also keeping up with his dream of becoming a mixed-martial-arts champion. "I bet they've got some kind of crazy, fucked-up Persian fighting style over there," Punkville said with a grin before leaving the United States for the Middle East in December.

"CompLexity," says Stryker, as the draft clock ticks down, "you have one minute."

Lake leans back in his chair and looks out at his team, and his star Danny "fRoD" Montaner, the Counter-Strike natural who's won the approval of his dad back home in Miami.

"After he saw me on TV the first time," fRoD says of his father, Miguel, "he told me, 'If this is what you want to do, I won't bother you anymore about going to college.'"

In the seats next to fRoD are Matt "Warden" Dickens and Tyler "Storm" Wood and another new CompLexity teammate, Swedish player Marcus "Zet" Sundström, a former member of Ninjas in Pyjamas.

In adding Rambo and the Swedish star Zet, CompLexity further separated itself competitively from the pack and is now peerless globally in Counter-Strike. And by adding a well-known European player like Zet, they've also enjoyed a popularity boost overseas. CompLexity is now the name in gaming. The downside of the 2006 postseason player shuffle, it goes without saying, is that two guys had to be cut.

Lake suffered over the decision but ultimately released two players he felt were least committed to the team's future, Justin "Sunman" Summy and Corey "Tr1p" Dodd.

Sunman was an aging former star whose competitive drive had been on the wane even during the 2006 season. In cutting Tr1p, though, Lake was parting ways with his strat caller and team leader.

After being cut, it didn't take long for the two ex–CompLexity players to find new teams. Both Tr1p and Sunman signed on with the Canada-based Evil Geniuses, and both players are here at the Playboy Mansion with the goal of getting drafted into CGS.

It all worked out for Tr1p and Sunman, but seeing those two players sitting a few rows behind their old CompLexity teammates was a bittersweet realization that for all gaming achieved in 2006, some things clearly would never be the same again.

Not that anyone would choose to return to the anonymity of the cellar-dweller past. Still, though, there was a certain purity in those ignored, unappreciated days. There also was a spirit of defiance, and a wonderful absurdity as well—that a group of people could be so consumed with a pursuit that nobody in the outside world gave a damn about. It was theirs. It belonged to the gamers.

With DirecTV appropriating the subculture, even now new seeds of rebellion are being sown in the shifting gaming underground. At LAN centers around the country and in online threads, the voices of dissent are rising.

One major objection from the hardcore community was CGS's decision to use Counter-Strike: Source, the graphically superior yet competitively ridiculed update over the classic version 1.6. For the gaming hard-core, version 1.6 was the one that felt right, despite its antiquated graphics and technical flaws. It was stripped-down, like street hockey, while Source was mocked as eye candy. Still, for DirecTV, it was a no-brainer. The newer Source looked better on TV. Plus, by agreeing to showcase Source, CGS had the blessing of Valve Software, opening the door to the development of licensed CGS versions of the game.

Another complaint of the hard-core community was CGS's shortening matches and deemphasizing the game's money system. Burks knew nobody would watch a match on TV lasting over an hour, and he had no intention of spelling out the dull minutiae of the purchasing of weapons. Still, to the grassroots, the streamlining of Counter-Strike was tantamount to dumbing down the game.

Somewhat separately, my own lament over what's been lost in gaming's leap to the airwaves is far less technical. It's more a gut feeling I get while seeing the players mugging for the TV cameras at the Playboy Mansion.

What's different now, even from CGI a year ago in San Francisco, is a sense that many of these guys were suddenly "acting" like themselves instead of just being themselves—as if they're exaggerating their own personalities for the audience. The cocky kids are acting cocky. The tough kids are acting tough. In short, it seemed that gaming was becoming reality TV.

Even Jason Lake, who complained once last season about being miked up for a match like a "goddamn Christmas tree," has begun playing for the cameras, too. At times this weekend, while filming promo footage, Lake seemed almost to be consciously recreating that "fiery coach" image he saw on the wall at DirecTV headquarters. At one point during an exhibition match shot a couple of days ago for CGS's intros, Lake paced behind his team then looked straight into the camera and bellowed, "Welcome to the show!"

It was a re-creation of Lake's most spontaneous, most enjoyably ridiculous moment of the entire past triumphant season—when he shouted that same battle cry at Alternate aTTaX in a moment of passion during the Intel Summer finals.

There's probably nothing wrong with Lake's re-delivering that line for CGS's cameras. It's certainly nothing any viewer would spot as rehearsed. But having spent time with this gaming crowd last year before anyone else was watching—before they were aware that anyone else was watching—somehow the whole thing didn't feel the same anymore.

The CGS draft was under way and the gamers were finally getting their due. They would have their chance to show the world what makes them special. Yet I stood there in the tent at the Playboy Mansion, struck with the realization that this story was over.

I recalled something that Mike Burks said a summer ago. At the time, he was speaking about his many years covering pro basketball. Now, in retrospect, his words rang true for Jason Lake and CompLexity, and perhaps for e-sports as a whole.

"There was this pattern thing for a while in the NBA," Burks said at the time. "Larry Bird's Celtics couldn't get past the Sixers, and then they did and won a championship. Chicago with Michael Jordan couldn't get past Detroit, and then they finally broke through, too.

"The coolest thing about sports," Burks said, "is a team's first year of success. The fans are into it, the players are into it, the media is into it. There's just such a genuine upswell of support and affection.

"Everything changes after that year. People want more money. There's dissension. Talk radio starts killing the team. That first year is special. It's unadorned. And if you're in the middle of it, it's the best feeling in sports."

With his two minutes winding down, Lake ceremoniously scribbles down his draft selection inside a folded card and hands it to a bunny. She delivers it to the commissioner, who announces, "With the second pick, L.A. selects Team CompLexity."

Warden, Storm, fRoD, Rambo, and Zet rise from their seats in the audience and ascend the steps to the stage. At the top they're greeted by a beaming Lake, who holds his arms out wide and says, "You're my boys."

Warden hugs Lake and says into his ear, "I'll never be able to thank you enough for changing my life."

His coach pats him on the back and answers "I never could have done it without you."

The five CompLexity players try on their official L.A. jerseys and ball caps and stand proudly before the cameras. They've finally hit the big time.

The draft continues, and other Counter-Strike teams are selected, as are players from the other games. As scripted, Moto selects Team 3D in the first round, and they too take the stage to don their new team jerseys and grin for the cameras.

JaX drafts his Money Crew, which now includes Dominator, who signed with the team after being cut from Team 3D. Dolven later drafts Pandemic onto the Carolina Core. And later, the Chicago Chimera selects Evil Geniuses, so Trip and Sunman wind up getting in on the action, too.

Throughout it all, standing unnoticed in the back of the tent, Craig Levine keeps a watchful eye on the production. One of Levine's many responsibilities tonight is to make sure the names of gamers selected are posted on monitors above the stage. It's seemingly technical work but a nonetheless fitting assignment, since Levine is the guy who's most responsible for getting all these kids here in the first place.

In retrospect, it was Levine who, in building Team 3D, gave pro gamers something to aspire to. "For years," Levine says, allowing himself a moment of reflection, "everyone looked at 3D as where they wanted to be. We were winning. We had fans. We had sponsors. We commanded the respect of the industry."

And it was Levine who sold DirecTV on the idea of putting Counter-Strike on the air. As their earliest e-sports consultant, he conveyed the game's special drama to Burks and taught him to appreciate it as sport. He was the one e-sports insider wise enough to recognize what changes were necessary to make the game watchable on TV, yet he still preserved its integrity.

It was Craig Levine who saved Counter-Strike.

"It's gratifying to see the whole thing succeed," Levine says overly humbly, "because *everyone* made sacrifices through the years."

Time will tell if the 3D-CompLexity rivalry endures within CGS, or if it's superseded by some unforeseen feud involving Dallas or Carolina or the other franchises. It's apparent now, though, that the true rivalry between Team 3D and CompLexity has come to an end. It's over because the battle between Craig Levine and Jason Lake has reached a civil and satisfying conclusion for both.

"You know," Levine summarizes, "for years, we were like bottom-dwellers scrounging for whatever we could get, trying to grab everything we could because we didn't know how long it would last. Thankfully, that time has passed."

Lake adds of the rivalry that was: "After beating them at CGI, I knew it was over. I knew Craig would still succeed, but I also knew I'd earned my place at the table and no one could take it away. If I beat Craig, it's only because I'm still here. And for a while, he was doing the best he could to drive me away."

To Lake, the necessity of challenging Levine and Team 3D's dominance in Counter-Strike was never in question. A champion must be challenged, period. To the onetime Iowa State University frat boy, it was like being back at his favorite college bar, People's, the one with the old pool table with the ratty red felt.

Lake saw Levine running the table, so the competitor in him just had to put a quarter on the rail and offer a challenge. More than $400,000 worth of Lake's quarters later, he finally beat him. Even if Levine was already playing a different game.

Lake had his triumph on the big stage, his number-one team in the world, a $100,000 emergency parachute from DirecTV, and most important, two healthy kids at home in Atlanta and a wife who's willing to put up with his "videogame thing" awhile longer.

For his trouble, Levine received a bigger monetary payoff than Lake from DirecTV. Could it have ended any other way? Levine got $125,000 for Team 3D, and he's now positioned to make millions through consulting and his ESEA Web site.

In the end, they both won, and not least of all because they pushed each other to greater heights.

"After three long years," Lake says, in reflection, "it's like the poker cards were put back in the deck, and it was time to just respect each other for what we accomplished.

"Our game was over."

# Acknowledgments

**M**ANY PEOPLE CONTRIBUTED TO THIS BOOK WITH THEIR wisdom, generosity, and encouragement. I would like to express special gratitude to a few whose assistance was invaluable.

First, I am forever indebted to my agent, Stacey Glick, who contacted me out of the blue and suggested I write a book about gamers. I am also indebted to my editor at Viking, Alessandra Lusardi, whose insight made this final version far better (and a good amount shorter) than its original draft.

In between, and in less-than-particular order, were many others who deserve thanks: Gotfrag's Lee Chen, Trevor Schmidt, and Jason Bass for their expertise; Mike Burks, Alex Gomez, David Hill, Eric Shanks, Steven Roberts, Roderick Alemania, Caley Cronin, and Christian Averill for the access; my parents Walter and Judy for the biologically obvious and for their extra help in the summer of '06; and much further back Marion Roaman for that copy of *The Stranger*.

At the *New York Post*, extra thanks to editor Stephen Lynch for the assignment that was the seed of this project, as well as Barry Gross, Lauren Ramsby, Chris Shaw, Isaac Guzman, Robert Walsh, and above all Jon Blackwell for their support.

Gratitude to Chris Bunting, Ralph Russo, and Jeremiah Murphy for their feedback; Jon Boal, Artem Agafonov, and Ken Lam for their footage and camaraderie.

Also, a note of appreciation to Andy Billing, Salli Frattini, Jim and Sonae Lee, Frank Nuccio, Angel Munoz, Matt Ringel, Laurent Genin-Satoh, Corey Dunn, George Nikitin, and Josh Geha.

During my cross-country research trip, many offered hospitality and road maps, particularly Danielle Lake in Atlanta, the Kim family in Dallas, the Dickens family in Houston, the Wood family in Little Rock, the Montaner family in Miami, the Sievers family in Iowa, Stephen Summy in Pennsylvania, Corey Dodd and friends in Fargo, and Joey Valvo and Chez in L.A.

Likewise, a big thank you to the McMichael family and Mama T for opening their homes to me during rewrites.

The telling of this story begins with the cooperation and trust of all the e-sports loonies who allowed me into their world, especially Craig Levine, Alex Garfield, Alex Conroy, and most of all Jason Lake, who fittingly took the greatest leap of faith. Without you guys, there's nothing.

To Shaye, may what was discovered here at least bring some balance to what was lost.

And most of all, to Maureen and John, know that without your unquestioning support, this book would not have been possible.

# Index